£3.99

G000126100

)

BYRON
and his Children

BYRON
and his Children

Susan Normington

ALAN SUTTON PUBLISHING LIMITED

First published in the United Kingdom in 1995 by
Alan Sutton Publishing Ltd · Phoenix Mill · Far Thrupp · Stroud
Gloucestershire

Copyright © Susan Normington, 1995

British Library Cataloguing in Publication Data

Normington, Susan
  Byron and his Children
  I. Title
  821.7

  ISBN 0-7509-0601-4

Typeset in 10/13pt Baskerville.
Typesetting and origination by
Alan Sutton Publishing Limited.
Printed in Great Britain by
Butler & Tanner, Frome, Somerset.

Contents

List of Illustrations

Preface

George Gordon, 6th Lord Byron, is widely known for his passionate love affairs and his commitment to the cause of Greek freedom, but outside academic circles his poetry is largely unread and most of his popular reputation is founded on the words of his discarded lover, Lady Caroline Lamb, 'Mad, bad and dangerous to know'.

Byron and his Children shows that although he was incapable of steadfast love for any woman he became deeply attached to his children, linking the effect of his childhood experiences with his attitude towards them. Byron's father, a compulsive lecher and gambler, died when he was three leaving him to be brought up by his mother, a careful Scot. This proud, passionate woman unwittingly placed him in the hands of a nurse who humiliated and abused him. He felt embarrassment and shame over his lame foot and, because of it, was cruelly baited at school.

Byron and his Children highlights the gentle side of his character. He celebrated his first, illegitimate, child with the words, 'I hail thee, dearest child of love, Fair cherub, pledge of youth and Joy.' He tried to veil his affection by nonchalance only to be stunned when his third child, Allegra, died. He pined for his only legitimate offspring, Ada, separated from her by his self-imposed exile, but foreseeing a time when she would come to know and love him. His prediction came true twenty-eight years later when she chose to be with him in death – their coffins touching deep in the Byron vault at Hucknall Torkard.

Acknowledgements

The author is grateful to the following for permission to reproduce illustrations: by courtesy of the National Portrait Gallery (55); The Keepers and Governors of Harrow School (28); City Librarian of Nottingham (7, 29, 37, 45); John Murray (Publishers) Limited (38, 52, 53, 54, 58, 59, 60, 62, 64, 65, 66); Mr G.C. Burgess (68). The following illustrations are reproduced from *Illustrations of the Life and Works of Lord Byron*, by Edward and William Finden, John Murray, 1833 (2, 4, 5, 6, 8, 9, 10, 11, 12, 13, 14, 15, 20, 21, 22, 26, 32, 34, 35, 36, 39, 42, 43, 48, 50, 57); *The Works of Lord Byron*, Rowland Prothero (ed.), 6 vols, John Murray, 1901 (3, 16, 41); *The Byron Gallery*, C.R. Cockerell, 1833 (40); *The Last Days of Lord Byron*, W. Parry, Knight and Lacey, 1825 (49); *The Life, Letters and Journals of Lord Byron*, Thomas Moore, John Murray, 1838 (67); *The Two Duchesses*, Vere Foster (ed.), Blackie & Son, 1898 (17, 19, 31); *Astarte*, Ralph Milbanke, Earl of Lovelace, Christophers, 1921 (23). The rest are engravings or from private collections. The author is most grateful to John Murray for allowing her to quote from *Byron's Letters and Journals*, edited by Leslie A. Marchand, 12 vols, 1973–82 and from *Ada, Countess of Lovelace*, Doris Langley Moore, 1977. She would also like to thank Cambridgeshire County Council's Libraries and Information Service, in particular the librarians at the Huntingdon and Ramsey Libraries for their help and interest, Mr G.C. Burgess for permission to use his family papers and Vivienne Morgan for her unstinting help in researching the possible Byron-Marshall connection.

CHAPTER ONE

From Aberdeen to the House of Lords

Byron leant gently over the back of the nurse's chair where she sat rocking the sleeping baby. He gazed lovingly at the child remarking that there were no violent Byronic traits to be seen in her calm, sweet face. Hesitatingly, almost fearfully, he asked if she was perfect. The nurse carefully unwrapped the shawl and exposed the baby's healthy little legs and feet. He was pleased but flustered, explaining that he had wanted to reassure himself that all was well because if anything had been wrong with her it would have to be set right immediately.[1] Little Augusta Ada Byron had been born into an unhappy household. Within weeks her parents were to separate and she would never see her father again. It was as though Byron's young life was to be repeated.

George Gordon Byron was born to the former Miss Catherine Gordon of Gight on 22 January 1788 while his father, Captain John Byron, known as 'Mad Jack', was living in France out of range of his creditors. Catherine travelled to England and, with the help of her family lawyer, John Hanson, rented a furnished apartment in the newly expanding section of London just off Oxford Street and waited for the birth of her baby. It took place in the back drawing room on the first floor of a building in Holles Street. Mrs Byron was well attended through her ordeal by Dr Denman, Mr Combe, a male midwife and Mrs Mills, a nurse, all hired by Hanson.[2] The baby was baptized on 29 February at Marylebone parish church attended by two godfathers, the Duke of Gordon and Colonel Duff of Fetteresso.

George, as his mother called him, had inherited his father's looks. Jack Byron was irresistible to women, with his long straight nose, blue eyes and dimpled chin. At twenty-two he had run off with a married woman, Amelia, Marchioness of Carmarthen, the only child and heiress of the last Earl of Holderness and Baroness Conyers, worth £4,000 a year in her own right. Of the three children of their passionate union only one survived, Augusta Mary. Amelia, weakened by childbirth, caught an unspecified illness and died, taking her £4,000 with her.

Captain Byron moved briskly into the busy marriage market based in Bath, on the lookout for what his son later called a 'golden dolly'. Catherine Gordon was no match for his stock-in-trade of good looks and charm and soon fell deeply in love. She was a well-built girl with plump arms and a sturdy neck. Dresses did not flatter her and not even delicate floating gauze shawls could mask her ample chest or hide the ripples on her midriff. She had few social graces but a sensible head, a good heart and a fortune. On 13 May 1785 the couple were married in St Michael's Church, Bath (an unusual choice for the bride as it was in Bath her father had drowned himself). Captain Byron's creditors were quick to scent money and immediately pressed their claims; within two years the penniless couple were forced to flee to France. In 1787 the estate of Gight was sold to Lord Haddo for £17,850, every penny going towards paying off more of Mad Jack's debts. Catherine, still blindly in love, acknowledged her husband had 'his foibles – they deserve no worse name'.[3]

When George was two Catherine moved to Queen Street, Aberdeen, to be close to her family. They were followed soon afterwards by her feckless husband. This was to be the only family life that Byron ever knew and it was shortlived. His parents fought. Mrs Byron frequently concluded her arguments by hurling cups, saucers and even fire-irons at her husband's head. Drawn together by animal magnetism alone and unable to live in peace Mrs Byron was forced to move to new lodgings at the other end of Queen Street taking George and his nurse May Gray. During a short period of truce the couple had taken it in turns to visit each other and politely take tea, but Jack Byron soon tired of this and would only communicate with his wife by letters – begging letters. The besotted woman rewarded these with small sums of ready money out of her income of £150 a year.

In 1790 Mad Jack returned to France to live with his sister, Frances Leigh, at Valenciennes, saying ungallantly that his wife, 'Catherine the Curst', was 'very amiable at a distance; but I defy you and all the Apostles to live with her two months, for if anybody could live with her it was me.' He resumed his life of vice, squandering any of his wife's money he could get his hands on, but it was not enough and, after lingering in debt and misery, he died of starvation and tuberculosis on 2 August 1791 at the age of thirty-six. The news of his death left Mrs Byron distraught and her uninhibited cries of grief could be clearly heard up and down Queen Street. She wrote to her sister-in-law, 'I do not think I shall ever get the better of it, necessity not inclination parted us.'

George's sweetness and playfulness made it almost impossible not to be fond of him, but he suffered from fits of ungovernable rage which matched his mother's. One day he bit a large piece of china out of a saucer and on another occasion, in one of his 'silent rages', he seized his frock with both hands and tore it from top to bottom, then stood in sullen stillness waiting for retribution.[4] Mrs Byron enrolled him at a day-school run by Mr Bowers. 'I have sent George to you that he may be kept in abeyance,' she said. The fee for a year was a guinea, a cheap price to pay for regular peace and quiet.

Many years later Byron recognized, with alarm, similar symptoms in his own daughter Allegra and put her in a convent school when, like him, at the age of four she had become 'quite above the control of the servants'. He hoped that at school she would have 'her learning advanced and her morals and religion inculcated'.[5]

George's right foot was twisted out of its natural position and a source of embarrassment at school and at home. His mother frequently hurt his feelings when in her paroxysms of rage she called him a lame brat and further confused his emotions after the storm subsided by cuddling him, devouring him with kisses and swearing his eyes were as beautiful as his father's. Determined to cure the foot, she took him to Dr Livingstone in Aberdeen who in turn consulted the celebrated Dr John Hunter in London. Together they devised methods of bandaging it or placing it in a metal contraption. Caught up in a maelstrom of emotions George turned to his new nurse, May Gray, who while she worked on his foot at bedtime told him stories and legends or sang in an attempt to keep his mind off the pain. She taught him to repeat the first and twenty-third psalms and to enjoy Old Testament stories, but she also inculcated in him her own dour doctrine of Calvinism.[6]

George entered Aberdeen Grammar School when he was six and rose from being twenty-third in a class of thirty-eight boys in April 1794 to fifth in a class of twenty-seven boys by the time he left in April four years later. He was lively, high-spirited and hated bullying. He severely beat a boy who had insulted him and when he arrived home hot and breathless, his red jacket and nankeen trousers dusty and creased, he told his mother he had been paying a debt, for he was a Byron.

George was not quite eight when he fell in love with his seven-year-old cousin Mary Duff. The memory of her dark brown hair, hazel eyes and pretty face and childish caresses remained with him. 'How the deuce,' he asked himself many years later, 'did all this occur so early? Where could it originate? I certainly had no sexual ideas for years afterwards; and yet my misery, my love for that girl were so violent, that I sometimes doubt if I have ever been really attached since.'[7]

The death of his second cousin, William Byron, at the battle of Calvi in 1796 brought George closer to the peerage, but he was shocked two years later to learn that the 5th Lord Byron had died and he had inherited the title. On the morning his new name, 'Dominus Byron', was first called out at school assembly he was unable to answer '*Adsum*' as usual but stood silent for a moment before bursting into tears.[8]

At the end of August 1798 all the preparations for moving south to his ancestral home were complete and a few days later the coach carrying the new Baron of Newstead and Rochdale, his mother and May Gray, rattled up to the tollhouse outside Newstead. Mrs Byron leant out of the window, her plump face gleaming with pride and happiness, 'Who owns Newstead Abbey?' she asked the toll-keeper, at the same time waving her hand in the general direction of the estate.

'They say', replied the woman, 'it is a little boy who lives at Aberdeen.'

'And this is he, bless him!' cried out May Gray, kissing the boy sitting on her lap.[9]

The trio drove up the winding drive and past the large lake to the sweeping steps of the abbey where John Hanson and his wife stood waiting to welcome them. Hanson had been retained by Mrs Byron to manage Byron's Newstead and Rochdale estates.

The group toured the neglected abbey, inspecting the cloisters, the deserted cells and rooms, the fine stone hall and old kitchen. They wandered through the stone-vaulted crypt, admired the broken west façade of the Priory Church and the great park. The surrounding hills looked barren with hardly a tree to be seen for miles except for solitary clumps of Scotch firs. The oaks had been sold for timber by the 5th lord who had done his best to ravage the estate, intending to leave a worthless inheritance to spite his son who had married against his wishes.

George was fascinated by the abbey and its Gothic ruins and glamorized the stories he heard from the tenants about the 5th lord, known locally as 'Wicked Lord' or 'Devil Byron'; he treasured the sword used in the notorious duel between him and William Chaworth, a distant relation and neighbouring landowner. The duel fought by Byron and Chaworth had occurred during an evening meeting of the Nottinghamshire Club on 26 January 1745 in the Star and Garter tavern in Pall Mall over an argument about the best way of preserving game. Chaworth bolted the door of a dimly lit room, turned, and the Wicked Lord, his sword half drawn, called, 'Draw!' Chaworth drew catching his sword in Byron's waistcoat. Unscathed, Byron shortened his sword and plunged it in Chaworth's body then raised the alarm. The landlord found them in each other's arms, Chaworth bleeding from a wound 6 inches deep. Both men surrendered their swords and the Wicked Lord was heard to say, 'Good God! that I should be such a fool as to fight in the dark.' Chaworth lingered until nine o'clock the following morning. In his dying moments he forgave the 5th lord saying he hoped the world would too. Chaworth's uncle did not agree and he successfully urged that Byron should be prosecuted.

The 5th lord was sent to the tower to await trial by 'God and his peers' for wilful murder. A state trial with the possibility of an execution was a spectacle worth seeing and tickets sold for 6 guineas each. Proceedings began on 16 April in Westminster Hall in the presence of the cream of society. 'It was a great sight,' said Thomas Percy. The prisoner was found innocent of murder but guilty of manslaughter. Horace Walpole commented that 'The prisoner behaved with great decorum, and seemed thoroughly shocked and mortified. Indeed, the bitterness of the world against him has been great, and the stories they have revived or invented to load him, very grievous.'[10]

The 5th lord returned to Newstead and was appointed master of the local Stag Hounds. He lived with his servant lover, 'Lady Betty', raising money by selling the pictures from the house and the deer and timber from the park. He gained a reputation for devil worship. But, like all the Byrons, he was loved and respected by his tenants for his friendliness and willingness to redress their grievances.[11]

He died in the neglected abbey with the sword that had killed Chaworth lying in his bedroom, leaving the title and run-down estates to the 'little boy who lives at Aberdeen' who was so impressed with his great-uncle's exploits that he took the sword to his own bedroom.

Byron was tutored in Nottingham by a local schoolmaster, Mr Rogers, an American loyalist. Treatment on his foot was renewed and an expert, Mr Lavender, was consulted. He rubbed the foot in handfuls of oil, twisted the ankle with brute force and screwed it up in a wooden vice. Mr Rogers said, 'It makes me uncomfortable, my Lord, to see you sitting there in such pain and I *know you* must be suffering.' 'Never mind, Mr Rogers,' replied Byron, 'you shall not see any signs of it in *me*.' He developed a profound dislike of Lavender, who was pompous as well as cruel, and one day he wrote out all the letters of the alphabet putting them together randomly and inventing false words and sentences. He showed them to Lavender asking him gravely what language it was. Unwilling to admit his own ignorance, and to Byron's delight, the quack replied, 'Italian.'[12]

Mrs Byron had sent May Gray to Nottingham to look after her son but she proved to be an unhappy custodian. Young and unsupervised she threw over all her early religious principles and lost her fear of hell fire. She neglected Byron, brought men into their rooms at night, forcing him to put himself to bed. During drunken frenzies she beat him so hard that even his bones ached. She encouraged Lavender in his habit of sending the boy to fetch tankards of ale from local taverns and made him pay for them with counterfeit sixpences which Lavender had made.

When Mrs Byron was told of her son's sufferings at the hands of Lavender, she allowed him to visit John Hanson's family in Earls Court, London, to consult Dr Matthew Baillie, the anatomist. He commissioned yet another instrument to straighten both the leg and the foot. It was not as painful as Lavender's machine but it was difficult to force Byron to wear it and Mr Sheldrake in the Strand made him a special shoe which alleviated the more obvious limp and dragging motion.[13]

Hanson persuaded the Earl of Carlisle, a remote cousin, to become Byron's guardian.[14] He consented reluctantly. Both Lord Carlisle and Hanson agreed it would be better if Byron was removed from his mother's volatile influence and with her agreement he was sent to Dr Glennie's school in Lordship Lane, Dulwich, then a small village 7 miles outside London. Byron became very bored repeating the work he had done in Aberdeen but Dr Glennie found him 'playful, goodhumoured, and beloved by his companions. His reading in history and poetry was far beyond the usual standard of his age.'

Unable to stay away from her son Mrs Byron rented a house in Sloane Terrace and, against Dr Glennie's advice, she brought the boy home for weekends and sometimes longer periods. Dr Glennie disapproved of the young people she introduced to Byron. 'How could she?' he exclaimed. 'Mrs Byron was a total stranger to English society and English manners; with an exterior far from prepossessing, an understanding where nature had not been bountiful, a mind almost wholly without cultivation and the peculiarities of northern opinions, northern habits and northern accent. I trust I do no great prejudice to my country-women if I say Mrs Byron was not endowed with powers to retrieve the fortune, and form the character and manners, of a young nobleman, her son.'[15]

On several occasions Dr Glennie argued with Mrs Byron but, unlike her son, her rages were not silent and she broke out into such loud fits of temper that it was impossible for the other children and servants not to be aware of what was going on. Dr Glennie heard a pupil remark, 'Byron, your mother is a fool,' to which the downcast boy replied glumly, 'I know it.' Lord Carlisle refused to put up with such outbursts and withdrew all contact with Mrs Byron. To Dr Glennie's last appeal to mediate he said, 'I can have nothing more to do with Mrs Byron – you must now manage her as you can.' However, he did not leave her to starve and when she was in financial distress he supported the petition to the king which Hanson had drawn up and on 2 October 1799 George III signed a warrant for the grant of an annuity of £300 back-dated to 5 July.[16]

May Gray's services were now no longer required and she returned to Scotland; it was not until after she had left that the full enormities of her behaviour in Nottingham were revealed. Hanson gently drew from Byron the details of her sluttish, drunken occupations but more horrible than these confessions was the revelation that she had been in the habit of coming into his bed and sexually abusing him.[17] As a parting gift, presumably at the instruction of his mother, Byron gave her a full-length miniature of himself and a watch. This early lesson in dual standards must have puzzled him.[18]

When he was twelve Byron fell in love with another cousin, thirteen-year-old Margaret Parker. He described her as 'one of the most beautiful evanescent beings'. Two years later she fell ill with consumption and died. Byron spent Christmas with the Hansons and in the New Year Hanson accompanied him to Harrow to meet the headmaster, Dr Joseph Drury. Lord Carlisle believed that Harrow was a suitable school and Hanson secured £500 for Mrs Byron to cover the fees. Byron entered the school after the Easter holidays.

Lord Carlisle summoned Dr Drury to London a few months later to discuss his ward's financial prospects and to find out how he was progressing. Dr Drury made no comment on the financial state of his pupil but on his progress he said, 'He has talents, my Lord, which will *add lustre to his rank.*' 'Indeed!' exclaimed his lordship, giving Dr Drury the unpleasant feeling that Lord Carlisle had hoped for a different reply.[19]

Looking back on his childhood Byron remembered with astonishment the intensity of his feelings towards the sufferings he endured because of his foot; 'My poor mother, and after her my school-fellows, by their taunts, led me to consider my lameness as the greatest misfortune, and I have never been able to conquer this feeling.' He compensated at school by being haughty, quick to take offence and overly impressed with his newly inherited title. He took refuge in solitude and was often seen sitting alone with a book on a grave near Harrow church. He discovered the pleasure of swimming and used to go on horseback to swim in the pool called the duck puddle 2 miles from Harrow.[20]

Although Byron was not unhappy at school he was not convinced that boarding schools were the right way to educate boys; indeed, it was his account of his life at Harrow which later influenced Lady Byron to refuse to allow their grandsons to attend one. He later wrote,

One of the most striking results of the English system of education is, that while in no country are there so many instances of manly friendships early formed and steadily maintained, so in no other country, perhaps, are the feelings towards the parental home so early

estranged, or at best, feebly cherished. Transplanted as boys are from
the domestic circle, at a time of life when the affections are most
disposed to cling, it is but natural that they should seek a substitute for
the ties of home in those boyish friendships which they form at school,
and which, connected as they are with the scenes and events over
which youth threw its charm, retain ever after the strongest hold upon
their hearts.[21]

Byron's principal school friends were 'P. Hunter, Curzon, Long and
Tattersall,' while, 'Clare, Dorset, Charles Gordon, De Bath, Claridge, and
John Wingfield were my juniors and favourites, whom I spoilt by
indulgence'.

With this in mind it might seem strange that Byron should later put his
natural daughter Allegra into a convent school at the young age of four,
but at the time he feared for her safety in Ravenna which was a hotbed of
Carbonari uprisings. He justified his action by saying he had 'no reason
to look upon my own personal safety as particularly insurable; and I
thought the infant best out of harm's way, for the present.'

Hanson found a tenant for Newstead, Lord Grey de Ruthyn, who
signed a lease which covered the rest of Byron's minority and included a
clause which allowed Byron to hunt, fish, course and shoot on the estate.
Grey also extended an invitation to his landlord to stay at Newstead
during his vacations should he wish.

In July 1803 Mrs Byron moved to Burgage Manor in Southwell, a town
not far from Newstead, but Byron found life there dull and took up Lord
Grey's offer to stay at the abbey.

He had met Mary Ann Chaworth, great-niece of William Chaworth, the
dead duellist, soon after he arrived from Scotland and, with time on his
hands, he rode to her home at nearby Annesley Hall to renew their
acquaintance. Her mother made him welcome and he soon became a
regular visitor.

He liked to sit in the rose-garden, under Mary's sitting-room windows,
fantasizing about the Chaworth–Byron duel and comparing their past to
that of Romeo and Juliet. He walked with her in the French garden and
lingered on the terraced walk with its heavy stone balustrade and
sculptured urns. He showed off by shooting holes in a wooden door and
had already begun to cultivate his reputation for oddity by carrying a pair
of the Wicked Lord's pistols in his pocket.

Mary's mother organized an outing to Castleton Caves in Derbyshire.
The caves are deep and dark with a river running through them and the
only way to cross the river is by a boat which can hold only two people
lying down side by side. Byron shared Mary's boat and never forgot the

intense sensations of pain and pleasure he experienced at being so close to her and said they were so profound, he could never describe them adequately.

The seventeen-year-old Mary Chaworth soon became irritated by the silent adoration offered to her by the fat fifteen-year-old schoolboy. She thought he was self-satisfied and found his vanity offensive, especially after he had told her, several times, he was a good-looking fellow. She was looking forward to her marriage to John Muster of nearby Colwick Hall. Muster rode, fenced, boxed, played tennis, swam, shot and played cricket. Quite a contrast to the love-sick schoolboy.[22]

The six-week summer dream ended abruptly when Byron heard that Mary had remarked to her maid, 'Do you think I could care anything for that lame boy?' Although it was late at night he instantly dashed out of the house and, without clearly knowing where he was going, ran and did not stop until he found himself at Newstead.[23]

Byron wrote to his mother imploring her not to send him back to Harrow and to let him stay for one more day. On 4 October Mrs Byron wrote desperately to the school, 'The truth is, I cannot get him to return to school, though I have done all in my power for six weeks past. He has no indisposition that I know of, but love, desperate love, the worst of all maladies in my opinion.' She wrote to Hanson on 7 November, 'Byron is really so unhappy that I have agreed much against my inclination, to let him remain in this County till after the next holydays.'[24] Byron did not return to school until January 1804.

In November Lord Grey invited him to Newstead and on moon-lit nights they amused themselves by shooting roosting pheasants. Despite a difference of almost seven years they got on so surprisingly well that Byron intended to prolong his stay until after his birthday, but something occurred that so horrified and disgusted him that he left Newstead vowing never to have anything more to do with Lord Grey. He never revealed the cause of the break saying that it was far too serious a subject to talk about. It might have been because Grey made unacceptable advances to him, or that he was disgusted by Grey's robust debauchery with the servant girls, or, more probable, that he suspected Grey of having designs on his mother. He had noticed that she was flattered by Grey's attentions, and occasionally flirted with him; Byron knew she had lied about her age and he feared she might be in love. Mrs Byron was confused by her son's mysterious behaviour but he continued to be rude to Grey despite her threats and stormy tempers. Lord Grey remained unaware of his offence and Byron never enlightened him. He said the only person he could have told the secret to was his half-sister Augusta.

Augusta had been brought up by her maternal grandmother at Eckington, north of Chesterfield and it was not until after the old lady's death in 1801 that Mrs Byron dared to contact her to try to make an opening in the charmed aristocratic circle for her son. Lady Holderness had considered Mrs Byron uncouth and there had been no contact between half-brother and sister since infancy. They met again at General William Harcourt's house in Portman Place during one of Augusta's visits to London. They enchanted each other. Augusta soon became his confidante and a friend who could be relied on to side with him against his mother. Flighty and a gossip, she told him of a visit she had made to Margaret Parker, and how the dying girl blushed to the roots of her hair at the mention of his name.[25] Byron, who knew nothing of her death, was deeply shocked.

In November 1804 Mrs Byron's friendship with Lord Grey seemed serious and Byron looked on it with distaste. He did not want to spend Christmas anywhere near them or Southwell and he appealed to Augusta for help. She contrived that he should spend it in London with the Hansons, explaining that it would give him the opportunity to see his guardian Lord Carlisle. In January she told Hanson, 'Lord Carlisle was *very much* pleased with my brother, and I am sure, from what he said to me at Castle Howard, is disposed to show him all the kindness in his power. I know you are so partial to Byron and so much interested in all that concerns him, that you will rejoice almost as much as I do that his acquaintance with Lord C. is renewed. In the mean time it is a great comfort for me to think that he has spent his Holydays so comfortably and so much to his wishes.'[26] Byron was in London from 5 December, not returning to Harrow until February, and during those weeks he tasted London life and London vices, sowed wild oats and made his first sorties into sensual pleasure. After an episode with one young woman, Ellen, he was inspired to write

> Oh! might I kiss those eyes of fire,
>   A million scarce would quench desire:
> Still would I steep my lips in bliss,
>   And dwell an age on every kiss:
> Nor then my kiss should sated be;
>   Still would I kiss and cling to thee;
> Nought should my kiss from thine dissever:
>   Still would we kiss and kiss for ever;
> E'en though the numbers did exceed
>   The yellow harvest's countless seed.
> To part would be a vain endeavour:
>   Could I desist? – ah! never – never!

Mrs Byron had hoped he would spend his seventeenth birthday at home but Byron disappointed her and returned directly to Harrow. She knew Augusta was undermining her influence and attempted unsuccessfully to break the alliance but, unknown to her, and with the help of Hanson, they contrived to meet again in London at the end of July before Byron returned to Southwell.

Byron sympathized with Augusta's courtship with their cousin, George Leigh, and wished her happiness although he was scathing of love itself. Leigh, the son of Frances Leigh, at whose house in Valenciennes Jack Byron had died, was a colonel in the 10th Light Dragoons and cut a great dash. General Charles Leigh, his father, considered Augusta's income too small and opposed the marriage but she resolutely clung to her desire to marry George, facing down opposition from almost everyone including Mrs Byron, whose experience with handsome, penniless young men should have been heeded.

Augusta was attractive, and had a strong family likeness to the Carlisles. Her large eyes were set in a long oval face, with full lips, good teeth and a slightly receding chin. Her small head was covered with dark brown hair which fell round her long neck and fashionably sloping shoulders. She was a striking and interesting-looking girl with a good ear for music, a pretty voice and a fine though freckled complexion. She was shy and gentle with strangers but considered lively and impudent when at ease. Lady Harriet Cavendish thought she was 'a tall, reserved, alarmed lady' who lacked spirit, and considered her romance with the dashing George Leigh a bit of a joke. She sympathized with her sister Lady Georgiana Morpeth one day, 'for your being left with Miss Byron . . . which in point of insipidity must be cosa da morire'.[27]

In 1807 the Prince of Wales gave George a house and the duty of running his stud based at Six Mile Bottom just outside Newmarket. This enabled Augusta Byron and George Leigh to be married on 17 August and move to Cambridgeshire and into the long rambling house that was their new home.

Three months later Lady Harriet Cavendish reported to her sister, 'Colonel Leigh is said to be always in Town and it is another subject upon which people are tempted to be ill-natured, but to be sure with some reason, for he certainly is "le moins marié que possible" and everybody, excepting his wife, meets him at every place in England save Six Mile Bottom.'[28]

Byron moved into his rooms at Trinity College in October 1805 and for the first few days felt very lonely, but he soon began to enjoy the independence. He ordered wine and furniture, had his portrait painted wearing his elaborate university gown and kept a servant and a horse. All these luxuries were paid for by Mrs Byron with the £500 she had been awarded from the Court of Chancery to pay for his school fees and which she now handed over to him completely. She applied for an increase from the Civil List to cover the loss of the £500 but was refused and her pension was reduced by £200. She pathetically told Hanson that even in her reduced circumstances her house 'will always be a home for my son whenever he chooses to come to it'.[29]

By November Byron had worked himself into a rage because his mother had not paid for his furniture, gown and books and would not allow him to have his rooms papered and painted over the Christmas break. When it seemed likely that she might come to Cambridge to clear things up he told Hanson he would risk rustication or expulsion from the university rather than meet her.

Determined to emphasize his independence he took rooms at 16 Piccadilly with Mrs Elizabeth Massingberd, a widow living with her daughter, who had let rooms to Mrs Byron in the past. On 27 December Byron wrote to Augusta saying he had been extravagant and consequently was in need of money. Although he would not take any from her, he would be grateful if she would agree to stand joint security with him for a couple of hundred pounds from moneylenders. He forbade her to tell Hanson, his mother or Lord Carlisle what he was doing or the extent of his debts. Augusta eventually went to Lord Carlisle for advice, but he did not want to know anything about it and told her to contact Hanson; but by this time it was too late. Byron was in the hands of the moneylenders with Mrs Massingberd and her daughter standing as security for him and gaining a handsome profit for themselves.

With his borrowed money Byron paid off a few creditors and then wrote an insulting letter to his mother informing her that he intended to leave Cambridge and travel abroad. The wretched woman wrote to Hanson, 'I beg you will not mention to my son, having heard from me, but try to get out of him his reason for wishing to leave England, and where he got the money. I much fear he has fallen into bad hands.'[30] Byron remained in London squandering the money on women, taking fencing lessons from his former fencing master from Harrow, Henry Angelo, and sparring with Gentleman Jackson, the famous boxer. Stories of his exploits reached Southwell and Mrs Byron became distraught with worry. She saw Byron following his father's path, ending in penury and an early grave. 'That boy will be the death of me, and drive me mad! Where can he get hundreds? Has he got into the hands of moneylenders? He has no feeling, no heart.'[31] Mrs Byron was right to worry; Byron told John Pigot that he regularly patronized a French 'entremetteuse' and 'the adventures of my life from sixteen to nineteen and the dissipation into which I have been thrown in London have given a voluptuous tint to my ideas.' He vigorously played the field and used these experiences in his poetry. He celebrated the charms of Ellen, Caroline, Mary Chaworth, Marion, Eliza, Julia Leacock and several unidentified ladies.

Byron's friendship with Elizabeth and John Pigot had begun a little over a year before when Mrs Byron invited them with a group of young people to her home in an attempt to help Byron make friends of his own age. He was shy and refused to come down to meet them until he had been sent for three times. Elizabeth described him as a fat, bashful boy who wore his hair combed straight over his forehead. He was stiff and formal at first but after she broke the ice with a joke his face lit up, his handsome mouth displayed a broad grin, and all his shyness with the Pigot family vanished forever. They lived just across the Green from Burgage Manor and Byron sometimes sought sanctuary there when he wanted to escape from his mother. He played cricket and swam with John. One day the pair borrowed a thimble from Elizabeth and amused themselves for hours by throwing it in the deepest part of the river and taking turns to retrieve it.[32]

Byron's prowess at swimming enabled him to save the life of a drowning fifteen-year-old choirboy, John Edleston, whom he dragged out of the Cam. Edleston was exactly to the hour two years younger than Byron, the same height, very thin with a fair complexion, dark eyes and light-coloured hair. They became great friends and although they met almost every day they never tired of each other's company. Byron compared their friendship to that of David and Jonathan.[33] Before leaving Cambridge to begin work in the family business in London Edleston gave him a small cornelian which Byron passed to Elizabeth Pigot for safe-keeping.

Byron occasionally rode out to see Mary Chaworth, who treated him like a younger brother, teasing and laughing at him but it was not a joke to him. He later claimed that no one could guess the depth of emotion he felt. Mrs Byron found Byron's series of unrequited loves amusing and a year or so after his last meeting with Mary Chaworth she came into the room where he was entertaining the Pigots and said, 'I have some news for you.'

'Well, what is it?' he replied.

'Take out your handkerchief first, you will want it,' she said.

'Nonsense.' He did it anyway to humour her.

'Miss Chaworth is married.'

He pushed his handkerchief into his pocket saying with affected nonchalance, 'Is that all?'

'Why, I expected you would have been plunged in grief!' she persisted. Byron said nothing for a moment then changed the subject.

She inflicted a similar piece of cruelty in announcing the marriage of Mary Duff. 'Oh, Byron,' she said, 'I have had a letter from Edinburgh, from Miss Abercromby, and your old sweetheart, Mary Duff, is married to a Mr Robert Cockburn.'[34] The announcement visibly affected Byron to the extent that it alarmed her, but not enough to prevent her repeating the news all over Southwell.

In early August 1806 Byron sparked off a massive maternal explosion which took place in front of the entire Pigot family, including the dog.[35] The precise cause of the row is unknown but Byron's technique in similar circumstances was either to leave the house immediately or to display dumb insolence, bowing to his mother the more deeply the higher her voice rose. With help from the Pigots Byron escaped to the Massingberds and as soon as he arrived at 16 Piccadilly he wrote to his school friend Edward Long suggesting they go on holiday together. Before he had received a reply his mother arrived in London. Despite their differences they loved and cared for each other. The Southwell apothecary used to tell the story of how one evening, after a violent quarrel, they had both come to see him asking if the other had been to buy poison and forbidding him to sell it. After a week Mrs Byron returned to Southwell and Byron joined the Longs at Littlehampton where he spent many hours swimming, often carrying Edward's younger brother Henry on his shoulders. They passed the time target shooting, aiming at oyster shells, playing cricket, making Henry run for the balls while Byron annoyingly called him 'young shaver'.

Byron spent a few days holiday in September at Harrogate with John Pigot who was studying medicine at Edinburgh University. The pair stayed at the Crown Inn and dined in the public room but retired to their room each evening soon after dinner. They made few acquaintances because Byron was so shy. Harrogate was crowded and Pigot decided to go to the ball-night for an hour or so to look over the local ladies, but he could not persuade Byron to go with him. Pigot wrote, 'Few people understood Byron; but I know that he had naturally a kind and feeling heart, and that there was not a single spark of malice in his composition.'[36]

The fashionable rage among the young was amateur dramatics. 'How do our theatricals proceed?' Pigot asked his sister. 'Lord Byron can say *all* his part and I *most* of mine. He certainly acts it inimitably. Lord B. is now *poetising*, and, since he has been here, has written some very pretty verses. He is very good in trying to amuse me as much as possible but it is not in my nature to be happy without either female society or study. . . .'

The actors in Southwell were anxious for the return of the travellers and John received a letter with the message:

Tell Lord Byron that, if any accident should retard his return, his mother desires he will write to her, and she shall be miserable if he does not arrive the day he fixes. . . . Till Lord Byron returns, nothing can be done; and positively he must not be later than Tuesday or Wednesday.[37]

Byron had promised to write the prologue for the play and he set to work as the carriage left Chesterfield and by the time they reached Mansfield it was complete. A leading citizen of Southwell, Mr Leacroft, offered his drawing room, converted into a neat theatre, and the long awaited performances took place at the end of September with Julia Leacroft taking a prominent part and flirting wildly with Byron. He enjoyed acting and repeatedly drew applause for his performances. His shyness had vanished and he attended assemblies and dinner parties and even felt hurt if he heard of a rout to which he had not been invited, though he still retained a horror of new faces and if he saw strangers approaching the Pigots' door he would instantly jump out of the window to avoid them.

He was on terms of playful familiarity with his mother now that they were seeing less of each other and he used to call her affectionately 'Kitty Gordon'. At the height of the theatrical rage he threw open the door of the drawing room with a flourish exclaiming, 'Enter, the Honorable Kitty.'[38]

On a summer evening in 1806 Elizabeth Pigot was reading aloud passages of poetry by Robert Burns when Byron suddenly blurted out that he too composed poetry and immediately wrote out in pencil the lines beginning, 'In thee I fondly hop'd to clasp'. From that moment the desire to appear in print took possession of him. He visited John Ridge a printer in Newark, asked Elizabeth and John to help him and swore them to secrecy. Elizabeth was to deal with the printer and John was to pass on to Ridge the poems as he received them from Byron. A set of poems for Ridge came with the message, 'to be printed separate from my other compositions, as you will perceive them to be improper for the perusal of ladies; of course, none of the females of your family must see them.'[39]

In November John Ridge had completed his work on the small volume of verse now called *Fugitive Pieces*. One of the first people to receive a copy was the Reverend John Thomas Becher, Vicar of Rumpton and Midsomer Norton, Nottinghamshire, a relative of Mrs Pigot and friend of Byron's. His reaction was swift. The stanzas addressed 'to Mary' were too full-blooded, particularly the verse beginning,

> Now, By my soul, 'tis most delight
>   To view each other panting, dying,
> In love's *extatic posture* lying,
>   Grateful to *feeling*, as to sight.

Becher urged Byron to recall all the copies and cancel the whole impression. Byron accepted the advice and arranged for all the copies that had already been sent out to be returned and destroyed. John Pigot tore out the relevant page and kept his copy, but to Byron's amusement Becher, who had volunteered to oversee the burning, did not commit his own copy to the flames. The revised edition, called *Poems on Various Occasions*, was published early in January. Byron sent a copy to John Pigot, commenting that this version was 'vastly correct and miraculously chaste'.

The poems were eagerly read in Southwell and they sparked off an orgy of speculation. Whisperers said Byron kept a mistress in the house in the Bullpit and made clandestine visits to her on horseback. The identity of Mary was never made public but the Pigots believed they could identify her. Byron strenuously denied the source of his inspiration for Mary was a local girl, claiming instead that the original was someone he knew in London who had given him her portrait and a long strand of golden hair.[40]

Byron often recorded special events and landmarks in his life in poetry. In 1807 he wrote 'To My Son!' Even his friend and careful biographer Thomas Moore remarked that 'it is not easy to suppose a poem so full of natural tenderness, to have been indebted for its origin to imagination alone'.[41]

> Those flaxen locks, those eyes of blue,
>   Bright as thy mother's in their hue;
> Those rosy lips, whose dimples play
>   And smile to steal the heart away.
> Recall a scene of former joy,
>   And touch thy Father's heart, my boy!
>
> And thou canst lisp a father's name –
>   Ah, William, were thine own the same,
> No self-reproach – but, let me cease –
>   My care for thee shall purchase peace;
> Thy mother's shade shall smile in joy,
>   And pardon all the past, my boy!

Her lowly grave the turf has prest,
   And thou hast known a stranger's breast.
Derision sneers upon thy birth,
   And yields thee scarce a name on earth;
Yet shall not these one hope destroy, –
   A father's heart is thine, my Boy!

Why, let the world unfeeling frown;
   Must I fond Nature's claims disown?
Ah, no – though moralist reprove,
   I hail thee, dearest child of Love,
Fair cherub, pledge of youth and joy –
   A Father guards thy birth my boy.

Oh, twill be sweet in thee to trace,
   Ere age has wrinkled o'er my face,
Ere half my glass of life is run,
   At once a brother and a son;
And all my wane of years employ
   In justice done to thee, my Boy!

Although so young thy heedless sire,
   Youth will not damp parental fire;
And, wert thou still less dear to me,
   While Helen's form revives in thee,
The breast, which beat to former joy,
   Will ne'er desert its pledge, my Boy!

Moore said that the only circumstance he knew that bore even remotely on the subject of the poem took place in 1805 when Byron approached his mother with an unusual request. He asked her to look after the bastard child of a friend who had died in January. The putative father, George Curzon, a fellow Harrovian, had been unaware of the girl's condition and she did not discover it herself until after his death; but she immediately rallied and declared Byron as the father. He emphatically denied the accusation, claiming that all he wanted was to ensure the child was brought up carefully and well looked after. Mrs Byron meekly agreed, a surprisingly altruistic gesture from a woman known for her volatile nature, short of money and in 1805 seriously at odds with her son. Moore's informant pointed out, 'such a request might well have discomposed a temper more mild than Mrs Byron's'. On the other hand it might have been the most sensible course for a woman whose under-age son had fathered a child.

Moore was told the baby died immediately after birth, but according to Byron's poem it was the mother Helen who died. The name Helen is very similar to Ellen, the name of the young girl whose kisses enraptured him in 1804. If baby William of the poem survived and passed into Mrs Byron's care, she could have had him fostered immediately by an honest couple living well away from Newstead, all the arrangements being made through friends or lawyers. However, as Byron speaks of a child that can 'lisp a father's name', it looks as though William was still in Mrs Byron's care when he was two years old or slightly older. She was either not able to find a suitable couple or she wanted to keep him a little longer, but it seems likely that he was fostered out in 1807 and the event was commemorated in Byron's usual fashion, by a poem.

Byron was gaining the reputation for kissing and telling and in January 1807 he fell foul of the influential Leacroft family. He had flirted and teased their daughter Julia, along with most of the Southwell girls, but Julia had taken his attentions seriously and led him to the brink of indiscretion before he saw her trap and withdrew. The Leacrofts, not without reason, accused him of giving her false hopes and damaging her reputation.[42] Captain John Leacroft, Julia's brother, called to ask his intentions and his father wrote an abusive letter. This incident permanently soured Byron's opinion of Southwell and ensured that in future he viewed the mothers of marriageable daughters with circumspection.

In April Byron congratulated John Pigot on passing his first medical examination adding, 'Since we met, I have reduced myself by violent exercise, *much* physic, and *hot* bathing, from 14 stone 6 pounds to 12 stone 7 pounds. In all I have lost 27 pounds, Bravo! – what say you?'[43] This was no mean accomplishment. He had inherited the tendency to put on weight from his mother and had been a fat adolescent. He achieved his weight loss by playing cricket daily while dressed in seven waistcoats and a greatcoat, then taking a hot bath. He ate only a quarter of a pound of red meat in any twenty-four hours, drank no beer and only a little wine. He took quantities of laxatives. His ribs surfaced and his clothes had to be taken in by nearly half a yard. Many of his Cambridge friends did not at first recognize the slim Byron – even Edleston walked past him in the street.

He completed his new collection of poems, *Hours of Idleness*, and left Southwell for Cambridge intending to pay his debts and leave the university. 'I do not know what to say about Byron's returning to Cambridge. When he was there, I believe he did nothing but drink, gamble and spend money,'[44] his desperate mother wrote to Hanson.

According to Ridge, seventy-five copies of *Hours of Idleness* had been sold and an order placed for fifty more. 'In every bookseller's window I see my own name and say nothing, but enjoy my fame in secret,' wrote Byron. 'So much for *egotism!* My *laurels* have turned my brain, but the *cooling acids* of forthcoming criticism will probably restore me to *modesty.*' Sales of the book continued to be amazingly good and Byron was encouraged by Crosby, Ridge's London agent. Mrs Byron proudly sent copies to Augusta, Lord Carlisle and Mr Beardall, a tenant on the Newstead estate. It is unlikely that Lord Carlisle ever saw the poems as Augusta told Hanson, 'I have never had the courage to shew them to Lord Carlisle for fear of his disapproving others.'[45] Read them or not, Carlisle wrote a gracious letter of thanks to the young poet who was sufficiently impressed to tell Elizabeth Pigot.

Byron continued losing weight and by the autumn when he returned to Cambridge, he weighed 10 stone 11 pounds, making him 3 stone 9 pounds lighter than he had been six months earlier. Disgruntled that the rules of Trinity College prevented him keeping his new bulldog, Smut, in his chambers he bought a tame bear, quartering it in the small hexagonal tower above his rooms. He took it for walks on a chain like a dog, enjoying the expressions on the faces of the passers-by.[46]

It was during this period in Cambridge that he met John Cam Hobhouse, Charles Skinner Matthews, Scrope Berdmore Davies, Francis Hodgson, and William Bankes forming friendships that lasted until his death.

He had been forewarned that the *Edinburgh Review* was about to print a damaging review of *Hours of Idleness*, and he wrote immediately to Becher asking him to prepare his mother for the worst. It was indeed a venomous attack and Mrs Byron felt it deeply. Byron pretended he was untouched but he was wounded to the quick. However, he claimed that after he had drunk three bottles of claret and written twenty lines of verse he felt much better.[47]

In the spring of 1808 he renewed his friendship with Gentleman Jackson and surrendered himself to a life of dissipation. He managed to break off whoring and gambling long enough to visit Harrow and take his MA degree at Cambridge. He hired rooms in Brompton for his mistress, Miss Cameron, and in July she accompanied him to Brighton with Scrope Davies and Hobhouse. A seaside holiday must have seemed very inviting that summer when temperatures were the highest ever recorded in England. From 11 July to the 19th the thermometer dropped below 80 degrees Fahrenheit only once and on the famous Hot Wednesday it climbed to 99 degrees.

To avoid rumours reaching his mother, Byron disguised Miss Cameron as a boy and introduced her as Gordon, his younger brother. This ruse fooled very few people and Lady Perceval suspected the real nature of the relationship when Miss Cameron replied to her exclamation of 'What a pretty horse that is you are riding!' by 'Yes, it was *gave* me by my brother!'[48]

The young men devised a game to amuse Miss Cameron but she cheated and Byron spoke sharply to her. She rose to leave the room threatening to kill herself. 'Stop a minute, madam,' said Byron ringing the bell to call Fletcher, his new valet. 'Place a bottle of laudanum, and my Turkish dagger on Miss Gordon's dressing table and fasten a rope to the top of the bedpost.' He turned to the sobbing girl, 'Now, madam, you have your choice of deaths.' Furiously she sat down again whining, 'You want me to kill myself, and I won't!'

Lord Grey de Ruthyn's lease on Newstead had expired in June and by September Byron was back. He managed to delay his mother's arrival by having some of the rooms renovated and persuading her that it would be both improper and uncomfortable to move in before the work was complete.

The new Mrs Chaworth-Muster gave a dinner party at Annesley in November and invited Hobhouse and Byron. He was shocked at the strength of his emotions when he saw Mary and she shared his disquiet. They both behaved so awkwardly that people looked at them in surprise. Byron received an even greater emotional shock when he saw Mary's child and within days he had recorded his feelings.

> When late I saw thy favourite child,
>   I thought my jealous heart would break:
> But when the unconscious infant smiled,
>   I kiss'd it for its mother's sake.

The lure of foreign travel gripped him. He made his will, placed his property in the hands of trustees and told his mother, 'If I do not travel now, I never shall, and all men should one day or another. I have at present no connections to keep me at home; no wife, or unprovided sister, brothers, &c. I shall take care of you and when I return I may possibly become a politician.'[49]

He instructed Hanson to sell some of his assets and unrealistically ordered all his debts be paid, but when he received Hanson's depressing financial report he declared he was undecided whether to blow his brains out or marry a Golden Dolly. Mrs Byron had no doubts: 'I wish to God he would exert himself and retrieve his affairs. He must marry a woman of *fortune* this spring; love matches is all nonsense. Let him make use of the talents God has given him. He is an English Peer, and has all the privileges of that station.'[50]

Byron spent the whole of December at Newstead alone apart from the servants, with nothing to do except lounge on the sofa and read. 'Poor soul!' said Nanny Smith, 'he could not go out much with the men; all the comfort he had was to be a little with the lasses.' His attention was diverted by one of the housemaids, Lucy, a pretty, under-age girl from Warwickshire, who became his special companion and pet. Lucy, like Julia Leacroft, read more into his favours than he intended. According to the housekeeper, Nanny Smith, Lucy hoped one day to become Lady Byron. She was encouraged in this fantasy by a squint-eyed fortune teller who told her, for two shillings and sixpence, to hold up her head and 'look high' for she would come to great things. As a sign of his approval Byron gave her a long gold chain. She confided to Nanny Smith, believing her future was assured, that if she became a lady and mistress of the abbey she would be a good friend to her.[51]

Bored with dalliance Byron ordered the flagstones in the cloister to be lifted, convinced that the monks had buried money. The unwilling servants dug but found only stone coffins full of bones. One of the coffins was placed in the great hall and several skulls were cleaned and put in his bedroom where Nanny Smith said they seemed to grin at her when she went in at night to close his windows.

In January 1809 he instructed Hanson to make preparations for the tenants on the estate to celebrate his coming of age. Quantities of ale were laid in and arrangements made to roast an entire ox. Byron spent his birthday in London and later recalled that 'the day I came of age I dined on eggs and bacon and a bottle of ale – For once in a way they are my favourite dish and drinkable; but as neither of them agree with me, I never use them but on great jubilees.'[52]

Mrs Byron commented glumly to Hanson, 'I was very sorry to hear of the great expense the Newstead *fête* would put him to. I can see nothing but the road to ruin in all this, which grieves me to the heart and makes me still worse than I would otherwise be (unless, indeed, coal mines turn to gold mines), or that he mends his fortune in the old and usual way by marrying a woman with two or three hundred pounds.'[53]

Byron continued his preparations to leave England, instructing Hanson to discharge the cook and laundry maid but 'the other two I shall retain to take care of the house, more especially as the youngest is pregnant (I need not tell you by whom) and I cannot have the girl on the parish.' He had already told Hobhouse that 'Lucinda is pregnant'. In February he countermanded his instruction to Hanson to arrange for Lucy to receive an annuity of £100. 'Lucy's annuity may be reduced to fifty pounds and the other fifty go to the Bastard.' Bastards were the responsibility of the parish where they were born and many tended to throw the mother out as soon as her condition was noticeable. The father could keep his name out of the parish records if he arranged to give the girl enough to keep her and the child before her condition came to the attention of the parish overseers. The Byrons were not unfamiliar with the system. A bastardy order had been served in Nottingham on the poet's uncle, George Byron, some thirty years earlier by Mary Goddard the mother of his daughter.

Once settled in London Byron wrote to Lord Carlisle asking if he would introduce him in the House of Lords. He replied courteously to his ward explaining the technicalities of taking a seat, but did not offer to introduce him. Byron, always quick to take offence, saw the reply as an insult.

Anxious to have the satire he had been working on since the autumn published, he turned to Robert Dallas, a distant relative. Dallas had approached him the year before with a flattering letter to which Byron had replied, 'Your name and connection with our family have been long known to me, and I hope your person will not be less so.'[54] Without waiting for another invitation he called on Byron. Dallas had been educated in Scotland, read law at the Inner Temple and travelled in France and America before returning to England where he now earned a living translating books on the French Revolution. He had published two volumes of poetry and had the necessary experience in publishing to help Byron. They agreed the title of the satire should be *English Bards and Scotch Reviewers*. Still smarting from what he considered to be a rebuff from Lord Carlisle Byron added to the satire the lines

> Lord, hymnster, petit-maître, pamphleteer!
>   So dull in youth, so drivelling in age,
> His scenes alone had damned our sinking stage.

In the second edition he added the even more vicious lines:

> No Muse will cheer with renovating smile
>   The paralytic puling of CARLISLE . . .

When he heard that the earl suffered from a nervous disorder and these lines might appear to refer to it, he regretted his action saying, 'I thank heaven I did not know it – and would not, could not, if I had. I must naturally be the last person to be pointed on defects or maladies.'[55]

The new edition was published under his name, not anonymously as the first had been.

Dallas was strolling down St James's Street on 13 March when he saw

Byron's carriage waiting at the door. He entered, Byron shook his hand, 'I am glad you happened to come in: I am going to take my seat, perhaps you will go with me.' Dallas noticed Byron was pale with a look of mortification mixed with indignation on his face as he entered the House of Lords. After the oath had been administered, the Lord Chancellor, Lord Eldon, left his seat and with a smile went to shake his hand. Byron bowed stiffly placing only the tips of his fingers into the chancellor's hand. Dallas was surprised at his cold reaction and Byron explained, 'If I had shaken hands heartily, he would have set me down for one of his party – but I will have nothing to do with any of them on either side; I have taken my seat, and now I will go abroad.'[56] He remained in a bad temper through the journey back to St James's.

He returned to Newstead intending to enjoy himself. He invited Hobhouse, Matthews, Wedderburn Webster, Scrope Davies and John Becher to join him and hired monks' habits complete with false tonsures, ropes of beads and crosses from a theatrical costumier. Nanny Smith said that there were sometimes as many as seven high-spirited young men in the abbey at once. They began the day at ten with breakfast which sometimes lasted four hours. In the afternoon they read, fenced, played at single-stick or shuttlecock in the great room or practised with pistols, walked, rode, played cricket, sailed on the lake, played with the bear or teased the wolf. They ate again between seven and eight, enjoying the fine French wines their host had promised. After dinner they passed round a human skull mounted in silver and filled with burgundy. Tea was served a few hours later followed by a supper of sandwiches. They retired to bed beween one and three o'clock in the morning to rise at ten and begin all over again.[57]

The favourite time to dress up and play the buffoon all over the house was at dusk, between dinner and tea. Matthews nicknamed Byron 'The Abbot' and consistently teased the serious Hobhouse. One evening, dressed in his monk's robes, Matthews hid in one of the stone coffins which lined the long gallery. A few minutes later Hobhouse walked through alone, holding a candle in his hand. The flickering flame threw grotesque shadows on the stone walls and as he passed the coffin Matthews let out a sepulchral groan, rose silently and blew out the candle. Unknown to the others, Byron's page, Rushton, was also in costume and under orders to haunt the house. He was so successful in scaring everyone that Byron had difficulty in stopping one of his guests taking a pot shot at him.

The young men's harmless jokes and high spirits were later translated into stories of wholesale orgies, complete with skulls, virgins and ghostly monks. Byron deliberately cultivated the illusion, writing in *Childe Harold,*

> Monastic dome! condemned to uses vile!
>> Where Superstition once had made her den
> Now Paphian girls were known to sing and smile;
>> And Monks might deem their time was come agen,
> If ancient tales say true, or wrong these holy men.

When Nanny Smith was questioned about orgies she responded, 'Sometimes he had young gentlemen of his acquaintance with him, and they played some mad pranks; but nothing but what young gentlemen may do, and no harm done.'

Byron was eager to travel but he could not raise enough cash and the departure date was postponed repeatedly. He eventually borrowed the money from Scrope Davies and on 19 June 1809 he set off for Falmouth accompanied by Hobhouse and Fletcher, the farm labourer from Newstead he had hired as his valet, on the first leg of their journey to the East. Byron reassured his mother that he would write and urged her not to worry. 'The world is all before me, and I leave England without regret, and without a wish to revisit anything it contains, except *yourself* and your present residence.'[58]

CHAPTER TWO

Travel, Sorrow and Sensual Comforts

No sooner had the travellers arrived in Lisbon than they left it for Cintra, the celebrated mountain village which Byron declared to be the most beautiful in the world. With all his worries behind him, he wrote to Hodgson,

> I am very happy here, because I loves oranges, and talk bad Latin to the monks, who understand it, as it is like their own, – and I goes into society (with my pocket-pistols), and I swims in the Tagus all across at once, and I rides on an ass or a mule, and swears Portuguese and have got a diarrhoea and bites from the mosquitoes. But what of that? Comfort must not be expected by folks that go a pleasuring.[1]

He was flattered by the attentions of the Spanish beauties who vociferously appreciated his good looks and did not seem to notice his limp. In his long letters to his mother he outlined all his conquests and expressed his admiration for the ladies of Spain with their 'Long black hair, dark languishing eyes, *clear* olive complexions and forms more graceful in motion than can be conceived by an Englishman used to the drowsy listless air of his countrywomen'. In Seville he was embraced by an enthusiastic admirer who cut off a lock of his hair and presented him with one of her own – 3 feet long. In Cadiz he went to the opera with the young daughter of Admiral Cordova who was so impressed by him that she offered him Spanish lessons.

In Malta Byron fell in love with Mrs Constance Spencer Smith. She was 'very pretty, very accomplished, and extremely eccentric', and unhappily married. The 23-year-old daughter of Baron Herbert was pausing in Malta on her way to England to join her husband. She had been accused of conspiracy by the agents of Napoleon Bonaparte, imprisoned and had made her escape down a ladder dressed as a boy. Her adventures were recorded by her rescuer, the Marquis de Salvo, in his book, *Travels in the Year 1806, from Italy to England*. Such daring exploits appealed to Byron's romantic nature and he persuaded her to run off to safety with him. At the last moment the scheme was dropped as not feasible, so the couple agreed to meet the following year at Malta. The year passed, Byron's passion cooled and the urgency of the affair died away in the 'sirocco, sun and sweat'.[2] The bitter-sweet days over, he was relieved to see Constance, clutching his valuable yellow diamond ring in her hand, sail away up the Adriatic to write her memoirs in Vienna.

Ali Pasha, the despotic ruler of most of what is now modern Greece, was a very fat, bearded and blue-eyed man whose benign looks belied the extreme cruelty he meted out to his enemies; but he provided a house, food and horses for Byron and Hobhouse when they arrived at his capital city, Yanina. Byron dressed carefully for his first audience with the Pasha in 'full suit of Staff uniform with a very magnificent sabre'. He was received standing, 'a wonderful compliment from a Mussulman', but he was even more flattered by the Pasha's comment that 'he was certain I was a man of birth because I had small ears, curling hair, & little white hands'.[3]

The following days were filled with excitement and adventure. He saw the remains of Actium near the bay where Anthony lost the world and the ruins of Nicopolis, a memorial built by Augustus to celebrate his victory. He went to a Greek wedding and was caught in a storm while travelling in a Turkish ship. Fletcher, like his hosts the Turks, did not consider travelling a form of amusement and became very agitated as the ship tossed in the storm. Fearing 'a *watery* grave' he called on his wife, the Greeks called on the saints and the Muslims called on Allah. The travellers managed to get lost in the mountains for nine hours in a thunderstorm, where Fletcher alternately feared dying of hunger or being attacked by bandits. Byron enjoyed himself so much that he had no inclination to return home and made up his mind to stay away until lack of money forced him back to England. His only concerns were that his mother remained in good health and Hanson continued to supply him with money.

In December Hobhouse and Byron settled in comfortable lodgings in Athens run by Mrs Tarsia Macri, the widow of a former British vice-consul. She eked out a frugal living by letting rooms, helped by her three daughters, Mariana, Katinka, and Teresa.[4] He spent the ten weeks he was in Athens visiting ancient monuments, seeing the sights and flirting with the girls, none of whom was over fifteen. Twelve-year-old Teresa became his favourite and it was for her he composed,

> Maid of Athen, ere we part,
>   Give, oh give me back my heart!
> Or, since that has left my breast,
>   Keep it now, and take the rest!

An opportunity to visit Constantinople arose and the travellers left Piraeus on 5 March. Byron wrote to his mother from Smyrna on 19 March complaining that Fletcher had not adapted to foreign life. 'English servants,' he declared, 'are detestable travellers.' Unfavourable winds delayed their voyage and Byron took advantage of the delay to swim the Hellespont. Tides and the strong north wind beat him back on his first attempt but on 3 May when the conditions were calmer he succeeded in swimming from Sestos to Abydos, crossing the 'broad Hellespont' in an hour and ten minutes. He was very proud and told his mother, at least three times, that he had swum the Hellespont 'in humble imitation of Leander, of amorous memory'. On arriving in Constantinople he was met by the British ambassador's secretary, Stratford Canning, who accompanied him on a formal visit to the admiral of the Turkish fleet. Byron was smartly turned out, his scarlet coat richly embroidered with gold with two heavy epaulettes and feathered cocked hat, the uniform of an aide-de-camp to which, of course, he had no right.

Mrs Byron passed on the news that Lord Grey had married Anna Maria Kelman. This was greeted with a sneer, Byron promising to bring back a daughter-in-law draped in pearls no smaller than walnuts but not as large as ostrich eggs. He would have been even more scathing if he had known that Lord Grey would be dead within the year, that Anna Maria was destined to marry the Revd William Eden and that the pair were to snoop and spy on Augusta's daughters at the request of Lady Byron.

He was irritated to hear that one of his tenants, Mr Bowman, had refused to marry his pregnant girlfriend, Miss Rushton. Byron wrote severely, 'I will have no gay deceivers on my Estate, and I shall not allow my tenants a privilege I do not permit myself, viz, *that* of debauching each other's daughters. God knows, I have been guilty of many excesses, but as I have laid down a resolution to reform, and *lately* kept it, I expect this Lothario to follow the example, and begin by restoring this girl to society, or, by the Beard of my Father! he shall hear of it.'[5] Quite an outstanding example of righteous wrath from a reformed rake who was accused of fornication at seventeen and went on to debauch his servants at the age of twenty-one. He was distressed to hear that Augusta was unhappy about his attack on Lord Carlisle in *English Bards and Scotch Reviewers*. 'Poor thing,' he wrote to Mrs Byron, 'I hope she is happy.'

Hobhouse and Byron parted at Keos after a sentimental leave-taking; Hobhouse then continued on to England. Despite the recent display of affection they were glad to see the back of each other. Byron had sometimes found the goodwilled Hobhouse obtuse and humourless and Hobhouse had found Byron's pranks tiring.

On his return to Athens Byron found Peter Browne, Marquis of Sligo, an old Harrovian and friend from his Cambridge days. He was cruising round Greece in a brig which had been adapted as a private yacht. The two young men paid a visit to Veli Pasha, son of Ali Pasha, who was vastly taken by Byron and developed the unwelcome habit of throwing his arm around his waist and squeezing his hand. It was with relief that they left his hospitality behind. But a familiar situation was waiting for Byron in Athens. Mrs Macri insisted that his attentions to Teresa were more than friendly and constituted a proposal of marriage. Without pausing Byron took flight and moved to a Capuchin convent noted for its wonderful view, the Hymettus before it, the Acropolis behind, the Temple of Jove to its right, the Stadium in front and the town to the left. 'Eh, Sir, there's a situation, there's your picturesque! nothing like that, Sir, in Lunnun, no not even the Mansion House,' Byron told Hodgson. The convent school was home to six high spirited boys, 57-year-old Louis Fauvel, the French Consul and Giovanni Lusieri, an employee of Lord Elgin, who was commissioned to gather and ship the famous marbles to England.

The days slipped past pleasantly, riding to Piraeus, Phalerum, Tucolimano and returning to the convent to dine on woodcock and red mullet. Byron watched amused as his servants paired off with local women. Fletcher, whose patience had already been strained by foreigners and their odd customs, was infuriated by the Albanian laundresses who playfully stuck pins into his rump whenever they had the opportunity.

Byron never lost his own playfulness and he slipped easily back into his schoolday pastimes with the six students, teaching them to box and organizing them in teams, Greek Orthodox boys against the three Catholics. The monks found it most amusing when the Catholic boys won. He liked to teach the boys and was curious to know what inspired children. During his later exile in Greece he asked Augusta to explain what motivated little Ada. 'What is her *tic*?' He deeply regretted that he was unable to be with her and watch her develop and learn, but he was confident she would be well educated as 'her mother is highly cultivated'.

On returning from his daily swim at Piraeus one day, he met a procession of Turkish soldiers moving towards the beach carrying a sack containing a girl who had been condemned to drown as punishment for infidelity. Horrified, Byron halted the soldiers and ordered the officer, at pistol point, to accompany him to the Turkish governor of Athens where he pleaded for the girl's life. After accepting considerable amounts of money, the governor agreed to free her on condition she should leave Athens. Byron took the frightened creature back to the convent and when it was dark sent her to Thebes where she would be safe.[6] He used this dramatic episode as the basis of *The Giaour*. Later, Lord Sligo wrote an account confirming the incident.

The social lioness, Lady Hester Stanhope, arrived in Athens and encouraged Byron to become a frequent visitor, but her enthusiasm for his company disappeared when she learned that the English flocked to her house only to catch a glimpse of him. She was conceited and did not care for Byron, saying his eyes were too close together. Her dislike was mild compared to her antipathy to other women. She declared to Hobhouse (their paths had crossed in Malta) that she would as soon live with a team of packhorses as with women. He thought her violent, peremptory and argumentative but she met her match in Byron who retaliated to her argumentative arrogance by using the same tactics which enraged his mother, those of laughter and mocking agreement. He refused her offer to accompany her to Constantinople and a few days later said he did not admire 'that dangerous thing, a female wit'.[7]

Nicolo Giraud, Lusieri's brother-in-law, accompanied Byron on a second excursion to Attica, but they got no further than Patras before Byron was laid low with a fever and confined to bed for five days. Unable to put up much of a fight in his weakened condition he was forced by the worried Giraud to see a doctor. For three days Byron suffered the fashionable cures of purging, induced vomiting and clysters (enemas). Giraud nursed him day and night until he, too, fell ill and endured a similar cure. They returned to Athens for the winter.

Fletcher's continued complaints no longer amused Byron. He particularly disliked having to ask for comforts for his servant which he himself was happy to do without – and it was a long list as Fletcher refused to eat the food, drink the wine, or sleep in the beds. He kept up a persistent keening for beer, beef and tea. He muttered and moaned under his breath about the distance he had travelled from the moment he had cleared the Channel. Finally, in November, Byron sent him home, instructing Hanson to pay him £50 and find him a farm on the estate.

Fletcher carried letters for Hobhouse and Hodgson together with Byron's firm refusal to sell Newstead to cover his debts. His letters were full of gossip about old friends. Athens was popular with the English and he attended many balls, dinners and what he called a 'variety of fooleries' with the ladies of Athens. He began a satire called *Hints from Horace and the Curse of Minerva*, an attack on Lord Elgin for removing the marbles from Greece.

In February 1811 he wrote to his mother threatening never to come home if Newstead was sold and at the same time saying he expected to see her in the course of the summer. He was worried about his health, gaining and losing weight in an erratic way, he suffered from a cough, catarrh, piles, pains in his side and venereal disease. By the middle of March he had recovered sufficiently to give a farewell supper to his friends, and on 22 April he boarded the transport ship *Hydra* for Malta. Mrs Macri, on learning he was leaving Athens and unable to make him marry her daughter, made him an unsuccessful offer, the opportunity of buying Teresa for 30,000 piastres. Lusiero and Giraud accompanied him as far as Malta. Lusiero was travelling on business for Lord Elgin and Giraud was to be placed in a school there at Byron's expense.

The oppressive heat in Malta combined with a mild attack of malaria and some grim financial news from England depressed Byron. Even the news from Mrs Byron that he had a fortune on paper of over £100,000 did not cheer him. What good was it if he could not raise a shilling in cash? However, in his typically generous fashion he told Hobhouse not to worry about repaying the £ 818 3*s.* 4*d.* he owed covering the cost of their travels but to pay his tradesmen instead.

Ironically the frigate *Volage* which carried Byron home also carried the last consignment of Lord Elgin's marbles, an export Byron detested as an act of sacrilege. Byron's own eclectic collection of souvenirs included four tortoises, four human skulls which he had fished out of sarcophagi, a delicate shawl and a quantity of attar of roses for his mother. He alerted her to his imminent arrival by advising her on his diet, 'I must only inform you that for a long time I have been restricted to an entire vegetable diet neither fish or flesh coming within my regimen, so I expect a powerful stock of potatoes, greens and biscuit. I drink no wine.'[8]

He landed at Sheerness on 14 July and settled in at Reddish's Hotel in Albemarle Street, London, later the same day. In the evening he was given a warm welcome by Scrope Davies who turned up on the doorstep drunk and full of new jokes.

The following day Robert Dallas called and found Byron animated and talkative. He told him that he had written a paraphrase of Horace's *Art of Poetry* which would make a good finish to *English Bards and Scotch Reviewers*. Dallas took it home and found it both disappointing and 'grievous'. At breakfast the following day he mentioned casually that he was surprised this was the only work Byron had written during his travels. Byron replied that he had occasionally written short poems and a great many stanzas but 'they are not worth troubling you with, but you shall have them all with you if you like.' He opened a small trunk and took out a number of verses which, he said, had been read by only one other person who had not liked them and Byron was sure Dallas would be of the same opinion.[9] Dallas read the work, *Childe Harold*, and was convinced it would sell. After discussing the merits of various publishers he approached Mr John Murray who had already expressed an interest in

Byron's works. Murray showed *Childe Harold* to William Gifford his friend and literary adviser; he in turn admired the work and recommended that it should be published.

Byron was in no hurry to see his mother and set off for Sittingbourne where he lingered for two days with Hobhouse who was waiting to be sent to Ireland with his militia regiment. He returned to London to sort out his financial affairs and then left for Harrow to spend a few days with Henry Drury. On 23 July he apologized to his mother for the delay, saying he would join her at Newstead before continuing on to Lancashire to settle the business of the Rochdale mines. In the meantime he urged her to consider Newstead as her home.

Mrs Byron had efficiently administered his estate keeping a firm hand on expenses and dismissing servants when necessary.[10] Byron did not know that her health had been failing for over a year. Whether her frailty was caused by hard work or a variety of illnesses induced by her excessive weight is unknown, but several weeks after he returned she began to fade. Before Byron had left for the East she had had a premonition that she would never see him again. On the day she received the letter announcing his return she said to Mrs By, her maid, 'If I should be dead before Byron comes down, what a strange thing it would be!'

Byron's debts now totalled over £10,000 including £1,800 to a firm of Nottingham upholsterers, Brothers. (He had commissioned work for Newstead before he left and settlement of their bill was well overdue.) A few days before Byron returned to Newstead Mrs Byron had received a threatening dun from Brothers which caused her to fall into one of her violent rages; in her weakened state such a paroxysm proved fatal. She took to her bed and lingered a short while until her faithful heart stopped beating.

On 1 August Byron heard that his mother was dangerously ill, but while he was raising the money to cover the cost of the journey from London to Newstead the news of her death was brought to him. He told Pigot, 'My poor mother died yesterday! and I am on my way from town to attend her to the family vault. I heard *one* day of her illness, the *next* of her death. Thank God her last moments were most tranquil. I am told she was in little pain, and not aware of her situation.'

That night as he sat in the darkened room with her body, Mrs By heard him sighing through the half-open door. She went in to comfort him and urged him not to give way to grief but he turned to her and burst into tears exclaiming, 'Oh! Mrs By, I had but one friend in the world, and she is gone!'[11]

On 7 August news of the death of the amusing Charles Skinner Matthews reached him.[12] Matthews had become entangled in weeds and

drowned while swimming alone in the Cam. Byron wrote desperately to
Scrope Davies, 'Some curse hangs over me and mine. My mother lies a
corpse in this house; one of my best friends is drowned in a ditch.' He
continued, 'My dear Scrope, if you can spare a moment, do come down
to me – I want a friend. Come to me, Scrope, I am almost desolate, left
almost alone in the world, I had but you and Hobhouse and Matthews
and let me enjoy the survivors whilst I can.'[13] To add to his sorrows, news
arrived of John Wingfield's death in March. Wingfield had been one of
Byron's fags at school and was serving with the Coldstream Guards in
Portugal when he died of fever after the battle of Coimbra.

Weighed down with grief Byron was unable to attend his mother's
funeral or even to follow her coffin to Hucknall Torkard church when it
was placed in the family vault. He stood at the abbey door and watched
her funeral procession until it had completely vanished behind the trees
and then he turned to his page, Rushton, the only person left in the
house besides himself, and sent him to fetch sparring gloves. They
sparred, but Rushton thought Byron was abstracted and more violent in
his blows than usual. After a short while Byron flung the gloves away and
went to his room.

Deep in depression and sorrow he drew up a draft will on 12 August
and sent it to Mr Samuel Bolton, Mrs Byron's solicitor in Nottingham.
After the list of legacies he left instructions that he was to be buried in
the garden vault next to his favourite Newfoundland dog, Boatswain, who
had died in his arms in 1808. He later instructed Mr Bolton that if his
body were removed from the vault by his heirs the estate should go to his
sister.[14]

Scrope Davies answered Byron's call for company and stayed with him
until the end of August, leaving an invitation to join him in Cambridge in
October.

On his own once more Byron recalled his mother's foibles with
affection and remembered how they used to tease each other.[15] He
suffered from bouts of remorse and misery as he went through her
papers and found all his letters carefully preserved. A fierce spasm of
grief rendered him 'subject to a kind of hysterical merriment, or rather
laughter without merriment, which I can neither account for nor
conquer, and yet I do not feel relieved by it'. His proud mother had kept
a scrap-book into which she had pasted all the literary notices that had
appeared on his poems and satires and she had written in the margins
her own observations which showed great sense and ability. Murray was
anxious to proceed with *Childe Harold* but the grief-stricken Byron felt
unable to cope with London life and placed all the negotiations into the
hands of Dallas. Although Murray warned Byron that some of his

outrageous political statements as well as his unorthodox attitude on morals might adversely affect sales, Byron refused to alter a word.

Little by little the acute pain passed and in September Byron wrote to Hodgson,

> I am plucking up my spirits, and have begun to gather my little sensual comforts together. Lucy is extracted from Warwickshire . . . the partridges are plentiful, hares fairish, pheasants not quite so good, and Girls on the Manor ****. Just as I had formed a tolerable establishment my travels commenced, and on my return I find all to do over again; my former flock were all scattered; some married, not before it was needful. As I am a great disciplinarian, I have just issued an edict for the abolition of caps; no hair to be cut on any pretext; stays permitted, but not too low before; full uniform always in the evening; Lucinda to be commander.[16]

He made no mention of Lucy's baby, which would have been about two years old when she returned to Newstead. He usually greeted the birth of his children with embarrassed delight and since he had told his friends of his prowess with Lucy it seems strange he did not inform them of the birth; but he told his wife, on their honeymoon, that he had two natural children.

Byron was plunged into sorrow again on hearing that his young Cambridge friend, John Edleston, had died of consumption in May. He asked Mrs Pigot if Elizabeth would return Edleston's cornelian promising to replace it, 'by something she may remember me by equally well'. He commented that this was the sixth death of a friend or relative that had taken place between May and August.[17]

Byron took up Davies's invitation to stay with him in Cambridge for a few days but the visit was overshadowed by Edleston's death and Davies's heavy drinking. By the end of October Byron was glad to escape to his old lodgings at 8 St James's Street to discuss with Dallas the progress he had made with Murray towards publication of *Childe Harold*.

The Irish poet Thomas Moore had taken offence at several references in *English Bards and Scotch Reviewers* and wrote to Byron spoiling for a duel. Fortunately the letter went astray, time passed, Moore married and mellowed and hinted he would be satisfied with an apology, which Byron gave him in a friendly letter. Moore and Samuel Rogers, the poet and man of letters, were curious to meet Byron and so Rogers invited him to dinner at his house in St James's Place overlooking Green Park. Thomas

Campbell, well known for his patriotic poems, was also present. He had called on Rogers on the morning of the dinner and contrived an invitation.

Rogers asked if Byron would like some soup. 'No,' he replied, he never took soup. Would he take some fish? 'No,' he never took fish. Would he take some mutton? 'No,' he never took mutton. Would he take a glass of wine? 'No,' he never took wine. What would he like to eat asked the desperate host. 'Nothing but hard biscuits and soda-water.' These were not available so Byron made a meal of potatoes mashed up in a large amount of vinegar.[18] A few days later Rogers ran into Hobhouse, 'How long will Lord Byron persevere in his present diet?' he asked. 'Just as long as you continue to notice it,' was Hobhouse's dry reply. This may have been a little unjust as Byron had in fact developed a theory that there was a connection between what people ate and how they behaved and on one occasion startled Moore, who was enjoying a steak, by asking, 'Moore, don't you find eating beef-steak makes you ferocious?'[19]

'Lord Byron is back, Mr Rogers told me, and very much improved, and regretting his satirical poem,' the Duchess of Devonshire reported to her son, Augustus Foster in Washington.[20] Byron had lampooned Holland House as the place where 'Scotchmen dine, and duns are kept aloof' in *English Bards and Scotch Reviewers* but the Hollands forgave him and he was flattered to become a regular at Lady Holland's dinner table. Lady Holland was a divorcee and the mother of an illegitimate son, so not completely accepted in society; her salon was dominated by poets and Whig politicians, men whose reputations were not easily damaged. Byron saw her as a victim of cant and humbug. He told Lady Blessington that 'the first dispute I ever had with Lady Byron was caused by my urging her to visit Lady Holland.'

Byron wanted to see Hobhouse at Newstead before Christmas and tempted him by describing his new establishment. 'I have Lucy, Susan a very pretty Welsh Girl, and a third of the Notts's breed, whom you never saw, all under age, and very ornamental. But my diet is so low that I can carry on nothing carnal.'[21] Hobhouse declined the offer but Hodgson and Harness, one of his protégés from Harrow, accepted his invitation to spend Christmas at Newstead. Harness was looking forward to seeing ghosts and taking part in orgies but it turned out to be a sober and rather dull holiday. Byron spent most of his time editing *Childe Harold*, while Hodgson edited copy for the *Monthly Review* and the disappointed Harness was left with nothing to do but study for his degree. They met at dinner and discussed poets and poetry, occasionally slipping into serious discussions on religion. Hodgson, due to be ordained the following year, tried to exorcize the miserable dogmas of Scottish Calvinism planted in

Byron's brain by May Gray. The evenings frequently ended with a toast to the absent Hobhouse. Outside the abbey the short dark days were gloomy and cold with snow on the ground but inside the restored and newly decorated rooms it was cheerful, bright and warm with blazing fires, comfortable furniture and the curtains glowing crimson in the candle light. The two visitors adopted Byron's habits of rising slowly and retiring late.[22]

Byron returned to his old pastime of dallying with the Newstead maids, Bessy from Nottingham, Lucy from Warwickshire and Susan from Wales. He turned his attention to the newest, Susan Vaughan, and six days after arriving at Newstead, he confessed to Hobhouse that he was occupied with 'a Welsh Girl whom I lately added to the bevy'. By the time he left for London, 11 January, he was besotted. He wrote to Susan three times that day, once from Nottingham, once from Newport Pagnell and once from London.

His obvious preference for Susan made Lucy and Robert Rushton jealous. They sneered at her and made snide remarks. She promptly reported their behaviour to Byron who reproved Robert, 'Susan is to be treated with civility, and not *insulted* by any person over whom I have the smallest control, or indeed by anyone whatever, while I have the power to protect her.' Byron had taken an interest in Rushton's education and although he was racked with doubt over Susan's probable faithlessness, he could not resist telling him in the postscript to the letter to 'attend to your Arithmetic'.[23]

Susan felt secure and triumphant, believing she had routed her enemies and concentrated on organizing a party to celebrate Byron's birthday, which coincidentally was the same as her own. The three pretty girls were dressed in white and Lucy and Susan, past and present favourites, wore their badges of office, gold chains that Byron had given them. It was a very jolly evening. Each guest sang a solo, the girls danced a reel and everyone enjoyed the generous supper of roast pork, pork pie, potatoes, celery, apple pie, mince pies, custard and cheese all washed down with large quantities of punch. A toast to their absent lord was proposed and followed by three hearty cheers.

Robert was furious when he learned of Susan's complaints and wrote to his master broadly hinting that Susan's favours were more available than Byron knew. Alarmed, Byron replied, 'If anything has passed between you *before* or since my last visit to Newstead, do not be afraid to mention it. I am sure *you* would not deceive me, though *she* would. Whatever it is, *you* shall be forgiven. I have not been without some suspicions on the subject, and am certain that, at your time of life, the blame could not attach to you.'[24] Susan had foolishly written letters to Robert which incriminated both herself and Lucy and he lost no time in passing them to Byron who immediately dismissed the two girls. He wrote to Susan, 'Do not attempt explanation, it is useless, I am *determined*, you cannot deny your handwriting; return to your relations, you shall be furnished with the means, but *him*, who now addresses you for the last time, you will never see again. God bless you!'[25] Susan returned to Wales and obscurity but Lucy kept in touch with Nanny Smith who was able to tell Washington Irving almost twenty years later that 'Lucy never had the fine fortune she dreamt of; but she had better than I thought for: she is now married, and keeps a public-house at Warwick.'

Byron felt the ridiculousness of his situation and told Moore that he was in a state of ludicrous tribulation, for not only was he suffering from wounded pride and a streaming cold but he had a kidney stone which had elicited the predictable medical response of cupping, clystering, purging and vomiting. This did not stop him attending the House of Lords regularly and carefully considering a subject for his maiden speech, which he wanted to make as soon as possible. He remembered the disturbances caused by disgruntled Nottingham frame-makers during his stay at Newstead and felt he could make a fine speech based on his local knowledge.

The problems of the British cotton and woollen industries caused by the French blockade had been made worse when, in February 1811, the Americans renewed the Non-Intercourse Act, intended to cut off the supply of raw cotton. This coincided with the introduction of new weaving frames which did the work of several men. Faced with losing their livelihoods many weavers became desperate. They armed themselves with axes and sledgehammers and crept out at night to smash the new frames. The violence grew and magistrates and militiamen who were called out to deal with the disturbances were terrorized, their livestock maimed and their hayricks burned by the followers of 'General Ludd', the mythical leader of the rioters.

On 27 February Byron delivered his maiden speech, urging conciliation and forgiveness for the frame-breakers; he ended:

Suppose one of these men, as I have seen them, meagre with famine, sullen with despair, careless of life which your lordships are perhaps about to value at something less than the price of a stocking frame; suppose this man surrounded by those children, for whom he is unable to procure bread at the hazard of his existence, about to be torn forever from a family which he lately supported in peaceful industry, and which it is not his fault that he can no longer so support; suppose this man – and there are ten thousand such, from whom you may select your victims, – dragged into court to be tried for this new offence, by this new law, – still there are two things wanting to convict and condemn him, and these are, in my opinion, twelve butchers for a jury, and a Jefferies for a judge![26]

The disturbances in the midlands ended in February, when the bill Byron had opposed was enacted and frame-breaking became a capital felony. Lord Holland, who had advised him on Parliamentary procedure, felt the speech was, 'full of fancy, wit and invective, but not exempt from affectation nor well reasoned, not at all suited to our common notions of Parliamentary eloquence'. When it was over, Dallas, who met Byron in the passage outside the chamber of the House of Lords, described him as glowing with success, repeating compliments which had been paid to him and listing the names of peers who wanted to be introduced. He ended by saying that the speech had given him the best advertisement for *Childe Harold*.[27]

On 10 March Murray put *Childe Harold* on the market and within a week Byron was famous. He was twenty-four years old, 5 feet 8½ inches tall with light grey eyes, a handsome though rather thick nose, white regular teeth and a pale complexion. His head was small, his forehead a little too narrow but high. He accentuated it by shaving the hair away from the temples leaving the other glossy, dark-brown curls to cluster over his head.[28] His voice was low and sweet with a delightful impediment in pronouncing r's. It also retained a slight and engaging brogue which led Claire Clairmont to remark that he had a Scottish accent, provoking him to exclaim in a mock rage, 'Good God, I hope not! I am sure I haven't. I would rather the whole damned country was sunk in the sea – I with the Scotch accent!'[29] He defied fashion by sporting long, loose trousers instead of knee-breeches and he preferred to wear softer collars than the starched cravats recommended by his new friend George Brummell.

The craze of the 1812 season was waltzing and dancing lessons were given at five o'clock in most of the fashionable houses. Many people, including Byron, believed it encouraged wantonness but he may have been influenced by his lame foot. By those used to the more formal dances of the past in which the only contact between partners was a light touch of the hand, the waltz was regarded as decadent. Not only were young men allowed to place their arms completely round their partners, but those partners were dressed in scanty, loosely fitting, flowing dresses, having discarded the protection of stays and petticoats (though the popularity of the avant garde garments, knickers, was growing). The Duchess of Devonshire would not allow waltzing at Devonshire House but

Lady Melbourne, who had never cared much for convention, had no such scruples. She allowed her daughter-in-law, Lady Caroline Lamb, to invite her friends to Melbourne House and it was at a waltzing party there on 25 March that Miss Annabella Milbanke saw Byron for the first time. He was surrounded by admiring young women and fêted by his hostess. 'I did not seek an introduction to him,' she told her mother, 'but I shall not refuse the acquaintance if it comes my way.' Byron had not noticed her at all. She had been in London since February staying with Lady Gosford in Cumberland Place. It was her second season and she was on the marriage market. She first heard of *Childe Harold* and its famous author on 15 March while dining at Melbourne House, the home of her aunt Lady Melbourne; finding herself unable to join in the conversation or offer an opinion on the fashion craze of the season she immediately obtained a copy and finished it two days later.[30]

Byron was quite oblivious of her until she was included in a supper party given by her cousin Lady Cowper. There she spoke to him for the first time, the subject of the conversation being Joseph Blacket, a cobbler turned poet. The Milbankes had encouraged him in his ambitions so it is not surprising that when his patroness's daughter asked for his opinion on her own verses, he found them 'sublime, with a peculiar strength of thought, full of natural and classical ideas'. Byron politely acknowledged her family's kindness to the poet while privately thinking Blacket would have done better to remain a successful cobbler and live, rather than be an unsuccessful poet and die at twenty-three.

> Stranger! behold, interr'd together,
>   The *souls* of learning and of leather.
> Poor Joe is gone, but left his *all*:
>   You'll find his relics in a *stall*.

Annabella began to stalk Byron, recording the functions they attended whether he noticed her there or not. She questioned Mrs Gally Knight, a near neighbour of Byron in Nottinghamshire, who poured into her ears local gossip and stories passed on to her by her son Henry, a contemporary of Byron at Cambridge. The whole interesting catalogue was rounded off with the intriguing suspicion that he was an infidel.[31] Annabella brooded about the state of his soul and its salvation. She described him to her mother as having rolling eyes and lips thickened with disdain, but after Lady Cowper's supper she thought she had never met anyone more agreeable in conversation, remarking that every now and again she perceived in him impulses of sublime goodness which burst through his malevolent habits. Later she confessed she considered it 'an act of humanity and a Christian duty not to deny him any temporary satisfaction he can derive from my acquaintance – though I shall not seek to encrease it, he is not a dangerous person to me.'[32] She believed she could reform *Childe Harold.*

Annabella was in London against the wishes of her parents who had begged her to wait until Easter when they would all come for the season, but Annabella, who was used to getting her own way, spoke sharply to her father and, ignoring his wishes, flounced off to London. No sooner had she arrived but she informed them of her delight at escaping from 'the dullities of Seaham' and rejoiced in her robust appetite during the journey. She dined at Wetherby on *fleecy* mutton chops, at Grantham she ordered them again and ate 'twice two, and frightened the waiters'.[33]

She was an heiress and her list of suitors included the Hon. George Eden, brother of Lord Auckland; Lord Jocelyn, treasurer to the Prince Regent; William Bankes, a friend of Byron with £8,000 a year; General Packenham, the Duke of Wellington's brother just returned from the Peninsula; Major Dickens, who never managed to get up enough courage to propose; and Francis Cunningham, who was completely ignored. The earliest and most persistent admirer, Augustus Foster, son of Elizabeth, Duchess of Devonshire, was sent to Washington by the Prince Regent as Minister to the United States of America before being able to press his suit to a conclusion. His half-sister, Mrs George Lamb, kept him informed of the state of the field. In November 1811 she had written reassuringly that she had seen the Milbankes but had 'heard nothing that need alarm you; great coldness to all the admirers'.[34] Augustus Foster clung to hope. His mother wrote, 'I shall almost hate her if she is blind to the merits of one who would make her so happy.'[35]

Meanwhile Annabella busily visited the British Museum, took notes at classes on mnemonics and geology and attended Mr Thomas Campbell's lectures at the Royal Institution. She said, 'My complexion has become so clear, my eyes so lively, and my muscles so round that I have not looked so well this year past.' She continued, 'I am quite the fashion this year. Mankind bow before me, and womankind think me somebody.'[36]

CHAPTER THREE

Childe Harold *Besieged*

Anne Isabella Milbanke was the only child of Sir Ralph and Lady Judith Milbanke of Seaham in County Durham, the long awaited and loved offspring of elderly parents. The pair had waited fifteen years for their first child and despite the initial disappointment that it was not a boy the baby became the topic of their conversation and letters forever. When Annabella, as she was called in the family, was not quite two her proud mother reported that she could talk, was very fat and tall. She had a robust appetite which enabled her to eat three or four times as much roast beef as her older friend Bell Baker. George Baker, a family friend and Bell's father, sent over some fruit from his hothouse at Elmore Hall and little Annabella gorged herself on the grapes, peaches and nectarines. She was omnivorous and amused Sir Henry Vane-Tempest by asking him to open a fresh bottle of claret a day for her when she was only five. She lived a healthy, happy life at Seaham, swimming, riding, following the hunt with her mother and walking with the guns. She romped and ran in the open air during the summer until she became quite brown.

Annabella spent her childhood either at Seaham Hall or at Halnaby Hall, 40 miles away on the south bank of the Tees just inside the Yorkshire border. Annabella preferred Seaham where she used to run across the sands and act out daydreams, casting herself as the centre of heroic episodes and displaying no interest at all in dolls or feminine pastimes; but as she grew older she enjoyed helping her mother visiting and caring for the labouring poor in the village, including Joseph Blacket, the poet.[1]

Her parents had been unable to deny her anything as a child and as a young woman they wanted to see her make a happy marriage. They were greatly disturbed at the tone her letters were taking when she described her feelings towards Byron. He was known to be a rake, a liberal and to profess unacceptable moral values; but his charm together with the exhilarating sensation of flirting with danger was a challenge to most women.

In early May 1812, Sir Ralph and Lady Milbanke arrived to chaperone Annabella, who had already formed cautious friendships with Mrs George

Lamb and Lady Caroline Lamb. Both were called Caroline and to distinguish them they were known in the family as Caro George and Caro William. Caro George, illegitimate daughter of the Duke of Devonshire by his wife's best friend, Elizabeth Foster, later his second wife, was married to Lady Melbourne's fourth son. Caro William was married to Lady Melbourne's second and favourite son, later to be Lord Melbourne and prime minister.

Augustus Foster still clung to the hope of an engagement with Annabella and his mother reported that at a reception for the Prince Regent the three of them, her daughter Mrs George Lamb, Annabella and herself had sat side by side on a sofa while 'Old twaddle Ralph' and Lady Milbanke made polite enquiries about Augustus, but 'the girl still never names you to me – tant mieux.'[2] She wrote later, 'I hope you don't make yourself unhappy about her; she is really an icicle.'[3] She added, 'She is good, amiable, and sensible but cold, prudent, and reflecting.' Augustus agreed half-heartedly. 'She is certainly rather too cold in her manners, and gives to reason too much empire over her mind, but she has good eyes, is fair, and has right ideas and sense and mildness. I don't think she will ever be able to love very warmly; but yet I believe she thinks she ought to wait till the spirit moves her, and the spirit perhaps may never come, as I fancy happens to many of her temperament.'[4] William Harness described her as 'almost the only young, pretty, well-dressed girl we ever saw who carried no cheerfulness along with her'. He continued, 'She moved slowly along her mother's drawing rooms, talking to scientific men and literary women, without a tone of emotion in her voice or the faintest glimpse of a smile on her countenance.'

In April Byron spoke in the House of Lords in favour of the Earl of Donoughmore's motion, the Catholic Claims Bill. His perfomance was considered theatrical and marred by his chanting tone which was the hallmark of old Harrovians.[5] Nevertheless, 'He continues to be the great attraction at all parties and suppers. The ladies, I hear, spoil him and the gentlemen are jealous of him,' wrote the Duchess of Devonshire.[6] Byron's upward passage through society continued. He was introduced to the Prince Regent and Sir Walter Scott but he remained uneasy in unfamiliar company where, to compensate, he assumed an air of melancholy abstraction which was seen as truly Byronic by some and as sullen bad manners by others.

Annabella asked Caro William to pass her poems to Byron for his comments. He returned them with the message that he thought they were better than those of her dead protégé, Joseph Blacket. He stopped Bessy Rawdon one day and abruptly asked, 'Have you seen Miss Milbanke lately? I wish when next you see her you would be so kind as to give her a hint not to send me any more of her foolish little rhymes.'[7] Annabella received little encouragement and after seeing Byron from afar several times she returned to Seaham.

Caro William's approach was more direct. After she had read a copy of *Childe Harold* lent to her by Rogers she summoned him to Melbourne House and demanded to see the author.

'He has a club-foot, and bites his nails,' said Rogers.

'If he is as ugly as Aesop, I must see him!' she replied.[8] William Lamb showed no interest. It was his affectation to appear indolent and worldly-wise in contrast to his frenetic wife.

Byron became the social lion of the season and the centre of attention at Lady Jersey's fashionable parties. He continued to dine at Holland House, the Whig stronghold in Kensington, where both Hollands attempted to reconcile him with his guardian, Lord Carlisle. He was bombarded by young women anxious to make an impression and he later told Lady Blessington that he had enough love letters from English ladies to fill a large volume. The recently widowed Lady Falkland believed all the references to love in *Childe Harold* referred to her and wrote pledging herself to him together with a lock of her hair. Byron's eyes wandered and he admired pretty Bessy Rawdon with her bouncing curls and fragrant nosegays and Mrs George Lamb's singing reminded him of Edleston's clear notes so strongly that it brought tears to his eyes.[9] He paid frequent visits to Melbourne House and made the 62-year-old Lady Melbourne laugh. In 1818, after her death, he said, 'Her mind and heart were as fresh as if only sixteen summers had flown over her.'

At twenty-seven, Caroline Lamb had been married to William Lamb for seven years and although the fire and joy had gone out of their marriage they were joined by their devotion to their backward son Augustus. The power of the poetry in *Childe Harold* seized the imagination of this vivacious, unstable woman and she set out to capture Byron. He first caught her eye at Lady Westmoreland's but, like Annabella, she refused to pay immediate homage. When Lady Westmoreland led her to where he was standing by a table at the side of the room surrounded by cooing ladies she turned on her heel. This aroused his interest, just as she had intended. A few days later they met again, this time at Holland House where a formal introduction took place and he gazed at her through his magnificent eyelashes giving her the benefit of what Bessy Rawdon called his 'dangerous underlook'. Caroline saw Byron as *Childe Harold*, the tragic hero and catch of the season, and she fell unhealthily and obsessively in love. Neither her parents nor her husband interfered as she threw herself at Byron's head. The Duchess of Devonshire merely told Augustus, 'Your little friend, Caro William, as usual, is doing all sorts of imprudent things for him and with him.'[10]

Caroline was clever, agreeable, absurd, amiable, perplexing and fascinating. She was small with reddish hair and described by members of her family as like a delicate Ariel, or a little Fairy Queen and she had a passion for wearing pages' uniforms. Lady Granville described her as 'the strangest person that ever lived, really half crazy. She was not good-looking but very clever and could be very amusing.' She was not the sort of woman Byron usually admired as she was thin and did not have the dark antelope eyes he liked.

The grand romance that Caroline demanded was soon a one-sided affair. She killed it with unreasonable demands, daily love letters, private assignations and public displays of jealousy. The couple spent their days quarrelling and reconciling. They openly rode about in Byron's carriage in defiance of convention and on one occasion, when Byron attended a great party at Devonshire House without her, Caroline loitered by the gates with the link boys until it ended, then tried to crawl into his carriage and was seen by Rogers with her body pushed through the window and her legs dangling outside.

Byron intrigued everyone with his conversation and bearing. Bessy Rawdon confessed, 'I was much interested in him – all the women adored him – I adored him, and partly on that account, and partly because his manners were affected, the men hated him.'[11] On 10 May, the Duchess of Devonshire wrote to Augustus, 'He is going back to Naxos, and then the husbands may sleep in peace,' adding, 'I should not be surprised if Caro William were to go with him, she is so wild and imprudent.' In early June she reported, 'Caroline W. Lamb is quietly, thank heaven! at Brocket with William and all of them.'[12] Byron left London with his cousin George Byron and Hobhouse to spend a few days at Newstead but he was not safe there, as on 10 June a letter arrived from Caroline delivered by a page whom Hobhouse suspected was the lady herself in a disguise.

He was back in town by the end of the month proudly writing accounts of his meeting with the Prince Regent to Lord Holland and Sir Walter Scott. 'The other night, at a ball, I was presented by order to our gracious Regent, who honoured me with some conversation, and professed a prediliction of poetry.'[13] As the summer passed Byron became deeply depressed at his growing debts but he was reluctant to sell Newstead. He had reached the end of his tether with Caroline and decided to give her the slip and visit Harrow with Hobhouse. Just as they were about to leave, at midday on 29 July, there was a knock at the door and, wearing an elaborate but unsuccessful disguise, Caroline walked in. She had come intending to make such a scandal that Byron would be forced to elope with her and she seized a court sword that was lying on a sofa and threatened wildly that there would be blood spilt. Hobhouse took charge and after a noisy scene he persuaded her to accompany him to 5 Grosvenor Gate where he left her in the care of her friend, Mrs Conyers.

Caroline was drawing further away from rational behaviour and two weeks after the failed elopement she sent Byron a lock of her pubic hair, together with a letter asking for a lock of his hair not necessarily from the same place.[14] There was no mistaking that by now Byron had reached the end of the involvement and wanted to be left in peace. The passion was spent and only the ridiculous left.

On 10 August Lady Bessborough, Caroline's mother, concerned for her daughter's health and fearing the Melbournes would run out of patience and ask for a separation, visited Melbourne House to persuade Caroline to come on a family holiday on their estate in Ireland. They were interrupted by old Lord Melbourne, a short, fat, disagreeable man, who thoroughly disapproved of Caroline. He spoke to her sharply and she, offended at his remarks, flounced off declaring she would run away with Byron. Seized with panic, Lady Bessborough ran to find Lady Melbourne but by the time the two women returned Caroline had gone. They went to Byron who was astonished by their story and had no idea where Caroline could have gone, but soothed them and promised to find her and bring her back. Later the same day Caroline sent a message to Lady Bessborough by a hackney coach driver and Byron seized the man forcing him with threats and bribery to take him to where she was hiding. Caroline had taken refuge in the home of a surgeon in Kensington who had taken her in believing she had been abandoned. Byron, pretending to be her brother, forced her into the coach and returned her to her parents' house in Cavendish Square. When she at last returned to her own home at Melbourne House she indulged in extravagant displays of remorse on hearing that her mother had broken a blood vessel. Her play-acting continued and she managed to postpone the date of the family's departure for Ireland, claiming she was pregnant, which, if not true, was especially cruel to William who loved children.

Newstead was put up for sale on 14 August at Garroway's Coffee House but despite Hobhouse's best attempts to drive up the price none of the bids was accepted. A few days later on the advice of Hanson, Newstead was sold to Mr Thomas Claughton, a solicitor from Haydock Lodge near Warrington.

Through all the excesses of his affair with Caroline, Byron had continued to be welcome at Holland House and invited to the country houses of the Earl of Jersey at Middleton and the Marquis of Lansdowne at Bowood.[15]

In the autumn, together with the Jerseys, Melbournes, Cowpers and Hollands, he enjoyed the hospitality of the Earl of Oxford at Eywood. Lady Oxford, formerly Jane Elizabeth Scott, a rector's daughter, was twenty-two when she married Edward Harley, 5th Earl of Oxford, who became a dull and complaisant husband. Lady Oxford was greatly influenced by the French Revolution and allowed her taste for rebellion and free love full expression by producing a pack of beautiful children known as the Harleian Miscellany. Byron's favourite was eleven-year-old Lady Charlotte. He paid tribute to her in the verses *To Ianthe*, which he included in the seventh edition of *Childe Harold*, and arranged for her to sit for a portrait by Westall to illustrate future editions. It was remarked by some uncharitable people that little Charlotte had a remarkable resemblance to Sir Francis Burdett, a close friend of her mother. Lady Oxford was forty when her affair with Byron began and it was her wise advice that enabled him to stand firm when he was subjected to a barrage of threatening letters from the tortured Caroline. Byron felt as lighthearted at Eywood as he did at Newstead and spent his days splashing about with the Harley children on or in the water and scrambling about in the woods. He rented Kinsham Court, a family dower house near Eywood to relax in and discreetly conduct his affair with Lady Oxford. She gained great influence over him and by skilful management avoided the publicity antics such as Caroline's had caused. In April 1813 they feared there would be an addition to the miscellany but to everyone's relief it was a false alarm.[16]

In the pleasant atmosphere of Eywood Byron took stock of his future. The sale of Newstead was not proceeding as it should and he was tired of skirmishing with Caroline. He decided to follow his father's example and his mother's advice – marry. He approached Lady Melbourne and intimated there was someone he was interested in and would be glad of her help in sounding the lady out. She was astonished when he revealed his interest was in her niece Annabella Milbanke. Byron had hardly spoken to Annabella and had no reason to believe his suit would be successful but Lady Melbourne made no attempt to dissuade him or suggest that her literal-minded, unsophisticated niece was not a suitable match. She was glad as she believed that once Byron was married, William Lamb would be spared more humiliation from Caroline. Byron had little knowledge of Annabella's fortune but he expected that as Lord Wentworth's heir she would bring a handsome amount to the marriage. He was not in love but thought Annabella was pretty enough to grow to love, though not so beautiful as to attract too many rivals. She was clever, amiable, sufficiently well bred and he had never seen a woman he esteemed so much. He believed marriage based on esteem and confidence was more likely to succeed than one based on romance alone. Lady Melbourne overstepped the mark when she approached Annabella, through Judith Milbanke, with an informal offer of marriage since Byron had intended that she should only reconnoitre the position for him. However, on 12 October Byron was rejected.

In the New Year of 1813 Byron moved into new lodgings at 4 Bennet Street, off St James's. He joined fashionable clubs and societies and developed an easy friendship with Thomas Moore. After speaking in the House of Lords one evening he dropped in on him while he was dressing for dinner. Byron strode up and down in the next room spouting forth detached sentences from the speech he had just finished. 'I told them', he said, 'that it was a most flagrant violation of the Constitution – that, if such things were permitted there was an end to British freedom.' 'But what was this dreadful grievance?' Moore asked. 'The grievance?' Byron repeated, stopping his pacing to think, 'Oh, *that* I forget.' Both men laughed.[17]

Moore organized a visit to dine with Leigh Hunt who had been sentenced to two years imprisonment for a libel against the Prince Regent. The visitors were surprised to see how comfortable he and his family were in the Surrey gaol. The cell walls were papered with a design of a trellis with roses, the ceiling was painted as the sky complete with clouds, the barred windows were hidden by venetian blinds and it was furnished with bookcases decorated with vases of flowers and his favourite busts. There was also a pianoforte. Further, he had the use of a garden with flower beds surrounding a small patch of grass, full of pansies and young trees. An apple tree flourished so well that during the second year of his sentence it produced enough fruit to make an apple pie.[18] The dinner was enjoyable but the camaraderie that had built up during the day was dispelled by the arrival of Hunt's literary cronies anxious to meet the author of *Childe Harold*.[19]

On 5 July Byron attended a small waltzing party given by Lady Heathcote which provided another opportunity for Caroline to make an exhibition of herself. Byron had asked her, in the heat of their passion, not to waltz with others in front of him. Seeing him standing in the middle of the room she approached him, asking aggressively if she could waltz *now*. Byron replied she could. She turned on her heel and walked away. His answer did not please her and a short time later, as he escorted Lady Rancliffe into supper, Caroline pressed a sharp knife into his hand saying, 'I mean to use this.' He replied off-handedly, 'Against me I presume,' and swept past her. What happened next was unclear but Caroline said that Byron's answer was so unkind that as she ran away from him in distress the knife somehow cut her hand and blood was smeared on her dress. When it was seen by Lady Rancliffe and Lady Tankerville they began to scream. Byron claimed to have been completely unaware of the seriousness of the situation until he was scolded by Lady Westmoreland several hours later.[20] Lady Melbourne believed that Caroline had gone to the party in order to cause a scene and deliberately danced in front of Byron to annoy him. The event got into the press and was embroidered almost out of recognition.

The idea of going abroad again had been at the back of Byron's mind for some time and although his affair with Lady Oxford had run its course he toyed seriously with the idea of accompanying the family on an expedition to Sicily. However, he decided to content himself by going to Portsmouth to say a last goodbye to Lady Oxford and Potiphar, their nickname for her complaisant husband. He was therefore a little irritated when Augusta arrived unexpectedly on the day of the Oxfords' departure.

She was going through another financial crisis and was on the run from debt collectors. Augusta, at twenty-nine, had been married for almost six years and had been out of touch with her brother for some time. Byron had not attended her wedding but he congratulated her on the birth of her first child, Georgiana Augusta, born a week after Colonel Leigh sailed for the Peninsula in 1808. Augusta appeared very happy with her handsome dragoon and she had written to Byron extolling the virtues of marriage. He was not impressed but invited her to come to Newstead and to attend him when he took his seat in the House of Lords. She did neither.

Just as Lady Holderness's death had opened the gate for Mrs Byron to approach Augusta so it was Mrs Byron's death that gave Augusta the opportunity to renew her friendship with her brother. Byron replied to her letter of condolence with news of Newstead, its servants and a report on his travels. She replied from Six Mile Bottom on her return from London where she had taken three-year-old Georgiana to consult a doctor; as usual during times of trouble George Leigh was not at home, leaving Augusta to cope with both a sick child and a new baby, Augusta Charlotte, born in February 1811. Leigh was living under a cloud. He had fallen foul of the Prince of Wales by dishonestly holding back money from the sale of one of his horses. Augusta wrote saying she had much to tell Byron 'but it is more easily *said* than *written*. Probably you have heard of many *changes* in our situation since you left England; in a *pecuniary* point of view it is materially altered for ye worse.'[21] It was one of Augusta's worst faults that she was never able to spell out unpleasant facts plainly, but Byron knew what she was alluding to. 'I don't wish to pry into family secrets,' he wrote, 'or hear anything more of the matter, but I can't help regretting on your account that so long an intimacy should be dissolved at the very moment when your husband might have derived some advantage from his Royal Highness's friendship, – However, at all events and in all situations, you have a brother in me, and a home here.'

When he told her that he was busy fortune hunting Augusta laughed saying she hoped her future sister-in-law would have more attractions than merely money; she added, 'I shall be daily expecting to hear of a *Lady Byron*, since you have confided to me your determination of marrying, in which I really hope you are serious, being convinced such an event would contribute greatly to your happiness PROVIDED *her ladyship* was the sort of person that would suit you; and you won't be angry with me for saying it is not *everyone* would; therefore don't be too *precipitate*.[22]

Once again Byron invited Augusta and her children to visit Newstead but Augusta was restricted to caring for Georgiana, Augusta and now little George Henry John Leigh, born on 3 June 1812. He was christened at Six Mile Bottom in the presence of his godfathers, the Duke of Leeds, and the rakish Sir Harry Fetherstonhaugh, a racing crony of his father.

In March 1813 Augusta wrote to her brother again to ask his help as Leigh had run up alarming gambling debts. George followed the races round the country with his band of disreputable friends, betting heavily and losing regularly. He was rarely home except during the racing season at nearby Newmarket. Byron was sympathetic but unable to help. Claughton had postponed payment of the deposit on Newstead and delayed subsequent payments for as long as possible, to the point where Byron had begun to doubt whether he would ever pay.

Augusta arrived in London on 27 June and Byron invited her to accompany him to Lady Davy's that same evening. With brotherly bossiness he told her to be dressed and ready to leave by ten, promising her an interesting evening and an introduction to Madame de Staël whom Lady Jersey had recently launched into London society at her reception a week before. Germaine de Staël was a plain, sturdily-built woman and non-stop talker. Her hair and eyes were black, her mouth wide, revealing two protruding front teeth, her complexion swarthy and her known aim in life was to marry off her daughter Albertine. She believed that Lord Alvanley, noted for his extreme ugliness, had an income of £100,000 a year and desperate to do the best by her daughter, she was heard to praise him to his face for his beauty.[23]

Byron and Augusta had much in common and the novelty of being together after having been parted for so long was very enjoyable. They shared a sense of humour and Augusta could make Byron laugh. Anxious to take her mind off her money worries and the children's illnesses he organized little outings for her, including a visit to a masque at Almack's, the fashionable assembly rooms in King Street. He was able to get her a ticket as Lady Melbourne's daughter Emily, Lady Cowper, together with Lady Jersey were the leading patronesses of the club. On another occasion, at Lady Glenbervie's, they were noticed by the sharp-eyed Miss Milbanke, sitting together on a sofa.

Hanson heard that Claughton had agreed to sacrifice the £25,000 he had pledged as down payment on Newstead and this reinforced Byron's thoughts of travelling again. It was too late to go to Paris with Hobhouse and the Oxfords had already sailed for the Mediterranean; Sligo's trip to Persia was cancelled and Byron refused the offer of passage to Greece on the *Boyne* for himself and one servant as lacking in style.[24] Under the threat of a lawsuit Claughton managed to raise £15,000 in two instalments. Byron promptly lent Francis Hodgson enough money to get married and gave £1,000 to Augusta and her shiftless husband. Then he indulged in a monumental shopping spree. As well as buying trunks for his new clothes and refurbishing his aide-de-camp uniform, he bought guns, snuff boxes, five telescopes, rings, an Indian sabre, four swords (decorated with his coronet and cypher) and small arms. He also acquired camping equipment, two four-poster beds, camp stools, two chairs, kettles, stove, saucepans and a hammock. His enthusiasm was infectious and in a weak moment Augusta promised to accompany him. However, she soon came to her senses, pointing out the dangers of the plague, which had recently broken out and, to Byron's annoyance, refusing to consider going without at least one of her children. She was also worried about leaving George Leigh to face their creditors alone at Six Mile Bottom.

With his usual desire to shock, Byron told Lady Melbourne that he planned to leave England and take Augusta with him. She worried about the indiscreet remarks about incest he had made at Holland House and warned him to be sensible, to take care and consider Augusta's reputation. During her London visit Augusta stayed with the Hansons in Bloomsbury Square, later moving to the home of her friend, the Honourable Mrs George Villiers, in Knightsbridge which left little leaway for any private displays of affection. However, where there is a will there is a way. Annabella, when she was building her case against Byron and Augusta, claimed to have seen a letter from Lady Melbourne, which has since never been found, warning him that he was on the edge of a crime 'for which there is no salvation in this world, whatever there may be in the next'.[25]

Augusta sent him a lock of her hair tied up with white silk, wrapped in a sheet of paper on which she had written 'Augusta' and the words:

Partager tous vos sentimens
ne voir que par vos yeux
n'agir que par vos conseils, ne
vivre que pour vous, voilà mes
voeux, mes projets, & le seul
destin que peut me rendre
heureuse.

Byron wrote on the outside of the packet:

La Chevelure of
the *one* whom I
most loved +[26]

Annabella was piqued that Byron had not renewed his advances and indeed had hardly noticed her at all during the 1813 season. Under the pretext of concern for his reputation she told Lady Melbourne that she had heard he had taken unfair advantage of Mr Claughton. The message was passed to Byron who offhandedly told Lady Melbourne to reply as she thought fit and proper and that Annabella was welcome to defend him if that would amuse her.

Seeing that she was unable to attract Byron's attention and kicking herself for refusing him when she had had the chance, Annabella wrote to him directly on 22 August 1813. It was an enormously long letter telling him that her regard for his welfare did not arise from blindness to his errors. 'I was interested by the strength & generosity of your feelings, and I honored you for that pure sense of moral rectitude, which could not be perverted, though perhaps tried by the practice of Vice.' She continued, 'No longer suffer yourself to be the slave of the moment, nor trust your noble impulses to the chances of Life.'[27] She ended by asking him not to reveal their correspondence to Lady Melbourne. Byron replied quickly, also at great length, saying he had preferred her to all other women and did so still and did not feel his self esteem wounded by her refusal. He accepted her guidance that she would not accept him as a lover but wanted him as a friend. Believing her engaged to someone else he felt it was safe to say, 'I must be candid with you on the score of friendship. It is a feeling towards you with which I cannot trust myself. I doubt whether I could help loving you, but I trust I may appeal to my conduct since our eclaircissement for the proof, that whatever my feelings may be, they will exempt you from persecution, but I cannot yet profess indifference, and I fear that must be the first step – at least in some points – from what I feel to that which you wish me to feel.'[28] Regretting her lie she wrote back, 'I will not regret the friendship which you deem impossible, for the loss is *mine,* as the comfort would have been *mine.*' They continued to exchange letters. He wrote in his diary in November, 'What an odd situation and friendship is ours! – without one spark of love on either side, and produced by circumstances which in general lead to coldness on one side and aversion on the other.'[29]

The prospect of travel faded and in September Byron accepted an invitation from James Wedderburn Webster to form part of a house party at Aston Hall, near Rotherham. It was, curiously, the house where John Byron had seduced Augusta's mother. He amused himself by flirting with Webster's wife, formerly Lady Frances Annesley, daughter of the Earl of Mountnorris, and by giving Lady Melbourne a running commentary on his progress. The infatuated Lady Frances fanned his passion by passing him rings and secret notes under her husband's nose. The affair came to a head when the couple were left entirely alone and Lady Frances, to Byron's embarrassment, dramatically offered herself to him saying she was completely at his mercy. The tone in her voice alarmed him and, as he later told Lady Melbourne, he magnanimously 'spared' her.

The Bride of Abydos was published on 2 December and was an immediate success. Six thousand copies were sold within a month. Byron had begun to write *The Corsair* and took it with him when he visited the Leighs. He could not decide on a name for his heroine. His first choice was Francesca, then Genevra, finally settling on Medora which was also the name of a promising filly belonging to the Duke of Rutland. During his stay at Six Mile Bottom there were two other visitors, a shooting friend of George Leigh and his wife, Lady Frances Shelley. She complained, 'It was a wretched small house, full of her ill-trained children, who were always running up and down stairs, and going into "uncle's" bedroom where he remained all the morning.' She thought Augusta considerably older than Byron and her manner decidedly maternal, observing, 'She has evidently great moral influence over him.'[30] After a family Christmas with the Leighs, Byron left for London on 27 December. In the New Year he fulfilled his promise to Augusta and took her to Newstead, which she had never seen. The weather closed in and they stayed there cozily snowbound until 6 February 1814.

Byron was seriously under siege. Rogers was amused at the way ladies tried to get themselves noticed saying, 'I would receive a note from Lady— requesting the pleasure of my company on a particular evening with a postscript, "Pray, could you not contrive to bring Lord Byron with you?"' Wedderburn Webster was pushing his sister-in-law, Lady Catherine Annesley, but Byron preferred her youngest sister Lady Juliana and was curious about Lady Adelaide Forbes. Lady Falkland wrote passionate letters offering to press him to her heart and Mary Chaworth, now separated from her brutish husband, tried to draw him into correspondence.

Byron wrote in his journal for 16 January 1814, 'A wife would be my salvation,' and commented that, 'I hate an *esprit* in petticoats. That she won't love me is very probable, nor shall I love her. But, on my system, and the modern system in general, that don't signify. The business . . . would probably be arranged between papa and me. She would have her own way; I am good-humoured to women, and docile; and, if I did not fall in love with her, which I should try to prevent, we should be a very comfortable couple.'[31]

But he could not find anyone who compared favourably to Augusta. She was loyal, sympathetic, playful, blessed with the ability to make him laugh and could match his talent in talking nonsense. These qualities endeared her to him, perhaps more than was healthy for either of them, and his open admiration did not pass unnoticed, nor did his reckless talk of incest. His childish desire to shock was taken seriously by some and one of Augusta's nephews was taunted at Eton and asked about the identity of Zuleika in the *Bride of Abydos*.[32] Therese Villiers, who had known Augusta since she was a child, said, 'I think I am justified in saying *very* confidently that her mind *was* purity and innocence itself.'.

Lady Holderness had taught Augusta to respect the morals and beliefs of the Established Church, she could freely quote the Bible from memory and tolerantly believed that most actions were harmless if they did not make other people unhappy. She was a resilient woman who hid her feelings. Although her family and friends despised Colonel Leigh as a helpless drone whose thoughtlessness and selfishness had ruined the lives of his wife and children, Augusta loved him. She had chosen him, waited for him and had longed to be his wife and they jogged along in apparent harmony. She helped him in every way she could, from answering his turf correspondence to shielding him from debt collectors. In return he trusted her unwaveringly, allowed her a free hand in most things and never objected to her visiting friends during the Newmarket races when he and his reprobate cronies took over the house.

Byron struggled back to London through the snow in February to find he was being bitterly attacked for *Weep, Daughter of a Royal Line* which he had published anonymously in March 1812 and incorporated into *The Corsair*.[33] The reference to the Prince Regent caused offence to the Tory press:

> Weep, daughter of a royal line,
>   A Sire's disgrace, a realm's decay;
> Ah, happy if each tear of thine
>   Could wash a Father's fault away!

Byron and Hobhouse resumed their social life of dining out and theatre- going and, at a reception on 24 February 1814, Byron introduced Hobhouse to the independent-minded Miss Mercer Elphinstone. She was known as the 'fops' despair' having seen off proposals and advances from the Duke of Clarence, Count Bothmer of the King's German Legion and the Count of Balmain. She was an heiress in her own right, attractive, intelligent with fine eyes. She always spoke her mind.

Byron gave away Hanson's daughter, Mary Anne, to the Earl of Portsmouth at their marriage, by licence, at the Bloomsbury Chapel on 7 March. He found certain phrases in the preliminary exhortation of the marriage service amusing and suffered a mild fit of the giggles when he united the couple's left hands instead of their right before stumbling back to the altar-rail. He noticed that the bridegroom, oddly enough, appeared to have learned the service by heart and at one point was a step ahead of the priest.[34]

The weather continued to be snowy and bitterly cold until 20 March when the sun broke through and guns were fired to celebrate Wellington's crossing of the Adour river. The following day Byron and Hobhouse were invited to a small party at Lansdowne House together with Lady Charlotte Leveson-Gower, a friend of Augusta and a niece of Lord Carlisle. She was not particularly pretty but she had the type of shyness which Byron admired in his sister and which he liked to compare to that of an antelope.[35] She was once described by Lady Harriet Granville as 'one of those people whom it is not merely difficult but impossible to get acquainted with'.[36] Byron drummed up enough courage to speak to Lady Charlotte's mother, but he stopped short of asking for an introduction to Lady Charlotte herself, remembering his attacks on Lord Carlisle with whom he had not yet made his peace despite the urgings of Augusta, the Lambs, Rogers and the Hollands.

Byron visited Augusta early in April to keep her company during George Leigh's absence in Yorkshire. The visit was marred by a fit of gluttony (he ate an entire collar of brawn at supper and suffered from it for a couple of days). Augusta was bedevilled by Leigh's debts and the problems of bringing up young children in an inadequate house on a vanishing income. As soon as Byron received Claughton's down-payment on Newstead he gave her £3,000 to pay off some of the debts. He remained puzzled as to how Augusta could continue to love the improvident Leigh – but she did, and would spring to his defence if he was attacked.

Annabella agreed with her parents that she would not take part in the coming London season but, desperate to see Byron, she coaxed her devoted parents to invite him to Seaham. On 13 April she wrote telling

him to expect a formal invitation from her father and that he was to
ensure Lady Melbourne believed the visit was only a casual one. Byron
had long ago disobeyed her and Lady Melbourne was well aware of the
progress of the strange courtship she had instigated.[37] Indeed, for Byron,
one of the great attractions of marriage was the possibility of calling her
'Aunt'. He delayed answering the letter until he knew her views as he did
not want to make a fruitless journey north.

On 20 May Byron was in Cambridgeshire attending the baptism of his
goddaughter. His fellow sponsors were the Duchess of Rutland, daughter
of Lord Carlisle and Mrs Wilmot, a cousin by marriage. The baby was
christened Elizabeth Medora; Elizabeth for the Duchess of Rutland and
Medora after one of the heroines in *The Corsair*, which had been partly
written at Six Mile Bottom the previous December. Whether the Duke of
Rutland's filly, Medora, which had just won the Oaks, influenced Colonel
Leigh's choice of a name is not known.

If any great secret weighed on Byron's soul he did not show it. The
evening before the christening he dined with Moore at Watier's, the
fashionable eating and gambling house where he had recently been
made a member. Moore ordered him two kinds of fish, as he knew Byron
would be hungry, having eaten nothing within the last two days except for
a few biscuits and chewing mastic to keep his appetite down. Byron ate
two or three lobsters washing them down with half a dozen small glasses
of white brandy and the occasional tumbler of very hot water. They drank
two bottles of claret each, gossiping until about four in the morning.[38]
On 1 June Hobhouse and Byron had supper at Lady Jersey's, on 9 June at
Lady Lansdowne's and on the 14th the pair went to Lady Rancliffe's party
where Mrs Rawdon gave Hobhouse a long inventory of her daughter's
charms even though the delightful Bessy was in the same room. On
18 June, at Earl Grey's, Byron managed to speak to shy Lady Charlotte
Leveson Gower. They were both tongue-tied. (On such occasions when
he was younger Byron used to gabble 'one, two, three, four five, six,
seven', to regain his nerve.) He was much taken by Lady Charlotte,
describing her to Augusta as 'shy as an antelope', a sure sign of favour.
On 24 June they met again. Byron assured the blushing girl that he was in
a greater fright than she was and the atmosphere relaxed and they talked
for half an hour. Her conversation and attitude charmed and reminded
him of the early awkward meetings he had had with Augusta. He asked
Rogers if there was any possibility of making peace with Lord Carlisle, 'as
I feel disposed to do anything reasonable or unreasonable to effect it'.[39]

On 1 July Byron and Hobhouse went to the Watier's masquerade at
Burlington House. Hobhouse disguised himself as an Albanian and Byron
as a monk. When Bessy Rawdon saw Byron she exclaimed to Hobhouse,

1 No. 16 Holles Street, London; Byron was born in the back drawing room on the first floor.

2 Aberdeen, where Byron and his mother lived until he was ten.

3 Newstead Abbey, showing the steps (later removed) where Byron sat waiting for
Annabella Milbanke's reply to his proposal of marriage.

4 Byron aged seven – the
portrait he gave to his nurse,
May Gray.

5 Harrow churchyard: ' . . . where I used to sit for hours and hours when a boy. This was my favourite spot.'

6 Byron at seventeen: 'The Adventures of my Life from 16 to 19 . . . have given a *voluptuous Tint* to my ideas.'

7 Mary Chaworth at seventeen: 'Our union would have healed feuds in which blood had been shed by our fathers.'

8 Mrs Catherine Byron: 'I am sorry to say the old lady and myself don't agree like lambs in a meadow, but I believe it is all my own fault.'

9 Byron at Cambridge: 'My life here has been one continued routine of dissipation . . .'.

10 The Maid of Saragoza: 'I find that reserve is not the characteristic of the Spanish belles, who are, in general, very handsome, with large black eyes, and very fine forms.'

11 Teresa, the Maid of Athens: '. . . the old woman, Teresa's mother, was mad enough to imagine I was going to marry the girl; but I have better amusement.'

12 Temple of Jupiter Olympus, Athens: 'Eh, Sir, there's a situation, there's your picturesque! nothing like that, Sir, in Lunnun, no not even the Mansion House.'

13 The Capuchin Convent, Athens, where Byron was 'vastly happy and childish'.

14 John Murray, '*To thee, with hope and terror dumb, The unfledged MS, authors come; Thou printest all – and sellest some – My Murray.*'

15 Samuel Rogers: 'Of the professions of esteem with which Mr Rogers has honoured me, I cannot but feel proud, though undeserving.'

16 Annabella Milbanke was twenty when she met Byron. She recorded: 'My complexion has become so clear, my eyes so lively, and my muscles so round that I have not looked so well this year past.'

17 Augustus Foster, Minister to the United States and Annabella's most persistent suitor.

18 Lady Melbourne, mother of William Lamb and friend of Byron: 'She was my greatest *friend*, of the feminine gender.'

19 The Duchess of Devonshire, who owned 13 Piccadilly Terrace.

'Does he not look beautiful?' Caroline Lamb misbehaved by parading backwards and forwards so often in front of Byron that he dreaded another scene. She first caught his attention by immodestly displaying her green pantaloons. He told Lady Melbourne that he had scolded her like a grandfather. Which was just what she was aiming for, of course.[40]

Byron wanted to take Augusta and the Leigh children on a holiday to Hastings and asked Hodgson, who was there visiting his prospective bride, to find him a house. He was very specific: he wanted one large enough to accommodate Augusta, her four children, three maids, his valet and footman and the temporary cook and housemaid; his own room must be as far as possible away from the women's and children's; and the house near to good bathing beaches. Hastings House was hired and became the base for three happy weeks of swimming, eating turbot, walking on the cliffs, tumbling down hills and making the most of the leisure and the sea.[41]

During their holiday the subject of Byron's marriage was exhaustively discussed. Augusta favoured her friend Lady Charlotte and put out careful feelers on Byron's behalf. Knowing the antagonism towards him felt by the Carlisles she did not hold out great hope and agreed that, although she did not feel Annabella was the best choice for Byron, she was willing to consider her in the event of failure with her favourite.

Annabella had not seen or heard from Byron for some time and, fearful he had escaped, wrote to him on 6 August 1814. She put her case as delicately as she could:

Some time ago I had meant to acknowledge clearly, knowing that you would not mistake the motives of my acknowledgement, that I had been deceived (and too willingly, inasmuch as you were concerned) in thinking I had ever formed a decided attachment. The reasons which led me to believe the character of one person suited to my own, have disappeared with opportunities for fuller investigation . . . nothing could now induce me to marry him.[42]

Byron replied, tongue in cheek:

I did – do – and always shall love you . . . but I was informed that you were attached, if not engaged – and very luckily – to a person for whose success all the females of the family where I received my intelligence were interested. What your own feelings and objections were and are I have not the right and scarcely the wish to enquire. . . . You would probably like me if you could; and as you cannot, I am not quite coxcomb enough to be surprised at a very natural occurrence.[43]

Annabella's reply to Byron's letter was so ungracious and verbose that he assumed that his suit was at an end and briskly replied, 'Very well – now we can talk of something else.'[44] Realizing she had made a mistake Annabella took another tack and decided to flatter his vanity by asking him to recommend books of modern history for her to read.

He arrived back in London on 11 August to the good news that *Lara*, which he had written in May, had sold 6,000 copies in four days. The unhappy news was that the sale of Newstead had fallen through, though Claughton had forfeited his £25,000. On 21 August Byron, Augusta and the children left for Newstead to spend happy days reading, swimming, boating and relaxing. Byron fished in the lake catching carp and lots of perch while Augusta and the children flourished.

He replied to Annabella's exhaustive literary letter on 25 August giving her suggestions for a reading list and answering personal questions on his health, ending with a postscript regretting he would not be able to visit Seaham during the present year. She answered again at great length.

Augusta still persevered in her attempt to entice Lady Charlotte to be her sister-in-law and was disappointed but not surprised when she backed away and accepted a proposal from Henry Howard, the future Earl of Surrey. They married in December. 'You see,' said Byron, 'that after all, Miss Milbanke is to be the person; – I will write to her.' Augusta urged him to think again, pointing out that Annabella had no great fortune, she was well educated and tended to be a blue stocking, just the type of woman he most disliked. Nevertheless he wrote a letter but before sending it, he showed it to Augusta. She said, 'Well, really this is a very pretty letter; – it is a pity it should not go. I never read a prettier one.' 'Then it *shall* go,' said Byron.

He was uncertain what reply he wanted from his 'pretty' letter, which was less of a love letter and more of a probing one. 'I neither wish you to promise or pledge yourself to anything; but merely to learn a *possibility* which would not leave you the less a free agent.'

Having convinced himself that 'a wife would be the salvation of me' and thrown the die he became agitated and would sit on the steps outside the abbey and watch for the post. He told Augusta he was sure he would be refused, and then speculated on what he should do if he were accepted. Predicting failure, he planned to leave England in October with Hobhouse. They would go to Italy; he had always wanted to see Venice and the Alps.[45]

Annabella wrote back a short note of explosive joy, saying she was almost too agitated to write but, 'It would be absurd to suppress anything – I am and have long been pledged to myself to make your happiness my first object in life. *If I can* make you happy, I have no other consideration.

I will *trust* to you for all I should look up to – all I can love.' She efficiently made two copies of her letter sending one to Newstead and the other to his rooms at Albany explaining that she wished to spare him a moment's suspense. Enclosed with the London letter was an invitation from Sir Ralph to visit Seaham once again.

Byron and Augusta were having dinner with a friend when Annabella's letter arrived. Simultaneously the gardener handed Byron his mother's wedding ring, freshly dug up from under her window. With the unopened letter in his hand, Byron exclaimed, 'If it contains a consent, I will be married with this very ring.' He read the letter then handed it silently across the table to Augusta. He looked so pale that she thought he was going to faint. He said, 'It never rains but it pours.'

CHAPTER FOUR

'Marry not,' says he

Byron set off for London on 21 September determined to put his affairs in order before visiting Seaham. He wanted to make a settlement of £60,000 on Annabella, but to do that he needed to sell Newstead. In town he ran into Hodgson who, after several glasses of claret, became outraged at what he perceived as the greed of the Milbankes, and said they must be the most 'royally selfish persons' to accept such a sacrifice. Byron was still uncertain of Annabella's assets, but knew that Sir Ralph had lost a great deal of money fighting election campaigns – he had represented Durham for twenty-two years, most of them spent on the opposition backbenches. Byron contacted Hanson and was intensely irritated that a meeting to draw up the marriage settlement could not be arranged immediately with Sir Ralph's agent.

The Milbankes broke the news of the engagement to their relations in a series of letters. 'It has taken place with the entire approbation of her father and myself, to which is added my brother's kindest sanction,' wrote Lady Milbanke.[1] A formal announcement was placed in the 5 October edition of the *Morning Post* and was met by astonishment in some circles. Lady Granville thought it 'wonderful of that sensible cautious prig of a girl to venture upon such a heap of poems, crimes and rivals',[2] a view secretly shared by Byron, who was taken aback by his success. 'I certainly did not dream that she was attached to me, which it seems she has been for some time. I also thought her of a very cold disposition, in which I was mistaken,'[3] the surprised groom wrote to Moore. 'By the way, my wife-elect is perfection, and I hear of nothing but her merits and her wonders, and that she is "very pretty".' Her expectations, I am told are great: but *what*, I have not asked. I have not seen her these ten months.'[4] He felt foolish and apprehensive about the wedding. 'I must not marry in a black coat, they tell me, and I can't bear a blue one,' he complained to Lady Jersey, continuing, 'Pray forgive me for scribbling all this nonsense. You know I must be serious all the rest of my life, and this is a parting piece of buffoonery.'[5] The news was noted laconically in Hobhouse's diary on 30 September. The following day he congratulated his friend and agreed to stand as groomsman at the wedding.

Annabella described her engagement as 'an event that affords me the best prospect of happiness. The attachment had been progressive for two years and I now own it with feelings of happiness that promise to be durable as they are deep . . . for his despondency I fear I am but too answerable the last two years. . . .'[6] It was a bold attempt to hoodwink herself and others into believing that Byron had played the pale and anxious suitor for two years while in fact it was she who had relentlessly pursued him.

She took offence when friends wished her happiness on her coming marriage, bridling at, as she saw it, the implied suggestion that she could be anything else. She analysed her feelings and Byron's intentions, sending reports to her maiden friends, Selina Doyle, Joanna Baillie and Emily Milner. Augusta wrote her a charming letter saying how much she was looking forward to the day when she could call her 'sister', but by October, when the marriage settlement had still not been agreed, nor Newstead sold and Byron's courage was slipping away, the Milbankes became impatient. Colonel Leigh told Augusta that someone was running a book at Newmarket on whether or not the marriage would take place, though Byron was paying out on bets he foolishly made in Brighton when he had taken a guinea each from several gambling cronies at odds of 150:1 against him ever marrying. As soon as the announcement of his marriage appeared in the Durham papers they rushed to claim their winnings.

The departure of Byron and Hanson for Seaham to complete the arrangements for the marriage settlement was delayed by a crisis in Hanson's family. His daughter's husband, Lord Portsmouth, was somewhat feeble-minded and Portsmouth's brother and heir, Newton Fellowes, was attempting to have the marriage annulled on the grounds of his insanity. As groomsman to the marriage Byron had agreed to provide contrary evidence, but he became increasingly uneasy as the days slipped by and Hanson dithered and procrastinated. When Hanson pleaded illness as an excuse for more delay Byron's patience snapped. He wrote sternly on 25 October pointing out that the delays had caused him to miss meeting Lord Wentworth at Seaham, had displeased the whole of the Milbanke family and left Annabella confused, and any more could give the Milbankes an excuse to break the engagement.

Augusta tried to reassure Annabella and did her best to further her brother's cause, but she neglected to make sure he bought Annabella an engagement ring, an omission noted with fury by Lady Milbanke. While Augusta was trying to lull Annabella's fears, George Leigh was urging Byron to take his time, leading him to suspect that Leigh feared Byron's new wife would stand in the way of Augusta's inheritance.

Byron did not dare wait any longer for Hanson and quitted London for

Seaham on 29 October leaving instructions for him to make his way to Durham as fast as possible. He spent the night with the Leighs at Six Mile Bottom,[7] not leaving until late the evening of the following day when he dragged himself up as far as the Haycock at Wansford. The next night he slept at Newark and from there he wrote to Lady Melbourne confessing he was in a bad temper and that he had heard that Mary Chaworth was still seriously ill. She had been on his mind since he had heard that she had become insane in Hastings in the same house in which he and the Leighs had spent their happy holiday only two months earlier.[8] She still had a sentimental hold over him and he was appalled that her hunting husband would leave her alone in London while he followed the hounds in Yorkshire.

It was 1 November when he finally arrived at Seaham and the extraordinary length of time it had taken him to travel from London did not pass without comment. Lady Milbanke, in particular, was impatient and annoyed.

Annabella had set the stage and planned to meet him alone. When she heard his carriage wheels on the gravel she dropped her book, put out her candles, left her chamber and hurried to the drawing room.[9] Byron was standing by the fireplace and remained motionless as she approached holding out her hand. He took it in his, bent and kissed it and stood silently next to her for a moment before saying in a low voice, 'It is a long time since we have met.' Her pent-up emotions overpowered her and after asking if he had seen her parents she fled from the room to call them only to find that they had already met on the doorstep. The family returned to the drawing room and Annabella took her seat next to Byron, watching him out of the corner of her eye, as he played nervously with his large watch chain. The stilted conversation restricted itself to generalities and after a little while Byron enquired what time Annabella got up in the morning. She said they assembled at about ten. The couple shook hands and parted. Annabella got up early the next day and waited for Byron until, just before midday, she went for a walk on the beach, alone.[10]

Byron wrote regularly to Lady Melbourne reporting on the habits of her brother and his family. Two days after his arrival he told her that he liked honest, humorous, red-faced Sir Ralph despite his penchant for telling the same stories over and over again, but he instinctively disliked Lady Milbanke, finding her tiresome, pettish but clever. However, it was clear to see they were both devoted to their clever daughter.

Uncertain of his real affection Annabella began one evening to probe into his motives, feelings, sensibilities. She asked him to tell her frankly if for any reason he had changed his mind, because if he had she would release him from the engagement. An ardent lover would have embraced her and protested undying love but Byron, startled, fell back limp on to the sofa and several minutes passed before he recovered, murmuring indistinctly, 'You don't know what you've done.'[11] Annabella told herself that he was struck with despair at the idea of losing her. It did not occur to her that he saw the tantalizing door of freedom swing open before him, but honour demanded that he should not take the first step.

Byron was not convinced she was truly in love with him, telling Lady Melbourne, 'Annabella is the most silent woman I ever encountered which perplexes me extremely. I like them to talk, because then they think less. . . . However, the die is cast; neither party can secede; the lawyers are here. . . .' But his doubts grew and a few days later he wrote, 'Do you know I have grave doubts if this will be a marriage now? Her disposition is the very reverse of our imaginings. She is overrun with fine feelings, scruples about herself and her disposition (I suppose, in fact, she means mine) and to crown all, is taken ill once every three days with I know not what. . . .' He concluded, 'In short it is impossible to foresee how this will end *now*, any more than two years ago; if this is a break, it shall be her doing not mine.' Meanwhile, he tried 'the calming process so renowned in our philosophy'. This consisted in exchanging words for gestures, a caress for a frown or a kiss for a cross word. 'Entre nous it is really amusing,' he wrote, 'she is like a child in that respect – and quite *caressable* into kindness and good humour.'[12] The first experience of his touch frightened the inexperienced Annabella, releasing emotions and desires she did not understand and making her embarrassed to be alone with him. Her modesty was affronted but at the same time she was doubtful how long she could withstand him. The strain became too much and she ordered him to leave without informing her parents of her delicate reason. On the day he left she wrote, 'I wish we were married, and then I could do my best, and not quarrel with myself for a thousand things that you would not mind. I expect you will write me a lecture – and it shall be studied *con amore*. I must write to our sister – plead for me with her – and plead for me too with my Lord and master – beseeching him still to "love and cherish" his undutiful wife.' On the following day she ended another letter, 'Will you take me to your heart? my home "till Death do us part" – and don't turn me out of doors in revenge as you threatened.' Even Byron agreed that 'being under the same roof and not being married . . . well, past experience has shown us the awkwardness of the situation.'[13] He asked her again if she was quite sure she loved him. 'Why do you doubt it?' she asked signing her letters 'Wife'. Byron played along, calling her 'Sweetheart' and 'Mignonne'.

By the time Byron reached Six Mile Bottom he had made up his mind to break off the engagement. However, Augusta urged him to be careful and to think again. Leaving the Leighs in sombre mood he went to Cambridge to place his vote for Mr Clarke, Fellow of Trinity, for the professorship of anatomy. On entering and leaving he was applauded by the students in the gallery, a most unusual and flattering occurrence. Before he left Cambridge he accepted Augusta's advice and wrote to the confused Annabella, 'Don't scold *yourself* any more – I told you before there was no occasion – you have not offended me. I am as happy as hope can make me – and gay as Love will allow me to be till we meet, and ever my Heart – thine.'[14]

Once in London he settled into the familiar routine of theatres and dinners with Moore. Hanson was so deeply embroiled in questionable legal disputes which surrounded the marriage of his daughter to Lord Portsmouth that it was impossible for Byron to rent his Hampshire house, Farleigh, as he had planned. This was a disappointment as he had hoped to live economically in the country with Annabella until Newstead was sold and his financial position improved.[15]

Annabella became tired of waiting and on 2 December pointedly announced that the wedding cake was being prepared. He dashed her hopes the following day; the paper-work would not be completed for at least ten days and, even more disheartening, he asked for a quiet wedding in her parents' home. This was disappointing news for Lady Milbanke too and denied her the pleasure of overseeing a splendid wedding to which all northern society would have been invited. On 8 December the news arrived that the negotiations with Claughton had broken down completely. 'Things must come round in the end,' Byron wrote, 'for even if N[ewstead] and R[ochdale] are both sold at a loss, they will at least leave us clear, and your settlement secured into the bargain. Well – "to marry or not" that's the question – or will you wait? Perhaps the clouds may disperse in a month or two. Do as you please.' This was hardly the letter of a passionate lover, but Annabella chose to ignore the way out he was offering and, as Byron later told Medwin, 'She married me from vanity and the hope of reforming and fixing me. She was a spoiled child.' Certainly she had received enough clues to deduce that Byron did not love her as most young men love their brides, nevertheless she insisted on entering a marriage with a reluctant bridegroom. Hobhouse later remarked tartly, 'Miss Milbanke may have been deceived in the expectations she formed in uniting herself with Lord Byron, but she was not deceived by Lord Byron, she was deceived by herself. A little less passion and a little more reflection would have convinced her of the propriety of accepting Lord Byron's proposal of delay.'[16]

Byron went to Doctor's Commons to apply for a wedding licence with Hanson; as it was handed to him he asked, 'Pray, sir, what is the proportion of those who come here first to make marriages, and then afterwards to unmake them?'[17]

Hobhouse and Byron left London for Seaham at midday on Christmas Eve and parted at Chesterford, Byron heading for Six Mile Bottom and Hobhouse for Cambridge where he spent a merry Christmas with Scrope Davies. He noted in his journal that he dined at Trinity College on Christmas Day and 'Heard they have been throwing a collector of property tax out of the window at St. Ives'.

Byron spent a gloomy Christmas with the Leighs overshadowed by his wedding and marred by George's constant complaints of illness and demands for medicine. However, he left unwillingly on Boxing Day to meet Hobhouse at three in the afternoon to begin their slow way to Wansford where they stayed the night. 'Never was a lover less in haste,' Hobhouse noted in his journal. The next day saw them crawling through the snow and bitter cold from the warmth of the Haycock towards Newark. Byron confessed to Hobhouse that he did not love Annabella, had not wanted to marry while his financial state was so precarious, and had given the family every opportunity of delaying if not breaking the engagement, but Annabella would not let go. At Newark Hobhouse settled down happily to read his new copy of Gibbon's autobiography while the bridegroom became 'more and more *less* impatient'. On 28 December they reached Ferrybridge. They dragged themselves to Thirsk the next day and arrived at Seaham Hall at eight o'clock on 29 December to find that the family had withdrawn for the night.

The servants admitted the guests and roused the Milbankes but Lady Milbanke, furious with Byron for the time he had taken to travel from London, refused to come down. Hobhouse had nothing to say as he thought he would have 'looked foolish in trying to find an excuse for our want of expedition'.

The guests were first shown to their rooms and then invited to reassemble in the library. Hobhouse was the first to come down, followed by Annabella, who shook his hand, and Sir Ralph who tottered in a few minutes later. Hobhouse thought Annabella looked dowdy but acknowledged she had excellent feet and ankles; he thought the upper part of her face more handsome than the lower but found her attitude frank, open and without any little irritating airs or affectations.

When Annabella heard Byron leave his room she ran to meet him, spontaneously throwing her arms around his neck and bursting into tears. The couple entered the library and were joined by Mr William Hoar, the Milbankes' cheerful solicitor from Sunderland and the

Reverend Thomas Noel, rector of Kirkby Mallory and illegitimate son of Lord Wentworth. The atmosphere relaxed. Sir Ralph told some stories and Annabella sat silently, modestly and appeared to Hobhouse to be a sensible and quiet girl dotingly fond of Byron, 'gazing with delight on his bold and animated face'. Byron, he noted, 'appears to love her personally, when in her company'.

The next day the settlements were signed in the morning and, at six o'clock, after dinner, there was a wedding rehearsal. Hobhouse stood in for Annabella and Hoar played the part of Sir Ralph. They then all shook hands and wished each other a Happy New Year before retiring for the night. Hoar left the following day and Hobhouse took the opportunity to walk on the beach. The dinner had not been quite so jolly as the night before but tolerable. Before going to bed Byron went to Hobhouse's room. 'Well, Hobhouse,' he said, 'this is our last night; tomorrow I shall be Annabella's.'[18]

Hobhouse got up and dressed for the wedding complete with white gloves and joined Byron who had been up some time walking in the grounds. They talked with Thomas Noel who had on his canonicals ready for the service before being joined by Sir Ralph and Lady Milbanke. She was so agitated she could not make the tea because of her shaking hands. The rector of Seaham, the Reverend Wallace, arrived and at half past ten the group broke up. Ten minutes later the groom and best man walked up the stairs to the first-floor drawing room where the two clergymen, Sir Ralph and Lady Milbanke were waiting. A table had been placed with prayer books in the bay window which overlooked the bleak winter garden. There were no flowers outside or on the makeshift altar. The chairs had been pushed back against the wall and hard hassocks placed in front of the table. Byron, dressed in his hated blue coat, took his place with Hobhouse on the right of the room near the fireplace. Then Mrs Clermont, Annabella's former nurse and companion, signalled to her that everything was ready. She came in alone wearing a dress of white Indian muslin over a petticoat of the same material. The hem of the petticoat and the detachable cuffs of the over-dress were embroidered with flowers and leaves. She also wore 'a white muslin curricle jacket – very plain indeed, with nothing on her head'.

Thomas Noel arranged Byron and Annabella behind their hassocks, Sir Ralph took up his place next to his daughter, Lady Milbanke and Mrs Clermont stood in the opposite corner and Hobhouse remained next to Sir Ralph. Annabella, noted Hobhouse, 'was as firm as a rock, and, during the whole ceremony, looked steadily at Byron. She repeated the words audibly and well. Byron hitched at first when he said, "I, George Gordon," and when he came to the words, "With all my worldly goods I

thee endow," looked at me with a half-smile. They were married at
eleven.' Hobhouse shook the new Lady Byron's hand and embraced his
friend who was kissed by Lady Milbanke. Annabella kissed her parents
and half-tearful left the room. but returned to sign the register which was
witnessed by Hobhouse and Wallace. She left again with her eyes full of
tears when she looked at her father and mother 'and thus she completed
her conquest – her innocent conquest,' wrote Hobhouse.[19] She recovered
after a few moments and took Byron's arm as they walked to cut the
towering wedding cake. Byron was calm and seemed his usual self.

Annabella changed into her travelling dress, 'a slate coloured satin
pelisse trimmed with white fur', and sat quietly until just before twelve
when Byron asked, 'Miss Milbanke, are you ready?'[20] Hobhouse escorted
her to the carriage and wished her many years of happiness. She replied,
'If I am not happy it will be my own fault.' Byron clasped Hobhouse's
hand through the carriage window and held on to it like a drowning man
until the carriage moved so fast that he was forced to let go.

Hobhouse left Seaham immediately, feeling 'as if I had buried a
friend'.

The carriage had not even left the grounds before Byron turned to
Annabella and asked her, through the cheers of the Milbanke peasantry,
'What could induce you to marry me?'

'Good heavens,' she replied, 'because I loved you.'

'No,' he said firmly. 'You have a spice of Mother Eve, you married me
because your friends wished you not to do so.'[21]

By the time they halted at a livery stable in Durham it had begun to
snow and they heard the bells ring out to celebrate the wedding of the
daughter of their former Member of Parliament. 'Ringing for our
happiness, I suppose?' Byron cynically asked. They sat silently until
suddenly Byron began to sing wildly to relieve his spirits. Later he
exclaimed, 'It *must* come to a separation! You should have married me
when I first proposed.' When they halted at an inn by the Rushford
crossroads Byron said, 'I wonder how much longer I shall be able to keep
up the part I have been playing?' They drank a glass of port and
continued their journey.[22]

Fourteen months later and for the benefit of her lawyers, Annabella
claimed that within an hour of leaving Seaham Byron had said, with a
malignant sneer, 'Oh, what a dupe you have been to your imagination!
How is it possible a woman of your sense could form the wild hope of
reforming *me*? Many are the tears you will have to shed ere that plan is
accomplished. It is enough for me that you are my wife for me to hate

you! If you were the wife of any other man, I own you might have charms.' (Byron's tone, as remembered by Annabella, was usually that of a Gothic villain, quite unlike the pattern of speech recorded by his friends.) He continued, she said, by saying he detested her mother and made fun of her small fortune, speaking to her as though she were destitute. Lady Anne Barnard, a childhood friend, asked why she did not return home immediately. Annabella explained, 'Because I had not a conception he was in earnest; because I reckoned it a bad jest, and told him so.'[23] Byron told Medwin, 'If I had made so uncavalier, not to say brutal a speech, I am convinced Lady Byron would have instantly left the carriage. She had spirit enough to have done so, and would properly have resented the affront.' Byron remembered sitting through the entire journey in moody silence, reading a book.

They crossed the Tees at Croft Bridge, passed through the village of Croft-on-Tees and out on to the Middleton Tyas Lane for the last one and a half miles. It was dark and still snowing when the carriage turned into Halnaby Hall where two Milbanke servants were waiting to open the gates. The other servants were lined up on the steps to welcome them. Minns, the butler, recollected Byron leaping out of the carriage and walking into the house leaving Lady Byron to shift for herself. She came up slowly, her face stained with traces of tears.[24] She shook hands with Mr Minns and asked him to provide refreshment for the waiting staff. But Jane Minns, his wife and Annabella's lady's maid during the honeymoon, remembered her leaving the coach as buoyant and cheerful as a bride should be, kindly and gaily responding to the waiting servants.

Mrs Minns led the couple through the fine marble hall decorated with stucco festoons and up the stairs to the first floor. Their bedrooms were small and on the north side of the house but there were warm and welcoming fires burning brightly in the grates.[25] Whatever bad feeling there may have been in the carriage was dispelled and Annabella was soon on remarkably good terms with her husband. Byron remembered and coarsely recorded in his memoirs that he had '*had* Lady B. on the sofa before dinner' on the day of their marriage.[26]

After dinner he began to tease and taunt her, asking if she planned to sleep in the same bed with him, saying with a look of aversion on his face, 'I hate sleeping with any woman, but you may if you choose,' adding that providing a woman was young, one was as good as another.

It was a cold January night and in their haste to get into bed they forgot to blow out the taper. Byron woke from a shallow sleep to find the light from the taper and the flames from the fire shining through the drawn red moreen bed-curtains, turning the bed into a red cave. Bathed in the scarlet light he fancied he was in Hades and that the sleeping

Annabella was Proserpina, and cried out, 'Good God, I am surely in hell!'[27] Instead of laughing, Annabella took offence. By now, thoroughly woken up and overcome with melancholy, Byron got up and wandered up and down the long gallery, eventually returning to bed to sleep heavily until twelve o'clock.

The weather was gloomy and the snow fell for hour upon hour. Byron woke to find he had a cold as well as a bride. He joined Annabella downstairs at midday and, according to Annabella, 'He met me repellently, and uttered words of blighting irony: "It is too late now. It is done, and cannot be undone."' She took him on a tour, inside and outside, of her home, a handsome red-brick house built during the Commonwealth with ornate chimneys and balustrades. Byron approved of the library and retreated there followed by Annabella. He hated to be watched but Annabella dogged his footsteps round the large house driving him from room to room to escape her loving eyes. He asked her to stop but she continued to follow him with canine devotion. She was not used to being ignored and like a spoilt child was reduced to depression and tears when Byron told her to stop being sentimental, making it clear that she was a nuisance. She came across him one day sitting next to the fireplace with his red portfolio near him. She fell to her knees in front of him and when he reproached her for not accepting his proposal sooner, Annabella replied, slipping her arms round his neck, 'You forget we *are* married, I believe.' Then, according to Annabella, he read aloud to her letters from Lady Melbourne including one in which she warned him that he was on the verge of an '"atrocious crime" for which there is no salvation in this world whatever there may be in the next.'[28]

Byron was delighted to receive a letter from Augusta and read out snippets, saying he thought Augusta's words describing her feeling during the hour of their marriage – 'As the sea trembles when the earth quakes' – were quite poetical. He asked Annabella what she thought of Augusta's opening sentence, 'Dearest, first and best of human beings'; Annabella did not record her reply. In later statements to her lawyer she said that Byron admitted that he had committed mysterious and atrocious crimes, that he was a villain, that he had two natural children, that if she had married him two years earlier she would have saved him and that there was insanity in his family. Her stolid reception of these outrageous confessions drove him to even more fantastic revelations. At one point she believed he had committed a murder.[29]

Annabella had read Dryden's *Don Sebastian*, and casually asked Byron about its subject, incest. 'Where did you hear that?' he asked angrily. Annabella looked up and saw he was holding over her the dagger which he usually wore. 'Oh, only from this book,' she replied and he put it down and said, 'If anything could make me believe in heaven, it is the expression of your countenance at this moment.'[30]

Incest as a poetical subject was not new. Sophocles, Shakespeare and Webster had used it and Byron and Shelley were to follow suit, but bearing in mind the grave suspicions which Annabella later claimed filled her heart, she took the strange step of inviting her new sister-in-law to visit them at Halnaby. However, 'poor Gussey' as she called herself, could not leave her children and Colonel Leigh, who amiably sent his best wishes and hoped that they would meet soon.

Byron frequently suffered from sleepless nights and used to pace the long gallery carrying his dagger and a pistol, only returning to bed when he felt he was able to sleep. One night he returned from his walk exhausted and Annabella placed her head tenderly on his chest. 'You should have a softer pillow than my heart.' he said. Annabella replied dramatically, 'I wonder which will break first, yours or mine.'[31]

The snow continued throughout the early days of the honeymoon, or 'treaclemoon' as Byron jokingly called it, and for the rest of her life Annabella felt miserable at the sight of falling snow. Annabella lacked a sense of humour and failed to understand her husband's love for jokes and the ridiculous. She was also burdened by enormous intellectual smugness which made it difficult to distinguish between truth and exaggeration. She never knew when her leg was being pulled, unlike Augusta who could laugh Byron out of bad temper and melancholy.

The honeymoon was not entirely gloomy. They developed pet names for each other, Annabella became 'Bell' or 'Pippin' for her pink cheeks and round face, Byron became 'Duck', a local endearment, and Augusta was called either 'Gussey' or 'Goose'. Annabella volunteered to make fair copies of Byron's work, *Hebrew Melodies* and *By the Rivers of Babylon* and *Herod's Lament* which were written at Halnaby. On Sundays she took him to the village church where they sat in the elevated, galleried Milbanke pew which was curtained off from the rest of the church. Byron spent most of his time in the library where he wrote cheerful letters to the outside world. He told Lady Melbourne that Bell went through the service very well, the kneeling was tedious and the cushions hard and the present scene at Halnaby was so domestic they might have been married for fifty years. 'Lady Byron is vastly well,' he told Moore on 10 January and by 12 January he was thinking about making provision for a son.

Isolated from her mother and other female friends, Annabella confided her troubles and slights to Mrs Minns. She accused Byron of intentional cruelty and she told the startled woman she was sure something most dreadful had passed between him and his sister. Mrs

Minns sensibly advised her to speak to her parents, but when they returned to Seaham Hall on 21 January Annabella kept her own counsel and her behaviour gave no indication that anything was wrong.[32] Nor did Sir Ralph and Lady Milbanke see anything suspicious during the six weeks the couple stayed with them.

The Milbankes had not wanted Byron as a son-in-law but had given way to Annabella's wishes. Sir Ralph told Mrs Clermont that Annabella persecuted them to allow her to marry him but, if he thought Byron had married to persecute her, he would curse him to his dying day. After the wedding the Milbankes made every effort to please the young couple and life at Seaham settled into a pleasant routine. Annabella told Augusta she had never seen her father and mother so happy, saying she believed her mother would go to the bottom of the sea herself to find fish for B's dinner.[33] Byron was content enough although Annabella thought he was determined to be miserable. His disquiet was the direct result of the uncertain state of his finances. He had no choice now but to sell Newstead, and he needed to sell it quickly.

Byron liked to write in his little dressing room but one night the room became so unbearably hot that he threw water on the fire to cool it down. This released fumes that almost suffocated him and he staggered into the bedroom in a stupor. Annabella quick-wittedly threw open the window and dowsed him in eau de Cologne. His admiration for her knew no bounds, he told Lady Melbourne that had he been single he would surely have died. When Annabella wrote her version of the incident she said that he was for a time under the impression that he was dying and broke out into the wild ravings of despair, saying, 'I have tried every thing – I will try virtue, I think. Perhaps I shall go to Heaven, holding by the hem of your garment.' An ending almost as good as those she had devised in the fantasy epics of her childhood.

Byron tried to teach her to talk nonsense with him and when he was on his own she heard him remonstrating with himself, 'Byron's a fool,' and 'Yes he *is* a fool,' or 'poor Byron – poor Byron.' As the days passed into weeks he became kinder, saying, 'You are a good kind Pip – a good-natured Pip – the best wife in the world.'[34] One evening they played the fool with Sir Ralph and Lady Judith, Byron wore his dressing gown inside out, and put on Lady Milbanke's long-haired wig, which he had whipped off her head, while Annabella strutted about dressed in his travelling cap and a long cloak wearing whiskers and mustachios stuck to her face. It was then he said to her, 'I think I love you.'

Preoccupied with money and restless at hanging fire at Seaham Hall, Byron wrote to Moore in early March, 'I am in such a state of sameness and stagnation – and playing dull games at cards – and yawning – and trying to read old Annual Registers and the daily papers – and gathering shells on the shore – and watching the growth of stunted goosebery bushes in the garden – that I have neither time nor sense to say more than yours ever, B.'[35] He was anxious to return alone to town to sort out his affairs and intended to pay a flying visit to Augusta on the way, but Annabella refused to let him leave without her. They left Seaham on 9 March and Byron told Moore that 'I have been very comfortable here, – listening to that d—d monologue, which elderly gentlemen call conversation, and which my pious father-in-law repeats himself every evening – save one, when he played upon the fiddle. However they have been very kind and hospitable, and I like them and the place vastly, and I hope they will live many happy months. Bell is in health, and unvaried good-humour and behaviour.'[36]

Annabella ignored Augusta's advice to find a small house in London and she refused her parents' offer of Halnaby Hall as a temporary home, though she knew that Byron wanted to live cheaply in the country. She asked Lady Melbourne to find them a house in London, telling her Byron would find it more amusing than the country. She emphasized that he needed plenty of 'space'. Lady Melbourne negotiated a one-year lease on 13 Piccadilly Terrace, a mansion which belonged to the Duchess of Devonshire who was living in France. The rent was £700, far more than Byron could afford.

As they left Seaham, Lady Milbanke managed to annoy Byron by calling out 'Take care of Annabella.' 'What on earth does your mother mean by telling me to take care of you? I suppose you can take care of yourself. I didn't want you,' he said grumpily. Annabella had learned to relax enough to laugh when he explained that the cause of his bad temper was that, 'I feel as if I were just going to be married.'

They travelled companionably together arriving at Wansford on the second night. There he said, 'You married me to make me happy, didn't you? Well then you do make me happy.' He spoke with passionate affection and she silently wept tears of joy.[37]

Augusta did not want visitors. Her aunt, Sophia Byron, was threatening to come, her husband was dithering over whether or not to accept an invitation to a shooting party in the north, she was short of money, her house was too small and it was full of children. She had suggested that Annabella and Byron rent a house nearby, but there was none to be had. The problem solved itself when Miss Byron did not come and George Leigh decided to go north. Augusta rearranged her inadequate house by taking the small spare bedroom for herself and leaving her bedroom and a drawing room for Byron to dress in. Knowing all the difficulties her stay would cause her unknown new sister-in-law, a more sensitive woman than Annabella might have taken the hint and postponed her visit.

When the carriage pulled up to the house Augusta was nowhere to be seen and Byron went in to prepare Gussey to meet her new sister-in-law. After waiting a few minutes Annabella joined him and almost immediately Augusta rushed down the stairs to welcome them warmly. She did not then kiss Annabella, an omission noticed by both Byron and his wife. The two women vanished upstairs and Annabella said how happy she was to be under Augusta's roof and they kissed affectionately. Although they knew each other by sight they had never spoken, but they had corresponded on the most intimate matters regularly since the engagement and almost every other day after the marriage. Byron was still annoyed when they came down and gave his sister a sour look which he explained away by saying he had just opened a letter about Newstead.

During the visit Augusta wrote to Hodgson saying, 'My bairns are well, and delighted at being able to scream "Oh, Byron!" again and approve of their new aunt. I am not quite sure that Georgiana is not a little jealous of this formidable rival in B.'s affections.'[38] Byron had once told Augusta he had the greatest respect for Herod but he was a patient, loving uncle to her children.

He could not put his increasing financial troubles out of his mind and he began to drink heavily. He frequently asked for brandy after dinner and he soon became very unpleasant. One evening he turned to Annabella and ordered her to bed, 'We don't want *you*, my charmer.' He was often belligerently drunk by the time he came to bed and on one occasion told Annabella, 'Now I have *her*, you will find I can do without *you* – in all ways.' And, 'I told you you had better not come here, and you will find it so.' He embarrassed Augusta by forcing her to show letters he had written before his marriage in which he clearly stated he did not love Annabella and discussed her fortune. He humiliated Annabella telling her he would have broken off the engagement if Augusta had not stopped him and said, 'It was all your doing, Augusta.' He turned to Annabella jeering at her foolishness in believing he had been dying for love of her.

One evening while looking at portraits of Byron, Annabella remarked that she would like to have one of him with his youngest niece. A few evenings later Byron electrified the two women by mischievously pointing to his goddaughter, Elizabeth Medora, saying 'You know that is my child.'[39]

Byron was in many ways jealous of George Leigh and this may have prompted the outrageous claim. Dressed in unfashionable baggy trousers fastened under the foot to hide his disability he was no match for tall

Colonel George Leigh of the 10th (Prince of Wales Own Royal) Hussars in his gold braided jacket with a red pelisse edged with white fur draped over one shoulder and scarlet shako with gold rosettes and cords. Byron remained confused and irritated by Augusta's obvious love for and loyalty to his shiftless cousin, and he was almost certainly drunk when he made the allegation. It was to cause great unhappiness for Augusta and provide valuable ammunition for Annabella, who told her friend the Reverend F.W. Robertson in January 1851 that Byron went on to calculate aloud the time of George Leigh's absence from home to prove Elizabeth Medora was not Leigh's child. However the 3rd Earl of Chichester, Augusta's nephew, commented, 'Although Colonel Leigh abominated Lord Byron he absolutely and totally denied and disbelieved in Mrs Leigh's guilt.'[40] As did the Prince of Wales, since Augusta had been appointed with his specific approval as a bedchamber-woman to his straight-laced mother, Queen Charlotte.

Augusta had grown to like Annabella, telling Hodgson, 'The more I see of her the more I love and esteem her, and feel how grateful I am and ought to be for the blessing of such a wife for my dear, darling B.' She comforted her, saying that Byron did love her and his troubles were caused by bad diet, overdoses of magnesia and drinking. The two women paced up and down the garden endlessly discussing every aspect of Byron while he deliberately behaved as badly as possible, drinking each night and playing them off against each other during the day. One of his favourite games was to stretch out on the sofa and demand they kiss him by turns. Annabella fretted at the thought that her kisses were returned coolly, those of Augusta warmly. He frequently cursed his marriage then politely apologized to Annabella saying he meant nothing personal. He drew unfavourable comparisons between the two of them and made adolescent remarks, speculating on whether or not they wore the new-fangled underclothes, knickers. This shocked and horrified Annabella so much that she was unable to write the words in her report to her lawyers and resorted to a special shorthand.

Byron had ordered two brooches, one for himself and the other for Augusta. They were made of gold and contained plaited strands of their hair and the letters A – B and +++. Byron teased Annabella saying to Augusta, 'If she knew what these mean! Do you remember our signs at Newstead?'

Each evening the brandy bottle came into play and each evening Annabella was dismissed to bed where she waited, dreading to hear his step followed by his curses aimed at Fletcher as he undressed. Some nights he recoiled from her accidental touch and on others he passionately assured her he wished the nights were longer than the days so it would extend the time they could be together. Annabella was greatly offended one night when he flinched from her inadvertent movement, snapping, 'Don't touch me.' He had told her on their honeymoon that he did not like to sleep the whole night through in the same bed with a woman and her touch may have reawakened memories of the detestable May Gray sneaking into his bed, but he did not explain. Annabella got up. 'Where are you going?' he asked. 'To my own room,' she replied. 'There', she recalled for her lawyer, 'I wept myself into some peace.'

Not all his venom was reserved for Annabella. He argued unpleasantly with Augusta over his boorish treatment of Lord Carlisle whose case she continued to support. He made the two-week visit a nightmare for both women and Augusta was pleased to see them leave on 28 March. 'I am sorry to say his nerves and spirits are far from what I wish them,' she told Hodgson, 'I think the uncomfortable state of his affairs is the cause; at least, I can discern no other. He has every outward blessing this world can bestow.'[41]

Byron's debts mounted when they took possession of their smart new London home overlooking Green Park. The rent, which remained unpaid for two years, was equal to the whole of Annabella's income, leaving nothing to pay staff or for the upkeep of two carriages. When they first moved to London they seemed to be a model couple, completely devoted to each other. People remarked on the attention Byron paid his wife commenting that he was often seen hanging over the back of her chair, introducing her to his friends and scarcely talking to anyone else; if she had to leave before he did he would lead her to her carriage and lovingly say goodbye.[42]

Annabella liked to buy flowers at Henderson's nursery just off the Edgware Road and Byron used to accompany her as far as Leigh Hunt's house, where he passed the time until she returned. Hunt, who had come out of prison in February 1815, was amused to watch him lightheartedly riding his son's rocking horse. On one occasion they had been so deep in conversation that Annabella had to send up to the house twice to let Byron know she was ready to go home. Catching a glimpse of her through the door Hunt thought she had a pretty, earnest look about her. Byron too looked well, a little fatter than the year before but handsome in his black jacket and closely buttoned white trousers, just like his portrait by Phillips.[43]

Byron was introduced to Sir Walter Scott by John Murray in April and although Scott was prepared not to like him he found Byron courteous and kind. Thereafter they met almost daily at Murray's and discussed religion and politics, but Scott thought he had no serious opinions on either and often seemed melancholy and gloomy. He sensed Byron had a tendency to be on the defensive and suspect people of being gratuitously offensive. He discovered the best way to treat these moods was to wait until they passed or find a natural topic of conversation when 'the shadows almost always left his countenance, like the mist rising from a landscape'. Scott gave Byron a handsome gold dagger formerly belonging to Elfi Bey and in return Byron presented him with the large silver sepulchral vase full of human bones that he had brought back from Athens in 1811.[44]

Byron had invited Augusta to stay at Piccadilly Terrace when she came up to London to go into waiting for the queen, and Annabella confirmed the invitation on 30 March. Later, when she tried to prove her suspicions of incest and justify her actions to her lawyers, as well as protecting herself against charges of pandering, she argued that to have refused to invite Augusta would have revealed to the guilty pair that she had guessed their secret. Byron's reaction to Augusta's presence was unexpected. He met her 'with lowering looks of disgust and hatred' and told Annabella, 'You are a fool for letting her come to the house, and you'll find it will make a great difference to *you* in all ways.'[45]

During the days they had spent alone at Piccadilly Byron was tender and kind to Annabella, who was beginning to show what he called 'gestatory' symptoms. He told Moore it was 'a subject upon which I am not particularly anxious', but he knew a baby would please the Milbankes. After Augusta's arrival Annabella was tortured by her own suspicions. She went to bed early and listened to them laughing as they came up the stairs and read all kinds of meanings into trivial episodes. She felt ill and uncomfortable and allowed herself to become overwrought. Whatever Byron did seemed sinister; if he laughed she did not like it, if he frowned she thought he was menacing, but most of all she was jealous of his easy relationship with Augusta.

Her uncle, Lord Thomas Noel Wentworth, became seriously ill in April and Annabella went to nurse him. Three days later Lady Milbanke arrived from Seaham and Byron wrote, 'Dearest, now your mother is come I won't have you worried any longer – more particularly in your present situation which is rendered very precarious by what you have already gone through. Pray – come home.'[46] On 17 April Lord Wentworth died, leaving the Kirkby Mallory estate and over £7,000 a year to Lady Milbanke who, under the terms of the will, resumed her maiden name of Noel. Annabella received nothing but would inherit everything on the death of her mother. As soon as rumours of her financial expectations became public 13 Piccadilly was besieged by debt collectors delivering duns and threatening executions.

Sir Ralph and Lady Noel remained in London until the beginning of August, but they were no richer than the Byrons as Sir Ralph had longstanding political debts, the Seaham property was mortgaged and the Durham Bank had failed. Annabella unsuccessfully tried to raise mortgages for both her parents and her husband. Byron became unpleasant, refusing the Noels' invitations and saying he wished they were dead. Augusta sided with Annabella declaring that she would not stay in the house to see Annabella so badly used, but it was not until the end of June, when his behaviour became even more outrageous, that Annabella put it down to Augusta's presence and asked her to leave.

As Annabella's pregnancy advanced it became a source of jokes. She told her parents she got stuck between two posts in Hyde Park and wriggled free. She complained that writing was difficult as she had not yet had the table 'cut like a shaving dish'.[47] In July plans were made for the birth of the baby. Sir Ralph and Lady Noel offered to move to their home at Kirkby Mallory in Leicestershire, leaving Seaham Hall available for Annabella's confinement, but by that time Byron's financial position was so serious they did not dare leave Piccadilly for fear bailiffs would break in and seize their furniture. Byron ordered Hanson to put Newstead on the market again and on 28 July he went to the auction at Garroway's with Hobhouse. Newstead did not sell, failing to meet the reserve price. Byron became depressed, and talked wildly of suicide. The few evenings he spent with friends were cheerless, although Augusta thought he looked well and was eating sensibly – 'meat, bread and biscuits' – and he had given up brandy and spirits, but Annabella was not 'looking well or feeling so'. Hobhouse noted the differences that were growing between them, 'He and she have begun a little snubbing on money matters. Marry not, says he.'[48]

Colonel Leigh attended an audience with the Prince of Wales who was more friendly than he had been before, promising to find a place or an appointment for him, but did not. In August Charles Leigh died leaving his affairs in turmoil and the will contested. Byron wanted to help but Augusta told Annabella that she was frightened that George might wheedle money out of Byron which she knew he could not spare. Nevertheless Byron went to Six Mile Bottom and found the children ill. He tripped over a mousetrap in his room, Augusta supported the Noels against his mindless abuse and she told him he was drinking too much. He left after five days without accomplishing anything except upsetting her.

He returned to Annabella in a kind mood but it soon changed and he sulked for days, totally ignoring her. On entering his study she asked: 'Am I in your way?' He replied, 'Damnably.' He was sorry afterwards, saying the exclamation escaped from him unconsciously and involuntarily because he did not like being interrupted when he was writing and Annabella did not respect this whim. By now Annabella resented all Byron's friends, the 'Piccadilly crew' as she called them. In her eyes they were comrades in crime rather than her husband's trusted companions of many years. She singled out Hobhouse for most of the blame.

During her unremarkable pregnancy Annabella religiously followed her doctor's suggestions, using them as reasons to refuse to ride in the carriage or take walks with Byron so that they were imprisoned in the sparsely furnished mansion, which Byron compared to a barrack. 'It was,' he said, 'an existence I could not support.' However, it would have been difficult for them to mix in society as they were desperately short of money, in mourning, and Annabella wilted if subjected to hot rooms and late hours. Byron was reluctant to go out too, remarking, 'I knew the society of London; I knew the characters of many of those who are called ladies, with whom Lady Byron would necessarily have to associate, and I dreaded her contact with them.'[49] Hobhouse and Augusta were concerned at their isolation and believed the occasional separation would do them good.

On one of the few occasions when they dined out, in September, they were observed by Mrs George Lamb: 'She is to lie in in November. He appears very happy, and is much improved by his marriage. George and he are the two new managers of Drury Lane, very eager about it, and, as it has hitherto gone on very well, it is only a great amusement to them.'[50] It was not an amusement to Annabella, who resented the time he spent at the theatre and more particularly with the actresses in the green room.

Whether out of boredom or bravado Byron began a tawdry affair with an obscure actress, Susan Boyce, whom he met in connection with his work on the Drury Lane committee. They quickly became lovers but as soon as Susan began to demand more commitment his interest cooled. He sent her money in 1821 when she was down on her luck, telling Kinnaird that 'she was a transient piece of mine – but I owe her little on that score. Advance the poor creature some money on my account. . . .'

On 9 November the bailiffs were sent in; one slept in the house permanently. Byron was distraught but tried to keep the news from Annabella. Later in a paroxysm of rage he told her that she had brought all their troubles on herself for marrying him against his wishes. He described his rages to Lady Blessington: 'Once the lurking devil in me is roused, I lose all command of myself. I do not recover from a good fit of rage for days after: mind I do not by this mean that the ill-humour continues, as, on the contrary, that quickly subsides, exhausted by its own violence; but it shakes me terribly and leaves me low and nervous after.'[51] Annabella wrote despairingly to Augusta, 'I am afraid *this* bailiff is a sad brute and will proceed to very great inconvenience. I have written to my Mother on the subject, who if she can, will certainly send me some money – but my father has been as nearly in Gaol as possible.' Four days later she invited Augusta back to Piccadilly, 'Let me see you the middle of next week – at latest.' When she arrived on 15 November Byron treated her with disgust, resuming the behaviour he had adopted at Six Mile Bottom, insulting both women. 'I was wretched,' said Annabella, 'but I thought her more so.' His drinking and wild behaviour frightened them and they began to believe the fury of his attacks must be a sign of madness. One evening on returning home drunk, he threw himself at Annabella's feet exclaiming he was a monster beyond forgiveness and he had lost her forever. Astonished, the tearful Annabella said, 'Byron, all is forgotten; never, never shall you hear of it more!' He leapt up and folded her in his arms bursting into laughter. 'What do you mean?' she asked. 'Only a philosophical experiment; that's all,' he said. 'I wished to ascertain the value of your resolutions!'[52]

On 25 November Hobhouse found Byron railing against marriage and talking of going abroad, saying the state of his finances was so bad as to drive him half mad, adding that he would not worry so much if only he were not married. No man, he claimed, could know what he had gone through and no man should marry. Marriage had doubled all his misfortunes and diminished all his comforts. 'My wife,' he added, 'is perfection itself – the best creature breathing; but mind what I say – *don't marry.*' His behaviour became more erratic and violent and the fearful Fletcher made sure that Byron never went into Annabella's room carrying his pistols. Augusta invited Mrs Clermont to stay saying, 'If he continues in this way, God knows what he might do!' She moved into the room next to Annabella. Augusta sat up with Byron each night when he came in fighting drunk and tried to calm him and prevent him from waking Annabella who slept in the room above.

Annabella continued to record her husband's drunken menaces, which at times appeared life-threatening and at others like foolish tantrums. On one occasion he threw his favourite watch, which he had taken to Greece, into the hearth and ground it to pieces with a poker. He regularly threatened suicide and madness and was unable to control his emotions at the theatre, almost having a fit of hysterics on seeing Kean perform. Annabella became convinced that Byron believed himself guilty of a terrible crime and she assumed it must have been a murder committed abroad while touring with Hobhouse in 1809.

Many of Byron's tirades were an attempt to spark an emotion other than self-satisfied forgiveness from Annabella, but she could never recognize when she was being teased. 'It is difficult to judge when Lord Byron is serious or not,' commented Lady Blessington, 'He has a habit of mystifying, that might impose upon many,' but by carefully looking at his face 'a sort of mock gravity, now and then broken by a malicious smile, betrays when he is speaking for effect, and not giving utterance to his real sentiments. If he is detected he is angry for a moment and then laughs saying that it amuses him to *hoax* people.'[53] Augusta more than once had said, half jokingly, 'Byron is never so happy as when he can make you believe some atrocity against him.' Hodgson's son commented that 'His extraordinary love of a bad reputation, of exhibiting himself in the most unfavourable aspect, amounted almost to insanity.' His overblown reaction to situations was well known to his friends. During a rant at Cambridge he ended with the melodramatic statement, 'I shall go mad.' Scrope Davies quietly remarked, 'Much more like silliness than madness.'[54] This behaviour must have been puzzling and hurtful to Annabella whom Harness described as 'a person entirely deficient in tact and reflection,' and who 'made no allowances for the unusual excentricities of genius. In some periods of our history she might have aspired to a real crown of martyrdom, for she was a Puritan in creed, and an unflinching advocate of her own views.'[55]

His antics so alarmed Annabella that she consulted Samuel Heywood, Serjeant-at-law, and an old friend of her parents, who advised her to stay with her husband until after the birth of her child. On returning from seeing him, Annabella announced to Byron that her labour had begun. According to the account she gave her lawyers, he said that once the baby was born she would not love him, as all women loved their children more than their husbands and as she left the room in tears he asked if she would continue to live with him. That evening Byron went to the theatre but 'the tenth wonder of the world' was not born until one o'clock the following afternoon, 10 December. A notice was placed in the *Morning Chronicle* announcing 'Sunday last, Lady Byron was safely delivered of a daughter, at his lordship's house, Piccadilly Terrace.'

Byron smiled at the baby as she lay on the bed beside her mother remarking, 'Oh, what an implement of torture have I acquired in you!' Mrs Clermont told Hobhouse that she had never seen a man so proud and fond of his child as Lord Byron. After being reassured that she had not inherited his club foot he worried about her eyes, which appeared to him to squint. He was not happy until Lady Noel had explained that most newly born babies gave that impression at first but it disappeared in time.

The baptismal registration took place on 20 December while Annabella was still confined to her room. The baby was named Augusta Ada but, when the actual christening took place in November the following year, Augusta was not one of the godmothers. No one had told her of the change or answered her letter of enquiry.

On 5 January Byron wrote to Moore, 'The little girl was born on 10th December last: her name is Augusta *Ada* (the second a very antique family name, – I believe not used since the reign of King John.) She was and is, very flourishing and fat, and reckoned very large for her days – squalls and sucks incessantly.' He added, 'Her mother is doing very well, and up again.'[56] Behind this scene of domestic bliss Byron continued verbally to terrorize Annabella, leaving her grateful for Augusta's sisterly protection. But Augusta's patience was wearing thin. She was expecting her fifth child in May and wanted to return to the relative calm of Cambridgeshire. Afraid to be left alone but too upset to speak to her, Annabella wrote, 'I never will nor can ask you to stay one moment longer than you are inclined to do. It would be the worst return for all I ever received from you. But, in this at least, I am "truth itself" when I say that, whatever the situation may be, there is no one whose society is dearer to me, or can contribute more to my happiness. These feelings will not change under any circumstance.' She ended, 'Judge for yourself about going or staying. I wish you to consider yourself, if you could be wise enough to do that for the first time in your life.'[57] Augusta was steadfast in emergencies and had acted with considerable courage during Byron's drunken rages. She had become fond of Annabella and decided not to abandon her now. Both women believed Byron was suffering from mental derangement and Augusta wrote to Hobhouse asking him to stand by Byron, 'he has so few *sincere* friends and well judging ones. I can never express what I feel about him, but believe me, I am grateful from my heart for your friendship and friendly forbearance towards his infirmities, of whatever kind they may be. His *mind* makes him the most unhappy of human beings.'[58]

Lady Noel had not been well for some time but had recovered sufficiently to return to Kirkby Mallory on 28 December. She knew the lease on the house in Piccadilly ran out in March and invited Annabella and the baby to stay with her at Kirkby Mallory. Together with her invitation to Annabella Lady Noel enclosed a letter to Byron specifically inviting him and expounding the amenities of the countryside.

After Ada's birth Byron's aversion to Annabella was plain to everyone in the house. She told him several times that she thought he was more fond of the baby than she was and added rather pathetically, 'fonder of it than you are of me'. He used to visit Annabella and the baby for a short time each day and on 3 January they had a serious quarrel. Their raised voices were loud enough for the nurse in the next room to hear every word. Among his unkind and childish threats Byron said he would bring his mistress into the house and he would do every wicked thing he could think of. He ended his outburst by saying that Annabella had nothing to complain of as he had neither confined her nor beaten her.[59] They did not speak for three days and then Byron asked Augusta to deliver a letter to her:

> When you are disposed to leave London, it would be convenient that a day should be fixed – & (if possible) not a very remote one for that purpose. Of my opinion upon that subject you are sufficiently in possession – & of the circumstances which have led to it – as also to my plans – or rather intentions – for the future. When in the country I will write to you more fully. As Lady Noel has asked you to Kirkby, there you can be for the present – unless you prefer Seaham.
>
> As the dismissal of the present establishment is of importance to me, the sooner you can fix on the day the better – though of course your convenience & inclination shall be first consulted.
>
> The child will of course accompany you – there is a more easy and safer carriage than the chariot (unless you prefer it) which I mentioned before – on that you can do as you please.[60]

Although Annabella knew they were living well beyond their means and must leave Piccadilly Terrace as quickly as possible, she replied sniffily the next day that she would obey his wishes and fix the earliest day that circumstances would allow for leaving London.

She did not leave immediately but consulted Dr Matthew Baillie, the same doctor who had treated Byron's foot when he stayed with the Hansons as a schoolboy. He advised her that Byron should not be left alone with any young woman. Augusta protested, saying that he might commit suicide if he was left without a woman to look after him, so they invited his cousin and heir, George Byron, to move in and protect them. Baillie suggested that Annabella should go away 'as an experiment' and should avoid subjects which she knew annoyed him. Annabella secretly searched through his papers and books, opening drawers and trunks hoping to find evidence of madness. All she found was a bottle of laudanum and a couple of books he thought too risqué for the library. She borrowed copies of the *Medical Journal* and made her own diagnosis – hydrocephalus. She scurried off to Hanson to see if she could find more signs of Byron's madness but was disappointed, as Hanson explained away each of her examples of insanity. He told her that Byron had been a nervous child and used to search his room carefully at night, to the extent of asking a servant to look under his bed. As he grew older, he

kept loaded pistols by the side of his bed and had for a short time had a
rope ladder in his room so he could escape in case of fire. As to the
laudanum bottle, Byron had carried one about with him for years. She
frightened Hanson with the violence of her emotions and fearing she
might be considering some kind of bodily restraint, he warned her that
such an action would be a mistake which might produce catastrophic
results. He said that he had never seen the least sign of insanity but
agreed Byron was prone to sudden bursts of violence and passion.
Hanson advised her not to take everything he said 'to the letter', which
was the advice that Byron had already given her – 'not to mind my words,
and then we may get along very well.' Annabella's agitation was so great
that Hanson asked if she was frightened of Byron, to which she answered,
'Oh, no, not in the least; my eye can always put down his!'[61]

On 14 January Byron and Augusta were sitting together when
Annabella came in and, repeating the gesture she made on the evening
he arrived at Seaham, walked towards where he was standing with his
back to the fireplace and held out her hand. 'Byron,' she said, 'I come to
say goodbye.' He put his hands behind his back and moved closer to the
mantelpiece. 'When shall we three meet again?' he quoted. 'In heaven, I
trust,' replied Annabella, humourless to the last.[62]

In her account of her last night at 13 Piccadilly she remembered only
falling into a sound sleep induced by deep sorrow, but Byron clearly
recalled it as the last night that they spent together fully as man and
wife.[63]

Ann Rood, Annabella's lady's maid had married the widowed Fletcher
and she accompanied Annabella and the new baby to Kirkby. The journey
was uneventful and although Ann Fletcher thought Annabella seemed
'low', her actions did not lead her to suspect Annabella was
contemplating leaving her husband or even that there had been any
disagreement. At the over-night stop at Woburn Annabella wrote to
Byron, 'The child is quite well, and the best of travellers. I hope you are
good, and remember my medical prayers & injunctions. Don't give
yourself up to the abominable trade of versifying – nor to brandy – nor to
anything or anybody that is not *Lawful & right.*' From Kirkby Mallory she
wrote,

Dearest Duck, – we got here quite well last night, and were ushered
into the kitchen instead of the drawing room, by a mistake that might
have been agreeable enough to hungry people. Of this and other
incidents Dad wants to write you a jocose account & both he & Mam
long to have the family party completed. Such a W.C! and such a *sitting-*
room or *sulking*-room all to yourself. If I were not always looking about

for B., I should be a great deal better already for country air. *Miss* finds
her provisions increased, and fattens thereon. It is a good thing she
can't understand all the flattery bestowed upon her, 'Little Angel'.
Love to the good Goose, and everybody's love to you both from hence.
Ever thy most loving, Pippin . . . Pip . . . Ip.[64]

Released from the tension of Piccadilly and enjoying the familiar
deference of her parents, Annabella's sorrows spilled out; but she did not
at first tell her parents the full story, letting them believe that Byron was
ill. The Noels at once, kindheartedly, offered to nurse him back to
health. He told Hobhouse, 'They want me to go into the country. I shall
go soon, but I won't go yet. I should not care if Lady Byron was alone, but
I can't stand Lady Noel.'[65]

Augusta sent bulletins on his behaviour to Annabella who hoped
Augusta and George Byron, together with the physician Le Mann, would
be able to persuade Byron to join her, but the reports from Piccadilly
Terrace were not favourable. Despite his promises, Byron continued to
drink and now feared he was losing his memory, having staggered in one
night, fallen up the stairs and left the doors open. Annabella bargained
with herself that if it could be proved he were mad she would not leave
him but if sane she could not forgive his brutish behaviour. Gradually she
revealed to her parents more and more details of her tormented married
life. They forced her to promise that if Byron were sane she would leave
him. On 18 January Le Mann reported that although Byron showed great
instability of temper he was not insane but suffering from bodily disease
'that may be easily overcome'.

Lady Noel immediately left for London taking with her a paper written
by Annabella outlining her grievances.[66] During the week she spent in
London Lady Noel consulted Sir Samuel Romilly, an eminent lawyer,
Serjeant Heywood, Colonel Francis Hastings Doyle, an old friend of the
family, Dr Stephen Lushington, a barrister, as well as Augusta, George
Byron and Mrs Clermont. Augusta was frightened that there would be a
'dreadful catastrophe' if Byron found out that the Noels were pressing
for a separation. 'So much the better,' Lady Noel said. 'It is not fit such
men should live.' Her language to Mr Le Mann was so extreme that Mrs
Clermont exclaimed, 'Pooh! do not be so violent, you talk like a child.'[67]
Le Mann's opinion was that Byron would soon be well enough to join
Annabella at Kirkby. On hearing this Lady Noel briskly retorted that the
doors would be shut against him should he attempt such a visit. Le Mann
said he had been working on Lady Byron's behalf, to persuade Lord
Byron to join her, but now he would not press him into taking such a
disagreeable step. He also refused to send any more reports on Byron's

health to Lady Byron, saying he did not want to be a party to treachery against his patient.

Lady Noel was much taken with the barrister, Dr Lushington. 'He seems the most gentlemanlike, clear-headed and clever man I have every met with – and agrees with all others that a proposal should be sent by your father for a quiet adjustment.' It was on his advice that Annabella refused to write or see Byron again as, he said, this might give him grounds to apply for restitution of conjugal rights. Lushington hinted that Annabella's health might be in danger bearing in mind Byron's affair with Susan Boyce and alerted her to Byron's rights as a father. Many years later both Byron's grandchildren agreed that without Lushington's influence a reconciliation might have been possible.

As soon as Lady Noel returned to Kirkby she reported to Sir Ralph who immediately wrote to Byron proposing a separation. When the letter arrived Augusta, guessing its contents and playing for time, sent it back unopened. Sir Ralph came to London intending to deliver a fresh letter by hand and Annabella made sure that Mrs Clermont kept an eye on her father so that he did not stir a step or write a line without legal counsel as she feared he might be won over. Mr Le Mann called on Sir Ralph at Mivart's Hotel hoping to dissuade him from pressing for a separation, and for a while it appeared as though he had been successful. Sir Ralph hesitated and left the room to speak to Mrs Clermont but when he returned he said it was too late – the step had been taken.[68] He wrote to Byron on 2 February,

> . . . circumstances have come to my knowledge, which convince me, that with your opinions it cannot tend to your happiness to continue to live with Lady Byron, and I am yet more forcibly convinced that after her dismissal from your house, and the treatment she experienced whilst in it, those on whose protection she has the strongest natural claims could not feel themselves justified in permitting her to return thither. . . . I therefore propose that a *professional friend* should be fixed on by you to confer with a person of the same description appointed by me that they may discuss and settle such terms of separation as may be mutually approved.[69]

Byron was quite unprepared for such an attack. Annabella's last letter had been affectionate and intimate and her behaviour during their last night had given him no reason to suspect she was other than a loving wife.

While still in a state of shock he solemnly swore to Hobhouse that he had parted with Annabella on friendly terms, had intended to accept the

Noels' invitation and had even ordered horses for the journey to Kirkby. Hobhouse believed he was the victim of a hoax and that five minutes alone with Annabella would clear the matter up. After reading the 'Dearest Duck' letter he was convinced that Annabella was not a free agent and that Byron's letters were being withheld. This view was strengthened by Ann Fletcher who wrote that Annabella had said, 'I still have hopes, for the letter has not been delivered', and on the morning of the day she expected her father's letter to have been delivered to Byron 'she was extremely distressed, and almost insensible', and asked Ann 'how soon she could pack up her things to go to town'. However, 'she gave no instructions to do so but said she would go to town, but was kept against her will.' On another occasion Ann was stopped by Lady Noel who said, 'You know you told Mrs Clermont that her Ladyship was in danger of her life while she remained in the house with Lord Byron. You know it was so.' Ann denied saying any such thing and reminded Lady Noel that the words were those of Mrs Clermont. Lady Noel became enraged repeating 'You know it was so.' Ann replied that she scarcely ever saw Lord and Lady Byron together more than once or twice a month and she had never seen or heard any unpleasantness, adding that Lady Byron frequently expressed great affection for Lord Byron. She told Fletcher that she had heard Annabella say 'that her father and mother had insisted that there should be a separation, and that she had passed her word to them that she would herself insist on it, but that she had desired her father and mother not to be too hasty'. When Ann asked 'if she would not retract it', Annabella replied, 'No; it was impossible.'[70]

Byron asked Augusta to press Annabella to confirm that it was her wish, not just that of her parents, that they should part. She replied, under Lushington's supervision, 'I will only recall to Lord Byron's mind his avowed and insurmountable aversion to the married state, and the desire and determination he has expressed ever since the commencement to free himself from that bondage, as finding it quite insupportable. . . . He has too painfully convinced me that all attempts to contribute to his happiness were wholly useless, and most unwelcome to him.'[71]

Hobhouse and Hodgson both wrote to Annabella asking her to reconsider. She replied to Hodgson,

> I married Lord B. determined to endure everything whilst there was *any* chance of contributing to his welfare. I remained with him under trials of the severest nature. . . . I may give you a general idea of what I have experienced by saying that he married me with the deepest

determination of Revenge, avowed on the day of my marriage, and executed ever since with systematic and increasing cruelty, which no affection could change. . . . My security depended on the total abandonment of every moral and religious principle. . . . I know him too well to dread the fatal event which he so often mysteriously threatens. I have acquired my knowledge of him bitterly indeed, and it was long before I learned to mistrust the apparent candour by which he deceives all but himself. He *does* know – too well – what he affects to inquire. I must add that Lord Byron had been fully, earnestly, and affectionately warned of the unhappy consequences of his conduct.[72]

Byron still could not believe her: 'Were you then *never* happy with me,' he wondered,

did you never at any time or times express yourself so? Have no marks of affection – of the warmest and most reciprocal attachment passed between us? or did in fact hardly a day go down without some such on one side and generally on both? . . . and had I not, had we not the days before and on the day when we parted, every reason to believe that we loved each other, that we were to meet again. . . . You are much changed within these twenty days or you would never have thus poisoned your own better feelings, and trampled upon mine.[73]

He had touched her heart and Ann Fletcher found her 'rolling on the floor in a paroxysm of grief', regretting that she had given her word to her parents to separate and was now unable to retract it.

Annabella, with Lushington's approval, replied,

I have determined, *if possible* not to indulge the language of feeling in addressing you, as it could only be injurious in our present relative situations. I wish that you had spared *me* by a similar conduct. By means of our authorized friends those points which require conversational discussion can be settled, and, whatever may now appear to you inconsistent, satisfactorily explained.[74]

Byron wrote again,

I have invited your return, it has been refused, I have entreated to see you, it is refused, I have requested to know with what I am charged, it is refused, is this mercy or justice? We shall see. And now, Bell, dearest Bell, whatever may be the event of this calamitous difference, whether you are restored to, or torn from me, I can only say in the truth of affliction, and without hope, motive, or end in again saying what I have lately but vainly repeated, that I love you: bad or good, mad or rational, miserable or content, I love you, and shall do to the dregs of my memory and existence.[75]

She regretted sending affectionate letters from Woburn and Kirkby ('I must have been mad to write the Kirkby letter') and with Lushington's help tried to explain them away:

My letters of January 15th and 16th: It can be fully and clearly proved that I left your house under the persuasion of your having a complaint of so dangerous a nature that any agitation might bring on a fatal crisis. My entreaties, before I quitted you, that you should take medical advice – repeated in my letter of January 15th – must convince you of such an impression on my mind. . . . I have *consistently* fulfilled my duty as your wife. It was too dear to be abandoned till it became hopeless. Now my resolution cannot be changed.[76]

She piously and long-windedly told Augusta that 'The present sufferings of all may yet be repaid in blessings. Do not despair absolutely, dearest; leave me but enough of your interest to afford you any consolation by partaking of that sorrow which I am most unhappy to cause thus unintentionally. You will be of my opinion hereafter; and at present your bitterest reproach would be forgiven.'[77]

In the third week of February Annabella joined her father and Mrs Clermont at Mivart's Hotel. On the day she arrived she met Lushington; she took with her all Augusta's letters which she intended to use as evidence to support her suspicion that incest had been committed between her husband and his sister. Lushington forbade her to return to Byron and instructed her to end direct dealings with Augusta. She signed a document he had prepared saying, 'if circumstances should compel Lady Byron to prefer the charge, she should be at full liberty to do so without being prejudiced by her present conduct.'

The strain on Byron was enormous. He ate only once in three days spending many hours in his room brooding. On one occasion he was heard weeping and those around him began to fear he might commit suicide. Annabella shrugged her shoulders when told of his state of mind, saying it was not her fault, she could not help it and must do her duty. While Ann Fletcher was brushing Annabella's hair one morning she asked if she was angry with her for telling the truth about what had happened during their stay at Kirkby. Annabella replied that she was not angry because it was true.[78] However, she denied Ann a reference when she left her service in 1819.

Rumours and stories had begun to circulate soon after Ada was born. At first they were trifling: 'the poor lady had never had a comfortable meal since their marriage'; 'Her husband had no fixed hour for breakfast, and was always too late for dinner.' As time passed the accusations became more serious, 'Poor Lady Byron was afraid of her life', 'Her husband slept with loaded pistols by his bedside, and a dagger under his pillow.' Hobhouse took Byron to task, listing his alleged crimes: great tyranny towards his wife, menaces, furies, neglect and real injuries, locking doors, showing pistols, frowning at Lady Byron in bed, and turning her out of the house. Byron became dreadfully agitated, vowing he had never lifted a finger against her and that the harshest thing he had ever said was that she was in his way. She also accused him of throwing soda bottles at the ceiling during her labour, but when the room was examined by Hobhouse the following day there were no marks on the ceiling. When asked about the truth of the cruellest story – that he had asked her during the birth whether the child was dead – he was horrified and said, 'She will not say that, though, God knows, poor thing! it seems now she would say anything; but she would not say that, no she would not say that.' His servants were summoned and examined by Hanson and their general reaction was that of surprise, 'What! is not my Lady coming back? Is anything the matter?' They blamed Mrs Clermont for most of the attacks on Byron. Mrs Milward, the housekeeper and married to the Noels' butler, was as astonished as the rest and stayed with Byron until he left Piccadilly for good.[79]

Augusta had wanted to go home for some time, for as well as looking after Byron she had been nursing Georgiana, now recovering under the kind care of Le Mann. George Leigh was impatient to have her home and two of the younger children at Six Mile Bottom had colds; but above all she was anxious to be in her own home to prepare for her new baby. Suddenly the old rumours linking Byron and Augusta were mysteriously revived. Hobhouse found Augusta in tears on 13 March. She told him that she had stayed in Byron's house long enough to prove that the rumour was a lie and that Colonel Leigh had handsomely discredited it in every way. She appealed to Annabella to publicly deny the rumour but was refused. The Dowager Duchess of Leeds urged her to leave Piccadilly and Lady Noel cattily remarked, 'So she ought, but she is a fool, and perhaps her brother's having left her all he has to dispose of may make her shy of offending him.' Augusta left Piccadilly and moved into her rooms at St James's Palace on 17 March.[80]

News of the separation travelled fast. On 27 February, Augustus Foster in Copenhagen wrote, 'I hear a report that Lord and Lady Byron have separated from incompatability. I should not be surprised, but hope it is not so.' The Duchess of Devonshire replied from Rome on 8 March, 'We are all astonished here at the separation of Lord and Lady Byron. . . . Nobody knew the cause when my last letters were written, but every body seemed to pity her. So do I too; but yet I think that, had I married a profligate man, knowing that he was so, and that I had a child, and was not ill used by him, I would not part from him.' Augustus was puzzled, 'Caroline seems quite shocked at Lord Byron's conduct to poor Annabel but don't give me the particulars. They were certainly two very opposite people to come together, but she *would* marry a poet and *reform* a rake.'[81]

Caroline Lamb wrote to Annabella hinting that she had information damaging to Byron and a meeting was arranged in great secrecy, attended by Mrs George Lamb. Caroline gleefully told them that Byron had admitted to her that he had taken part in criminal intercourse with his sister; that there was a woman who was expecting a child by him and if it were a girl it would be called Medora; that while at school he had practised unnatural crimes; that his page Rushton had been a victim of such a crime; that he had threatened her with violence should she reveal his crimes. Annabella wrote up her notes for Lushington, who was delighted. London soon buzzed with speculation fed by these juicy titbits and Annabella instructed Mrs George Lamb to be careful when spreading them to ensure they could not be traced back to her.[82] Caroline Lamb had little difficulty with manipulating the truth and was well known within her family for gifted lying; George Lamb once remarked, 'The only safe method is not to believe one word she says.' Caroline herself defined the truth as 'what one thinks at the moment'.

Annabella debated tactics with her mother and suggested delaying the separation proceedings in the hope of tiring Byron and goading him into doing something silly. Meanwhile she continued to write statements and comments for Lushington justifying her actions and laying the groundwork to prevent Byron or Augusta ever obtaining custody of Ada. Mrs Clermont wrote to Lady Noel,

> In regard to Mrs Leigh, you have, I think, been very unjust, as I am confident however maliciously he may act, it never has been her wish to take it (the child) from Annabella nor ever will be, although I fear she must have felt herself much hurt of late by a change of manner on this side. I know she had acted weakly but I do firmly believe her intentions have been good – nor can I ever forget the kindness Annabella experienced from her the latter part of the time she was in Piccadilly. Even for her life I believe we may thank Mrs Leigh.[83]

The campaign of vilification got off to a good start; on 22 March the Duchess of Devonshire wrote to Augustus, 'Lady Byron's fate is the most melancholy I ever heard, and he must be mad or a Caligula. Caro will have told you some of the stories. It is too shocking, and her life seems to have been endangered whilst with him from his cruelty . . . and now her sufferings.'[84]

On 17 March the legal preliminaries for the separation were agreed and Byron wrote the verses beginning 'Fare thee well!' which he addressed to Annabella summing up his grief, frustrations and regret. The paper was covered with tear stains by the time he had finished. He sent them to her with the letter, 'Dearest Bell, I send you the first verses that ever I attempted to write upon you, and perhaps the last that I may ever write at all. This at such a moment may look like affectation, but it is not so.' Annabella did not reply. She later claimed the poem was a piece of Machiavellianism on his part, to put her in the wrong because it was he who really wanted the separation.

Byron thanked Lord Holland for trying to negotiate a private and amicable arrangement and collected letters from friends that refuted a new charge of Annabella's that he had spoken ill of her. He sent them to her and she returned them through Augusta without any reply, which made him very angry. The following evening he composed 'A Sketch from Private Life', a vicious attack on Mrs Clermont whom he believed had been a prime mover in influencing Annabella to leave him. However, Mrs Clermont saw him quite clearly and wrote to Annabella, 'I have no doubt that, although he has been always wishing and endeavouring to drive you to a separation, his pride at least will suffer dreadfully; but he is a being whose whole talents seem to be employed in bringing unhappiness upon himself, and it is not in the power of any mortal to prevent him doing so.'[85]

When Hunt, Scrope Davies and Hobhouse came to dinner Byron showed Hunt, much to the latter's surprise, the Pippin letters. But, as Lady Blessington once remarked, Byron 'is an extraordinary person, *indiscrete* to a degree that is surprising, exposing his own feelings. . . . He is incapable of keeping any secret, however it may concern his own honour or that of another; and the first person with whom he found himself *tête-à-tête* would be made the confidant without any reference to his worthiness of the confidence or not.'

During his last days in London Byron amused himself with a pliant young woman who introduced herself on the pretext of taking up a theatrical career. She first approached him as a member of the committee of Drury Lane Theatre but when he offered to introduce her to Douglas Kinnaird, another member of the committee, she changed her tack. She said she was thinking of a literary career and wrote to him enquiring if it would be convenient for him to meet a lady who had business of great importance to discuss with him, and would he be home at seven o'clock that evening? Byron foolishly replied and the young woman, heavily disguised, presented herself at Albany. Fletcher at first refused to let her in, but she was so persistent that Byron relented. She at once threw off her disguise revealing herself to be an attractive girl with dark hair and eyes. She passionately declared that she cared for neither honour nor virtue if only she could be his. Byron was unimpressed. He was used to women throwing themselves at his feet daily; but this one persisted, boldly suggesting they leave town by stage coach, get off after 10 miles or so and return the following morning. Byron preferred a less elaborate scheme and agreed to meet her at a house in Albemarle Street. She revealed that her name was Claire Clairmont, she was seventeen years old, a champion of the rights of women, a friend of Mary Godwin, daughter of Mary Wollstonecraft and a disciple of Percy Shelley the atheist and proponent of free love. He took what she had to offer without thought or affection while she fell in love with his beautiful face.

Augusta accompanied Byron to Lady Jersey's party in the second week of April where they were cut by most of the women, led by Mrs George Lamb, and the men turned on their heels as soon as they saw Byron. As he leant dejectedly against a table the red-headed Margaret Mercer Elphinstone came up and said with a friendly nod of her head, 'You should have married *me*, and then this would not have happened to you.'[86] He valued her friendship and the courage she showed in defending him in public. Before sailing from Dover he handed a book to Scrope Davies asking him to give it to her and to tell her that if he had been fortunate enough to marry a woman like her, he would not have been obliged to exile himself from his country. On her part Miss Elphinstone did not forget him, telling Madame de Staël's granddaughter many years later that she was very proud of his friendship and above all she cherished his touching letter of farewell.

On Easter Sunday, 14 April, Augusta went to Piccadilly to spend a last evening with Byron before she returned to Six Mile Bottom to prepare herself for the birth of her fifth child, Frederick George, born on 9 May. It was a painful parting and they both wept. Augusta gave him a pocket Bible. He told Parry in 1824, 'I am sure no man reads the Bible with more pleasure than I do; I read a chapter every day, and in a short time shall be able to beat the Canters with their own weapons.' It was on his bedside table when he died.

Later Byron wrote to Annabella, 'I have just parted from Augusta, almost the last being you had left me to part with. . . . Wherever I may go, and I am going far, you and I can never meet again in this world, nor in the next. . . . If any accident occurs to me, be kind to Augusta, if she is then nothing, to her children.' He finished by giving her the carriage which took her from him to Kirkby and sent her an antique family ring which contained strands of Charles I's hair. 'The ring is of no lapidary value, but it contains the hair of a king and an ancestor, which I should wish to preserve to Miss Byron.' A few days later he received a terse note from Mr Wharton, a solicitor: 'Lady Byron has received from your Lordship a ring, which, according to your desire, will be preserved for your daughter.'[87]

The deed of separation was brought to Piccadilly at three o'clock on Sunday 21 April and shortly afterwards it was all over. Annabella left London the next day and Byron's friends and servants rallied round to make ready to leave. He took with him Berger, a Swiss guide, William Fletcher and Robert Rushton. He appointed a young doctor, William Polidori, to look after him. The following day Rogers came to say goodbye having just left Lady Byron who looked well but was 'torn here' and he touched his chest in the region of his heart. In the evening the Kinnairds came bringing him a cake and two bottles of champagne.

The next day the travellers were up at six and breakfasted but they were not ready to leave till half past nine. Hobhouse and Polidori left first in Scrope Davies's chaise, pushing through the crowd that had gathered about the front door. Byron and Scrope Davies, with Fletcher and Rushton on the box, travelled in Byron's new Napoleonic carriage, built by Baxter at a cost of £500. Everyone arrived safely in Dover at half past eight and dined together at the Ship. The following morning Fletcher told Hobhouse that the bailiffs had got into 13 Piccadilly and seized everything. Hobhouse, worried that they might pursue them to Dover, had Byron's new coach safely loaded on to the packet as soon as possible. Hobhouse was wise to be concerned as he later found out that the bailiffs had entered 13 Piccadilly ten minutes after they had left and declared they would have taken the carriage if it had been there. As it was they seized Byron's pet birds and squirrel.

It was impossible to sail the next day as the wind was contrary, from the east and strong, so, to kill time after dinner, they walked to see the grave of the poet and satirist Charles Churchill. To their amazement Byron lay down on it and gave the sexton who had led them there a crown to freshly turf it.

The following day, 25 April, they were up and breakfasted by eight and all on board except Byron. The captain said he could not wait and it was a little after nine when Byron got on board, having strolled down to the quay arm-in-arm with Hobhouse. When the packet began to move off

Hobhouse ran to the end of the wooden pier, 'as the vessel tossed by us through a rough sea and contrary wind, I saw him again; the dear fellow pulled off his cap and waved it to me. I gazed until I could not distinguish him any longer. God bless him for a gallant spirit and kind one.'[88]

CHAPTER FIVE

Augusta and Allegra

Annabella returned to Kirkby Mallory and Augusta Ada on the same day that Byron sailed into self-imposed exile. The little girl had been left with her grandparents during the two months her mother was in London supervising the separation and in that time she had become very close to Lady Milbanke. Annabella, determined that she should not be overshadowed in her absence, had instructed Lady Milbanke to show the baby her portrait regularly, saying at the same time, 'Pretty, pretty Mamma, give her a kiss.' Annabella was jealous of any affectionate feelings her daughter developed for other people and she made sure this did not often happen by changing her nurses and governesses regularly. However, she did little for her own cause when, with her unhealthy interest in all things medical, she decided to ease the baby's discomfort during teething by lancing her gums twice with such enthusiasm the nurse flinched. Not surprisingly, whenever she was left alone with her mother Augusta Ada yelled with fear.

To break the bond that had grown up between Augusta Ada and her grandmother, Annabella took the child with her when she went to Lowestoft in June. She boasted that the baby was so good humoured that 'It' would be a very agreeable companion. Augusta Ada was such a precocious, large, healthy child that strangers could be forgiven for thinking she was a year old, but even Lady Milbanke must have been surprised to receive a letter from 'It' describing the general excitement in Ely, Peterborough and Bury when it became known that Lady Byron and her daughter were passing through. 'It' signed the letter *Ada* and the name Augusta was dropped for ever.[1]

They spent a few days at Worlingham with Mary, Countess of Gosford, who was suffering matrimonial difficulties. Her husband had fallen under the influence of his sister, Lady Olivia Sparrow, a leading Evangelical and had taken up religion. 'It is the devil,' Annabella irreverently told her parents. Lady Gosford fled to Lowestoft and took a house next door to Annabella's which overlooked the sea. She was soon followed by her husband and it was under his influence that Annabella attended a Methodist meeting. She cultivated the local clergyman at Pakeford, the Reverend John William Cunningham, and visited the deserving poor with his family. Cunningham was also the vicar of Harrow and Annabella became such a good friend of his family that she was invited to stay with them at Harrow in September.[2]

While in Lowestoft Annabella indulged in one of her frequent bouts of illness. Throughout her life she wrote ceaselessly about the state of her health and, indeed, anyone with a less robust constitution would have collapsed under the draconian treatment she meted out to herself. She cupped and applied leeches fearlessly and for many years sustained a self-inflicted wound in her arm, into which she had placed a pellet to prevent it healing, to enable the 'poison' in her system to escape through the permanently open cut.[3] Her digestion was formidable and the number and quality of mutton chops punctuated the letters to her parents. She had been a plump little girl with a greedy appetite and it must have been very difficult, in adulthood, to maintain a pale and interesting look while consuming vast quantities of meat. At Lowestoft she ate 'nothing but meat, eggs, and biscuits – neither bread, butter, milk, tea, or strong drink'. This diet was leavened by long walks and sailing. She proudly denied sea-sickness claiming, 'It equalises my circulation and unloads my stomach.'[4]

In Lowestoft she reviewed her situation. During the separation she had concentrated on Byron's brutally indecent conduct, his unkind attitude to her and his foul language, but she still could not accept that he had not loved her and she thrashed about looking for someone to blame, speculating on the possibility that the rumour of incest she had instigated might be true. She had no proof except for Caroline Lamb's ravings, Byron's teasing, and her own fevered imagination; but she had convinced herself they were guilty before her marriage and that the habit was discontinued afterwards only because Augusta refused Byron's advances.

Annabella justified a campaign to force Augusta to confess her guilt by saying it was her Christian duty to rescue her from sin, redeem her and place her on the road to salvation. As well as the satisfaction of saving a sinner, Augusta's confession would ensure that she could never be considered as Ada's guardian.

The separation deed had not given guidance as to the custody of Ada but Annabella was advised by Sir Samuel Romilly to make her a ward of the Court of Chancery as it was doubtful if the Lord Chancellor would allow a child to be removed from its mother. On 8 March, without Byron's knowledge, this was done. Annabella celebrated with mutton chops and returned to Kirkby, bilious but well satisfied. Byron made no attempt to exercise his parental rights and on the day after the separation was signed he wrote to Augusta, 'All I have to beg or desire on the subject is – that you will never mention or allude to Lady Byron's name again in any shape – or on any occasion except indispensable business. Of the child you will inform me and write about poor little dear *Da* – and see it whenever you can.'⁵

Annabella enlisted Mrs Therese Villiers as her confidante in the moral war she planned to wage on Augusta. Mrs Villiers had been an intimate friend of Augusta and in February had written to Annabella asking her to deny the rumours and scurrilous stories circulating about her. Annabella replied primly, regretting that the suspicions existed and denying she was responsible. However, unwilling that Augusta should have a champion, she promptly called on Mrs Villiers at her home at 1 South Place, Knightsbridge and, after an interesting interview and several self-serving letters, Mrs Villiers abandoned Augusta's cause and entered into the conspiracy.

Lord Brougham had carried a grudge against Byron ever since he had called Mrs George Lamb a 'damned fool' without knowing that Brougham was in love with her. Brougham, with his twitching, trumpet-shaped nose and dingy complexion looked like 'something that had been dug up', according to Lady Granville, but as one of Lady Byron's legal advisers he was in a position to spread stories about the separation which 'were too horrid to mention'.⁶ Hobhouse recorded the gossip that 'Lady B. had said that B had boasted to her of going to bed with his sister. I implied that if he had she was more villainous in mentioning it than he in doing it.' He added 'Lady B. will not stick at a trick. I know from her having told B that she was in love with another man in order to hook him – she confessed this to B himself.' He also tartly told Caroline Lamb 'that I trusted that Lord Byron's enemies would condescend at last to perch upon a fact'.⁷

The gossip which was fuelling Augusta's troubles was no longer confined to London; snippets were being fed into the system by English travellers returning from Switzerland. Madame de Staël had welcomed Byron to Coppet, her home on Lake Geneva, with almost motherly solicitude and persuaded him to allow her to attempt a reconciliation. 'The separation may have been my fault,' Byron conceded, 'but it was her own choice. I tried all means to prevent and would do as much and more to end it – a word would do so, but it does not rest with me to pronounce it.' Henry Brougham got wind of what was being planned and reported to Annabella that Lady Romilly was bringing a conciliatory letter from Byron, adding that he hoped she would not take any notice of it. She did not.

Madame de Staël lent Byron a copy of *Glenarvon*, the novel written by Lady Caroline Lamb based on her love affair with him. It pilloried most of her family and friends and included the letter Byron had written when he was trying to rid himself of her attention. Murray told Hobhouse that the book would do Byron's sales no harm – quite the contrary.[8] When Madame de Staël asked if he was the original of the anti-hero Glenarvon, Byron replied coolly, 'C'est possible, Madame, mais je n'ai jamais posé.' Madame de Staël had 'made Coppet as agreeable as society and talent can make any place on earth', and Byron was distressed to hear of her death ten months later, 'not only because she had been very kind to me at Coppet – but because now I can never requite her.'

Byron was concerned about Augusta but could not understand from her vague hints what she was afraid of and certainly did not foresee the dangerous pitfalls his wife was devising. 'Your confidential letter is safe,' he wrote 'and all the others. This one had cut me to the heart because I have made you uneasy. Still I think all these apprehensions – very groundless. . . . Do not be uneasy – and do not "hate yourself" if you hate either let it be *me* – but do not – it would kill me; we are the last persons in the world – who ought – or could cease to love each other.'[9]

The conspirators waited until after the birth of Augusta's fifth child, Frederick George, in May. On 3 June they began their campaign of mental torture. 'Before your Confinement,' Annabella wrote, 'I should not risk agitating you, but having the satisfaction of knowing you are recovered, I will no longer conceal from yourself that there are reasons founded on such circumstances in your conduct, as (though thoroughly convinced they have existed) I am most anxious to bury in silence, which indispensably impose on me the duty of *limiting* my intercourse with you —'.[10] Augusta replied indignantly, insisting she had always put Annabella's happiness before anything else, telling Hodgson, 'No one can know *how much* I have suffered from this unhappy business – and, indeed, I have never known a moment's peace, and begin to despair for the future.'[11] When Hobhouse saw her in July 'she did not know what to say. Lady Byron corresponds with her again, in good terms, but not so affectionately as before.' Annabella, sensitive that her social position was several notches below Augusta and nervous of the latter's powerful aristocratic connections, had persuaded Lushington to withdraw his opposition to their contact, but he insisted that she keep copies of all their correspondence. Meanwhile Mrs Villiers was disappointed that Augusta appeared to pay more attention to the 'gauzes and sattins' she was to wear at the Prince Regent's fête than to confession; but Augusta did understand the seriousness of her position and felt she had no defence from the rumours except by accepting Lady Byron's protection.

Byron had himself told her, 'I think all these apprehensions – very groundless. Who can care for such a wretch as Caroline, or believe such a seventy times convicted liar? and in the next place, whatever she may suppose or assert – I never "committed" any one to her but *myself*. And as to her fancies – she fancies anything and everybody.'[12] Augusta still felt insecure and in her state of panic agreed to Annabella's condition that she would not see Byron as often as she had in the past, but she refused to give her word never to see him again. After completing her court duties she remained at St James's Palace and agreed to meet Annabella despite her husband's disapproval. George Leigh had never liked Annabella, thinking her cold and implacable, but he had not liked Byron either – even though, or perhaps because, he had received substantial financial support from him.

The two women met on 1 September in Annabella's lodgings at 1 Lower Seymour Street where, according to Annabella, Augusta made a full confession of guilt.[13] In an attempt to gain Annabella's good will she voluntarily showed her the letters Byron had written since he had left England and cringingly asked her advice on how she could stop him writing to her. The two conspirators rejoiced. 'I warned her,' wrote Mrs Villiers to Annabella, 'to be on her guard and the best precaution she could take was unbounded, unreserved confidence in you – that not a letter – a note – a word, should pass between her and him without being submitted to you – that you were her Guardian Angel and the only person who could assist her to counteract the execrable villainy of the other.'

In September Byron invited Augusta to visit him in the spring in Switzerland, promising that it would cost her nothing. 'You have no idea how very beautiful a great part of this country is – and *women* and *children* traverse it with ease and expedition. I would return from any distance at any time to see you, and come to England for you.' He then remembered Leigh: 'the great obstacle would be that you are so admirably yoked – and necessary as a housekeeper – and letter writer – & a place-hunter to that very helpless gentleman your Cousin.'[14]

A rumour reached Byron in Switzerland that Annabella intended to take Ada to the continent for the winter. 'I make it my personal and particular request to Lady Byron – that – in the event of her quitting England – the child should be left in the care of proper persons – I have no objection to its remaining with Lady Noel – & Sir Ralph,' he wrote to Augusta. He explained that he had no intention of ever removing Ada from her mother even though 'it is a very deep privation to me to be withdrawn from the contemplation and company of my little girl'. He continued, 'My whole hope – and prospect of a quiet evening (if I reach it) are wrapt up in that little creature Ada – and you must forgive my anxiety in all which regards her even to minuteness.'[15] The reply to his request was the message that 'Lady B. did not mean to quit England this winter.' Byron instructed Hanson to take 'the proper steps (*legal if necessary*) to prevent the possibility of such an occurrence. – If Lady B. – thinks proper now – or hereafter – to travel – that is no business of mine – but my daughter and only legitimate child must not be of the party – I do not wish to take her from the family – let her in such a case remain with Lady Noel – or my sister (or *I* will return immediately if necessary to receive her –) but let it be *immediately settled & understood that in no case is my daughter to leave the country.*' He did not receive a reply until well into the following year and it was brutally short: 'There never has existed nor does there exist, the remotest intention of removing Miss Byron out of the kingdom.' It was signed by Anne Isabella Byron and Ralph Noel. Byron received the news with fury telling Augusta, 'Give me but a *fair share* of my daughter – the half – my natural right & authority – & I am content; – otherwise I come to England & "law & claw before they get it".'[16]

During an expedition to Chamonix in September Byron bought pretty granite and spar playthings for Ada and Augusta's children. For little 'Da' he chose a ball of granite which he hoped she would enjoy rolling and playing with and a necklace of crystals. For the Leigh children there were packets of seals and necklaces. He told Augusta to make sure Georgiana got something she liked as a reward for the nice letter she had written to him. She had told him that she liked her little cousin with fair hair; 'How come Ada's hair *fair*?' he asked Augusta. 'She will be like her mother and torture me.' But he was glad to have news of her. 'Next to you – dearest – she is nearly all I have to look forward to with hope or pleasure in this world. Perhaps she also may disappoint & distress me, but I will not think so; in any case she will at least love me – or my memory.'[17]

Manfred, published on 16 June 1817 took as its subject the remorse of a man who had committed a crime for which he could neither forgive himself nor forget. Mrs Villiers wrote in great delight to Annabella, 'Did you see the newspaper of 23 June? There is a long critique of *Manfred* – the allusions to Augusta dreadfully clear. Lady Chichester brought it to me!'[18] The glee in Annabella's camp was short-lived as the public failed to see the connection and the queen did not withdraw her patronage, but Augusta was deeply hurt, frightened and confused. Her letters to Byron became quite incoherent forcing him to scold her, 'I repeat to you again and again that it would be much better at once to explain your mysteries than to go on with this absurd obscure hinting mode of writing. What do you mean? What is there known? or can be known? which *you* and *I* do not know better?'[19] He assumed her panic was caused by George Leigh's financial affairs and blunders but his patience was coming to an end. He told Murray, 'I can make out nothing from her letter – it is very foolish to torment me with ambiguities at this distance.' Augusta was worn out; she was expecting another child, her sixth in nine years. Amelia Marianne, known in the family as Emily, was born in November 1817 and Annabella was her godmother.

Neither Hobhouse nor Sir Francis Burdett thought it was necessary for Byron to exile himself but Byron felt he was ostracized and the separation gave him the opportunity to travel to Switzerland, as he had planned before his marriage.[20] Exactly one month before his arrival in Geneva on 25 May 1816 he had landed in Ostend at midnight and in good spirits. He declared Ostend a tolerable place and, according to Polidori, 'as soon as he reached his room Lord·Byron fell like a thunderbolt upon the chambermaid.'

The next day Byron, Polidori and his retinue boarded his huge new coach, a copy of one owned by Napoleon which contained a bed, a library, a plate chest and was large enough to dine in elegantly.[21] They travelled through Ghent, Antwerp and Malines, lost their way in the twilight not far from Ghent where Fletcher whined that he was afraid of being robbed. The gaudy coach was prone to broken wheels and springs which forced the travellers to stop at Brussels for repairs. On 6 May they moved on to Louvain and Cologne where they took to the Rhine, stopping only to admire Bonn, Koblenz, the Castle of Drachenfels and Mannheim. They arrived at Karlsruhe and paused for another two days while Polidori, who had been seriously ill with headaches and feverishness, recovered his health and Byron pounced on another chambermaid. They left Basle on the 20th and by the 25th had arrived at De Jean's Hôtel d'Angleterre at Sécheron, a mile outside Geneva.

Before retiring for the night Byron filled in the visitors' register, facetiously putting his age down as 100. The owner was not amused and sent him a note half an hour later asking him to correct it. Someone else had seen the entry and wrote next to it, 'I am sorry you are grown so old. Indeed I suspected you were 200 from the slowness of your journey. I suppose your venerable age could not bear quicker travelling.'[22]

The writer was the accommodating young woman from Albemarle Street who was already pregnant with Byron's child, conceived during the miserable days leading up to the signing of the separation. She had been persistent in her request to see Byron again and had wheedled an agreement from him that he would see her in Geneva, on condition that she travel in a respectable way and under proper protection. She had been waiting for her lover at the Hôtel d'Angleterre for almost two weeks.

Clara, or as she preferred to be known, 'Claire' Clairmont had accompanied Mary Godwin when she eloped to France in 1814 with the already married Percy Shelley. Shelley had instilled his theories of free love in both the young girls and Claire wrote to Byron from Paris on 6 May offering him not only herself but also Mary, telling him that once he had seen her he would fall in love with her, as she was both handsome and amiable. She ended the startling letter, 'Farewell, dear kind Lord Byron. I have been reading all your poems and almost fear to think of your reading this stupid letter, but I love you.'

Byron, anxious not to renew his acquaintance with her, did not return her message. Deeply disappointed and hurt, Claire wrote, 'I am sure you can't say as you used in London that you are overwhelmed with affairs and have not an instant to yourself. I have been in this weary hotel this fortnight and it seems so unkind, so cruel of you to treat me with such marked indifference.'[23] Eventually, after a day spent house hunting Byron and Polidori met Claire, Mary and Shelley. The two groups joined forces and for the next few days they ate breakfast together and discussed the houses that were available for rent, both parties being anxious to leave the expensive hotel and find cheaper accommodation. The Shelleys took a small house at Montalègre, close to the lake and near a small private mooring place. They celebrated together by taking a trip on the lake and returning to a convivial tea. Byron and Polidori took over the Villa Diodati on 10 June and it quickly became the headquarters of the young group. When the weather was bad they sat by the fire in the evenings talking of poetry and ghosts. It was agreed that each of them would write a ghost story but they soon gave the plan up, except for Mary who continued to develop her idea until she had completed *Frankenstein, or the Modern Prometheus*.[24] On fine nights they went sailing. Byron liked to play the fool; once he told them he would sing them an Albanian song and, leading them to believe it would be a sentimental ballad, he opened his mouth only to let out a strange wild howl and explode into laughter at the surprise on their faces.

Byron half-heartedly resumed the affair that Claire had initiated in London. He explained to Augusta, who had heard tales of multiple mistresses, 'As to all those mistresses, Lord help me, I have had but one. No don't scold; but what could I do? A foolish girl, in spite of all I could say or do, would come after me, or rather went before – for I found her here.' He continued, 'I was not in love . . . but could not exactly play the stoic with a woman who had scrambled eight hundred miles to unphilosophize me.'[25] He explained his position even more clearly to Kinnaird: 'I never loved nor pretended to love her, but a man is a man, and if a girl of eighteen comes prancing to you at all hours – there is but one way, the suite of all this is that she was with *child.*' He ended defiantly, 'This comes of "putting it about" (as Jackson calls it) and be damned to it.'[26] There was no mistaking Claire's condition at the end of July and on 2 August Shelley and Claire went up to Diodati to discuss what must be done.

Claire's unsophisticated worship bored Byron. He regretted he had given in to a moment of lust; the momentary feeling of intoxication Claire induced had cooled into indifference and was fast progressing into dislike. Claire, with her head full of Shelley's free-love lectures and Mary Wollestonecraft's views on the rights of women, had pushed herself into an impossible position. Instead of being a new woman, a fighter for the rights of women, fearless and independent, she had clipped her own wings, making herself dependent on a man who did not now, and had not ever, loved her.[27]

Byron proposed that the coming child should be placed in Augusta's care but Claire disagreed, saying children should always stay with one or other of their parents until the age of seven. He bowed to her wishes, stipulating that it would be best if the child stayed with him and she passed herself off as its aunt so, in that way, she could preserve her reputation. Claire left Switzerland with the Shelleys on 29 August and was bitterly disappointed that Byron would not spare the time to see her or even give her a parting kiss.

Byron's heart had hardened towards Claire and although he wrote to Shelley, who was now living in Bath with the two women, he never mentioned her or the coming child. She desperately craved a few kind words from him: 'I do not like to be the object of pity, and nothing makes me so angry as when Mary and Shelley tell me not to expect to hear from you. They seem to know how little you care for me, and their hateful remarks are the most cruel of all.' She continued, 'It is now the 17th of November; if you would write directly I should have the dear letter before I lie in, which would make me so happy – but if you will not, indeed I shall go quite out of my mind.'[28] Byron excused his cruelty, saying he was afraid to write in case she showed his letter to others and it caused more scandal. Her distress was so great that Shelley was forced to write, 'If you do not like to write to Claire, send me some kind message to her, which I will, to give suspicion his due, throw into the fire as a sacrifice.'[29]

Byron's second daughter was born at four in the morning of Sunday, 12 January 1817 in Bath. She was a beautiful baby with intelligent blue eyes, dark hair and an exquisitely shaped mouth and the Byron chin, complete with a dimple. Claire called her Alba, which may have been the feminine version of her nickname for Byron – Albé.

Mary's letter informing Byron of the birth of his child did not reach him until May 1817 but, despite himself, he was moved and contemplated the new child's future, jokingly telling Augusta he had a daughter by 'her who returned to England to become a Mamma incog . . . – & whom I pray the Gods to keep there . . . – I am a little puzzled how to dispose of this new production.' He went on to say that he would 'probably send for & place it in a Venetian convent – to become a good Catholic – & (it may be) a *nun* – being a character somewhat wanted in our family.' He added, 'although I never was attached or pretended attachment to the mother – still in case of the eternal war & alienation which I foresee about my legitimate daughter – Ada – it may be well to have something to repose a hope upon – I must love something in my old age.'[30] To Moore he wrote, 'Besides my little legitimate, I have made unto myself an *il*legitimate since (to say nothing of the one before), and I look forward to one of these as the pillars of my old age. . . . I have a great love for my little Ada.'[31]

In Bath Shelley's unconventional principles were widely known and he was suspected of being Alba's father although he had married Mary Godwin on 30 December 1816. The group moved to Marlow where they took a cold and damp house which soon caused Shelley's health to suffer. When Alba reached the age of one Shelley wrote to Byron to ask what his plans were for her. The warm blue skies of the south looked very inviting and, if Byron was willing to take charge of his child, they could all benefit from the trip to Italy to deliver her. Byron agreed to acknowledge Alba and bring her up himself. He wanted her to be named Allegra, a Venetian name, and her surname would be spelled *Biron* to distinguish her from 'little Legitimacy'.

On Alba's first birthday Claire wrote Byron a long, ill-advised letter full of fancies to induce him to see his daughter so she could attempt to revitalize her love affair:

> My dear friend, how I envy you! you will have a little darling to crawl to your knees and pull you till you take her up; then she will sit in the crook of your arm and you will give her a raisin off your own plate and a tiny drop of wine from your own glass, and she will think herself a little Queen of creation. But there is one delight above all this; if it please you, you may delight yourself in contemplating a creature growing under your hands; you may look at her and think; 'This is my work.'[32]

Alba was christened on 9 March 1818 with Shelley's two children at St Giles in the Fields, London. The Register Book of Baptisms shows that Alba became Clara Allegra Byron, daughter of the Rt Hon. George Gordon Lord Byron the reputed father by Clara Mary Jane Clairmont.

The father's residence was described as of 'no fixed residence. Travelling on the Continent'.

On 11 March Shelley, Mary, their children, two-year-old William and five-month-old Clara, together with Claire and Allegra and the Swiss nurse, Elise Foggi, and an English maid, Milly, left for Italy. The group arrived in Milan on 4 April and sent word to Byron asking to see him before they sent the child to him in Venice. It was over a month before a messenger arrived bringing a letter saying that he would only accept the child if Claire gave up her claim to her entirely. Shelley implored him to have compassion and Allegra's journey was delayed while Claire made an appeal, '. . . think if it is not a lamentable sight to see one human creature beg from another a little mercy and forbearance. You must know that you have all the power in your hands – I entreat you to spare me.' Shelley pressed her to think again before parting with Allegra, but Claire felt she could not deny her the chance of a brilliant future with her father. On 27 April, Claire's twentieth birthday, Allegra and Elise accompanied Byron's huge Venetian servant, Tita, to Venice with a tear-stained plea from Claire: 'I have sent you my child because I love her too well to keep her. With you who are powerful and noble and the admiration of the world she will be happy, but I am a miserable and neglected dependant. Dearest and best, I entreat you to think how wretched and alone I feel now that she is gone, and write to me that she is well, the darling bird!'[33]

Allegra first saw her father on 2 May and he found her healthy, capricious, noisy and, most important, everyone said she looked like him, except for Fletcher who thought she looked more like Annabella. For the first few days in Venice she lived with Richard Hoppner and his family, as Byron was concluding the transactions needed to lease the Palazzo Mocenigo on the Grand Canal. Hoppner had been British consul in Venice for four years and Byron found him agreeable and his Swiss wife pleasant. Byron became fond of his new daughter and within a couple of weeks he boasted to Hobhouse that she was a very fine child who was admired and caressed by the Venetians; however, she could not take the place of Ada.

Byron soon realized that his life at the Palazzo Mocenigo was not suitable for a young child and either he suggested to the Hoppners, or they offered, that she should go to live with them taking the maid Elise with her.[34] Richard Hoppner said later that Allegra was not by any means an amiable child nor were they particularly fond of her. Nevertheless Byron was pleased with her appearance. 'Her hair is growing darker and her eyes are blue – Her temper and her ways Mr Hoppner says are like mine – as well as her features. She will make in that case a manageable young lady.' He added sadly, 'I never hear anything of Ada.'[35]

When the news of Allegra's new home reached the Shelleys, through
Elise's whining, illiterate letters, Claire persuaded Shelley to take her to
Venice. They arrived on 20 August and Shelley immediately set out for
the Palazzo Mocenigo, arriving at three in the afternoon. Delighted to
see him, Byron took him riding on the Lido and put his villa at Este at his
disposal for a family holiday where Claire could indulge her maternal
instincts well away from him.[36] Claire spent the day with the Hoppners
who gave her highly coloured accounts of debauchery at the Palazzo
Mocenigo, from which they smugly claimed to have rescued Allegra,
emphasizing that she was now being properly fed and tastefully clothed.

At Shelley's command Mary hurried to Este bringing her feverish baby
Clare and her two-year-old son William. No sooner had she arrived than
Clare immediately succumbed to dysentery and, afraid to move her, the
parents dithered; by the time they arrived in Venice to look for
professional medical help it was too late. Clare died in her mother's arms
an hour after they arrived. Shelley returned Allegra to her father who
had again refused to see Claire, explaining in his half-joking way that 'I
declined seeing her for fear the consequence might be an addition to the
family.' Mrs Hoppner continued to send Claire letters guaranteed to
upset her, commenting on Byron's continued debauchery and the
unsuitable food his mistress, Margarita, was stuffing into Allegra.

In May 1819 Allegra attracted the attention of a rich English widow,
Mrs Vavassour. She was a northern landowner and not having a family of
her own wanted to adopt Allegra, but only if Byron would relinquish all
his claims. Claire was willing to consider the proposal but Byron would
only give consent for Mrs Vavassour to take Allegra to England and
educate her; he refused to surrender his rights as her father and the
scheme was abandoned in July. As the hot weather built up in Venice the
Hoppners tried unsuccessfully to persuade him to send Allegra to the
more healthy atmosphere of Switzerland, but Byron told Augusta,
'Allegra is well at Venice – There are also a fox, some dogs and two
monkeys, all scratching, screaming and fighting – in the highest health
and spirits.' The Hoppners left for Switzerland leaving Allegra, at Byron's
insistence, in the care of the wife of one of their servants.

The debauchery that the Hoppners made so much of began when
Byron arrived in Venice with Hobhouse in November 1816. They first
took rooms at the Hotel Gran Bretagna later moving into cheaper
lodgings.

Byron's landlord was a draper called Segati who had a pretty, 22-year-
old wife, Marianna, with whom Byron immediately fell in love,
'fathomless love', describing her as pretty as an antelope with large black
oriental eyes set in an Italian countenance and accomplishments to

furnish a new chapter for Solomon's song. Segati was very rarely about as he was busy running his business and Byron was happy and filled his days with books, Armenian lessons and Marianna. Hobhouse left for Rome without him. Byron explained to Augusta, 'you will easily suppose that I was not disposed to stir from my present position,' continuing, 'Thank heaven above – and woman beneath – and will be a very good boy. Pray remember me to the babes and tell me of little Da.'[37] He settled into Venetian life, describing himself as studious in the day and dissolute in the evening. The news from Murray was good. Some seven thousand copies of Canto III of *Childe Harold* and an equal number of *Chillon and Other Poems* had been sold. He enjoyed the winter carnival, attended the opera and continued to write. On 19 February he fell ill with a fever and suffered from half-delirium, burning skin, thirst, hot headaches, horrible palpitations and sleeplessness, but Marianna skilfully nursed him back to health.

He joined Hobhouse in Rome at the end of April and ran the gauntlet of twittering English tourists. While walking on the roof of St Peter's he was pointed out to Lady Liddell, a friend of Annabella's parents, who had never seen him before. She dared take only one horror-stricken look at him, her feet rooted to the spot. She cast her eyes down and snapped at her daughter Maria, 'Don't look at him, he is dangerous to look at.' His presence caused superstitious horror in faint-hearted ladies and in others a peculiar feeling of veneration. Lady Rosebery, later Lady Mildmay, was so terrified to meet him that, when he spoke to her, her heart beat so violently that she could hardly answer.[38] The attention of the expatriate British irritated him. 'I harm nobody – I make love with but one woman at a time and as quietly as possible and they lie through thick and thin and invent every kind of absurdity,' he complained to Scrope Davies.[39]

In June 1817 Byron signed a six-month lease for the Villa Foscarini on the bank of the Brenta river at the village of La Mira between Padua and Venice. It was a pretty villa, built on the site of a Capuchin convent near the ruined castle of Este, with a vine-covered pergola stretching from the hall door to the summer house. Byron and Marianne moved in to escape the heat of Venice taking Hobhouse with them. Monk Lewis arrived from London full of gossip, including Brougham's remark that Lady Byron's lawyers had declared 'their lips to be sealed up' on the cause of the separation. In a paroxysm of rage Byron composed a paper accusing the lawyers of conducting the proceedings in such a way as to make it impossible for any reconciliation to take place. He declared he would be happy to cancel the separation and go before any tribunal they cared to suggest to discuss the cause. He added, 'I have been, and am now, utterly ignorant of what description her allegations, charges, or whatever name they may have assumed, are; and am as little aware for what purpose they have been kept back, – unless it was to sanction the most infamous calumnies by silence.'[40]

On warm evenings Byron and Hobhouse rode along the bank of the Brenta, commenting on the charms of local girls. One evening they saw two unusually pretty ones among a group of peasants. The bold one called to Byron asking for money. He replied she was so young and pretty she could have no need of help from him. A few evenings later they encountered the same two girls and after passing the time of day Byron made an assignation for the following evening. The two girls were accompanied by a third woman who was 'cursedly in the way'. Hobhouse's choice took fright and ran off and Byron's fancy at first baulked slightly. However, when he told her that if she were really in need he would relieve her without any conditions, and it was up to her whether or not she made love with him, she made no objections. She cautioned that she was married and, while all married women had affairs, her husband, a baker, was ferocious. A few evenings later all was arranged with the baker and Margarita, now nick-named La Fornarina. Margarita Cogni was twenty-two, tall and swarthy, with a Venetian face and fine dark eyes. She was illiterate, fierce and overbearing. She used Byron's house as though it were her own and would knock down any woman she found there. She amused Byron and made him laugh which was one of his principal requirements from women. Their liaison lasted two years.[41]

By mid-November the cold wind made life uncomfortable at La Mira and Byron and Hobhouse returned to Venice where Byron took an active part in the Venetian social round, attending the opera, concerts and the widowed Countess Albrizzi's *conversazioni*. She ruled the most celebrated salon in Venice and attracted fashionable social lions as well as many pretty girls. Byron threw himself into the spirit of his second Carnival with verve. At one of the masques he met Elena de Mosta, a pretty, fair-haired, blue eyed girl, an unusual combination in Venice. She became passionately involved with him, insatiable for his love and refusing all his presents or gifts of money. However, she was tainted. Byron wryly remarked to Hobhouse that it was the first time he had contracted gonorrhoea without paying for it.[42]

The welcome news that Newstead had been sold for £94,500 arrived at the end of 1817 and allowed Byron to pay off some of his outstanding debts. He settled the balance of his rent for Piccadilly Terrace with the Duchess of Devonshire and paid the coachbuilder for his Napoleonic wonder.

Flush with new wealth Byron took a lease for three years on the Palazzo Mocenigo on the Grand Canal and acquired the services of Tita, or Giovanni Battista Falciere, a former employee of the Mocenigo family, who became one of his most devoted servants. Marianne was discarded and La Fornarina reigned in her place.

He was never free from English spies and gossips for long; Lady Calthorpe's daughter regaled her mother with her observations on Byron's life in Venice, and her tales were immediately passed on to Lady Noel. Byron's debaucheries and idiosyncratic behaviour were thoroughly discussed by his mother-in-law and her friends.[43] Byron did nothing to stop the stories of his eccentricities, even reinforcing them by boasting to Wedderburn Webster that for around £5,000 over the past two years he had kept a gondola, fourteen servants including a nurse for his bastard daughter, supported a small zoo consisting of two monkeys, two mastiffs, a dog called Mutz, four horses and a fox; he had lived in an enormous palace on the Grand Canal and rented a villa in the Eugean hills. He estimated that he could have lived well on half that amount if he had not spent so freely on women, roughly two hundred of them. It was difficult to say exactly, he bragged, as he had not kept count recently.

After months of procrastinating Newton Hanson and his father arrived in Venice bringing the final papers for the sale of Newstead. They were astonished at Byron's appearance.[44] He looked forty instead of thirty years old and his face was pale, bloated and sallow. He was fat with broad, round shoulders and even the knuckles in his hands were embedded in fat. Annabella's friends, the Montgomerys, had also seen him 'extremely fat . . . bloated and heavy', adding the two-edged comment that 'His face is much more like a full moon that ever *yours* was.'

Hanson drafted a codicil to Byron's will in which he left Allegra £5,000, to be paid to her on her twenty-first birthday or on the day of her marriage on condition that she did not 'marry a native of Great Britain'.

Byron was ambivalent about Allegra's immediate future. He had fallen in love with the young wife of Count Alessandro Guiccioli and could think of nothing else. He had seen her in the autumn of 1818 three days after her marriage to her 58-year-old husband at the house of the Countess Albrizzi, but it was not until April the following year, at an evening party of Madame Benzoni's, that they were introduced.

Teresa Guiccioli was the daughter of Count Ruggero Gamba Ghiselli of Ravenna and her husband's third wife. She was a chubby girl with a fine bust and rounded shoulders, good teeth and eyes. She had a delicate complexion and rich golden hair which she wore in ringlets. Byron was impressed with her conversation and appearance and described her as 'fair as sunrise and warm as noon'. She saw him as a celestial apparition and was irresistibly attracted to him. She agreed to see him alone the next day 'on condition that he would respect my honour', but when they met again, Teresa said, 'my strength gave way – for B. was not a man to confine himself to sentiment.'[45] They had ten days together before Count Guiccioli took Teresa to Cà Zen, his newly acquired estate near the mouth of the Po. On the journey to Ravenna a few days later Teresa had a serious miscarriage and arrived home half dead. Byron assured Kinnaird, his banker, that the foetus was not his. 'She was three months advanced before our first passade. . . .'[46] According to her doctors Teresa appeared to be developing the first symptoms of consumption. She was also weighed down with grief over the recent death of her mother, who had succumbed while giving birth to her fourteenth child.

On learning of her illness Byron left Venice for Ravenna and on his arrival he immediately sent word to Teresa through their go-between, the priest Don Gaspare Pirelli. He called on her the following day; alarmed at her pale appearance, he sent for Dr Agliette from Venice. The presence of Byron together with the doctor's care brought about an improvement in Teresa's health. Within two months she was able to accompany her husband on a tour of his estates.[47]

Byron felt uncomfortable cuckolding the count daily in his own house, but the situation was tremblingly delicious. There were no locks on the doors and he had to conduct his amorous manoeuvres in the Great Salon after dinner when the household were resting. It required the co-operation of a priest, a chambermaid, a young negro boy and Fanny Silvestrini, a governess and Teresa's confidante. Count Guiccioli, who must have known what was going on, confused Byron by seeking his friendship and taking him for rides in his magnificent coach and six. He asked if Byron could arrange for him to be made a British vice consul and Byron made unsuccessful enquiries on his behalf to Hoppner and Murray.

Teresa firmly resisted Byron's strenuous pleas to elope. She was determined to make him conform to the Italian custom of *serventismo*. This convention demanded that the lover pass himself off as the husband's friend and carry his mistress's fan and shawl, thus allowing him to accompany her in public without causing scandal. Teresa had already begun to treat Byron as though he were her accepted *amico* by referring to him as 'mio Byron' and going into his box at the opera alone. Byron thought of marrying her and wrote to Augusta, 'If you see my spouse, do pray tell her I wish to marry again, and as probably she may wish the same, is there no way in *Scotland?* without compromising HER immaculacy, cannot it be done there by the *husband* solely?'[48]

As Teresa recovered they entered into a period of happiness. They rode in the pine forests along the coast, Teresa frequently exasperating Byron by allowing her horse to bite his. She wrestled with the reins, being completely unable to guide her mount, and almost fell off, shrieking as she became entangled in the low branches and thickets, putting her elegant sky-blue riding-habits in danger of being ripped from her back. Her antics made Byron laugh and embarrassed the grooms. When apart they wrote each other little notes. 'Why not after dinner?' asked Byron, 'You well know *what* I "like" – every day in which we do not see and *love* each other, in deed as in our hearts, is (at least for me) the most irreparable of losses, one happiness the less. Tell me *when*.'[49] Confident of her hold over him Teresa began to flirt. Byron retaliated by taking an interest in one of her married friends, Gertrude Vicari, but after he was seen squeezing her thigh, Teresa made sure that Gertrude was sent to Bologna to be well guarded by her husband and her 'she-dragon mother-in-law'.

The count and Teresa moved to Bologna and Byron followed, taking rooms in a palazzo in Via Galliera not far from the Palazzo Savioli where the Guicciolis lived. To his surprise Count Guiccioli offered him rooms on the ground floor of his own palazzo.

When he was settled Byron sent for Allegra and was annoyed to discover that Elise had been dismissed and there was no one to accompany the child from Venice to Bologna. He was also irritated by the attitude of Hobhouse, Hoppner and Alexander Scott, another Venetian acquaintance, all of whom disapproved of his association with Teresa and thought he was making a fool of himself. Scott went so far as to warn him against putting Allegra into the hands of his 'Dama' as she might use the child as a hostage, forcing her to marry her brother, Count Pietro Gamba. Allegra eventually arrived, 'in good health – & very amiable and pretty at least thought so. She is English – but speaks nothing but Venetian – "Bon *di* papa" &c. &c. she is very droll – and has a good deal of the Byron – can't articulate the letter *r* at all – frowns and pouts quite in our way – blue eyes – light hair growing *darker* daily – and a dimple in the chin – a scowl on the brow – white skin – sweet voice – and a particular liking of Music – and of her own way in every thing – is not that B. all over?' he asked Augusta.[50] When Thomas Moore admired her, Byron, in his odd way, turned the compliment aside as though embarrassed, saying, 'Have you any notion – I suppose *you* have – of what they call parental feeling? For myself I have not the least.'[51]

The count's motive in allowing Byron to take rooms in his palazzo became clearer when he borrowed a large sum of money. When Byron refused to lend him any more Guiccioli lost his temper. In the resulting upheaval Teresa claimed she had suffered a relapse and must go to Venice to consult Dr Aglietti; her husband astonishingly insisted that Byron should escort her there because he had to go to Ravenna on urgent business. 'When I arrived at Venice,' Teresa said, 'the physicians ordered that I should try the country air, and Lord Byron, having a Villa at La Mira, gave it up to me and came to reside there with me.' She attributed her recovery entirely to Byron and his tender care.

Thomas Moore, on a short tour of northern Italy, visited the couple at La Mira. He was surprised to see how much weight his friend had put on, regretting that it had reduced his refined and spiritual look. He also thought his hair too long, his new whiskers unwelcome and his clothes foreign-looking but, despite everything, Moore conceded that Byron was still a very handsome man. His first impression of Teresa was not favourable, 'blond and young, married only about a year, but not very pretty'.[52]

Moore stayed in Venice for five days but 'So far from "seducing me to England",' wrote Byron, 'the account Moore gave of me and mine, was of anything but a nature to make me wish to return.' The visit was a great success. Byron told Murray, 'Moore and I did nothing but laugh.' On his last evening Byron met Moore, saying 'with all the glee of a school boy who had just been granted a holiday' that the contessa had given him leave to 'make a night of it'. They ate at Pellegrino's with Alexander Scott and went on to the Opera. The chief female singer's claim to fame, according to Byron, was that she had stilettoed one of her favourite lovers. Afterwards they sat in St Mark's Square and watched 'a sort of *cabaret*' and whiled the night away 'drinking hot brandy punch, and laughing over old times, till the clock of St. Mark struck the second hour of the morning'. Byron and Moore took a gondola and floated out on to the lagoon to see the beauty of Venice by moonlight. An hour later they parted at his palazzo, 'laughing as we had met; – an agreement having been first made that I should take an early dinner with him next day at his villa, on my road to Ferrara.'[53]

Moore arrived at La Mira at three o'clock to find Byron waiting for him in the hall. As he entered he caught a glimpse of little Allegra. She had just come in from her walk and was standing quietly with her nursemaid. He went across to talk to her and a few moments later complimented Byron on his child's good looks. Just before they sat down for dinner Byron left the room and returned a moment or two later holding a white leather bag in his hand. He held it out to Moore saying, 'Look here, this would be worth something to Murray, though *you*, I dare say, would not give sixpence for it.'

'What is it?' Moore asked.

'*My Life and Adventures,*' replied Byron. 'It is not a thing that can be published during my lifetime, but you may have it – if you like – there, do whatever you please with it.' He added, 'You may show it to any of our friends you think worthy of it.'[54]

Byron was tempted to accompany Moore to Rome but he realized he could not desert Teresa who had sacrificed her name and virtue for him. However, he was restless, beginning to resent her hold over him and to think again of returning to England or going to America or becoming a planter in Venezuela. Despite his unsettled mood he valued Teresa, telling Kinnaird that of all the women he had known Teresa was the most generous, 'I can assure you that she has never cost me directly or indirectly a sixpence – . . . I never offered her but one present – a brooch of brilliants – and she sent it back to me with her *own hair* in it (I shall *not* say of *what part* but *that* is an Italian custom) and a note to say that she was not in the habit of receiving presents of that value – but hoped that I would not consider her sending it back as an affront – nor the value diminished by the enclosure.'[55]

In early November 1819 Byron suffered another attack of fever and on recovering from a period of delirium he found Fletcher sobbing on one side of his bed and Teresa on the other. 'I have got *well,*' he told Augusta, 'but Allegra is still laid up though convalescent – and her nurse – and half my ragamuffins – Gondoliers, nurses – cook — footmen &c. I cured myself without bark – but all the others are taking it like trees.'[56] Only a few weeks before, he had written to Hoppner saying, 'Allegrina is flourishing like a pomegranate blossom', but now she had been diagnosed by Dr Aglietti as having 'doppia terzana'.

Count Gamba belatedly became worried about the effect the scandal was having on his daughter's name and, encouraged by Guiccioli, he brought the situation to a head. While Byron lay upstairs sweating in his palazzo, Guiccioli and Teresa argued violently in the room below. He presented his wife with an ultimatum: she must choose between him and her lover. She chose Byron, who was flattered but saw the dangers of an elopement far more clearly than she did. The scandal would horrify the Gamba family and seriously reduce her five sisters' chances of making good marriages. He used all his charm to persuade her to stay with Guiccioli, broadly hinting, because he knew she would not have gone without hope, that he would see her again. After ten days of bickering Teresa agreed to accept Guiccioli's written terms, which forbade her to have any contact with Byron. Pleading and tearful she allowed herself to be taken to Ravenna.[57]

In July 1819 Byron had generously offered to support Augusta and her family if they joined him but heard nothing. In September he wrote, 'You say nothing in favour of my return to England. Very well, I will stay where I am, and you will never see me more.'[58] He had still not put the idea of returning home completely out of his mind but he continued to toy with the thought of emigrating to Venezuela. 'I should not make a bad South-American planter, and I should take my natural daughter Allegra with me and settle,' he told Murray. Alone and out of spirits in the great rooms of the palazzo, he reflected on how he had left England on account of his own wife and would now 'leave Italy because of another's'. He described Teresa to Augusta as 'a kind of Italian Caroline Lamb – but very pretty and gentle – at least to me – for I never knew so docile a creature as far as we lived together.' He went on, 'All this – and my fever – have made me low and ill – but the moment Allegra is better – we shall set off over the Tyrolese Alps and find our way to England.' He promised to talk to her of his American scheme when they met. He knew nothing of the terror Augusta felt when she received his request to address her next letter to him at Calais, where he planned to stop before leaving for home. She wrote in a panic to Lady Byron, 'I'm sure I do not know how to address a letter to *Calais* – it being out of the question to *give him welcome to England.* Alas! how melancholy if that should be so – Luckily – (or *un*luckily perhaps) I do not die easily – or I think this stroke would about finish me.'[59]

Teresa, desperate without Byron, suffered a relapse into consumption so serious she was able to persuade her father to invite him to Ravenna, having miraculously convinced her parent that their relationship had been Platonic from the beginning. Byron told Murray, 'Pray let my sister be informed that I am not coming as I intended. I have not the courage to tell her so myself.' By the end of December he was in Ravenna and soon after had taken a suite of apartments in the Palazzo Guiccioli. Augusta breathed a sigh of relief.

Teresa had become fond of Allegra, and tended to spoil her, taking her for rides in Count Guiccioli's coach and six almost daily and to the carnival cavalcade in February. Allegra had plenty of toys – the Hoppners had sent her a box-full and Teresa was generous. Although Byron assumed a mask of indifference about her before his friends he frequently could not end his letters without a comment on her progress. In March 1820 Allegra was 'prettier but obstinate as a mule, and as ravenous as a vulture: health good, to judge of the complexion – temper tolerable, but for vanity and pertinacity. She thinks herself handsome, and will do as she pleases.'[60] In April she had 'increased in good looks and obstinacy'.

Claire bombarded Byron with letters, using the Hoppners as go-betweens. In March she asked him to send Allegra to the Shelleys in Pisa but Byron refused. He disapproved of the way the Shelley children were brought up and he feared for Allegra's health. 'Have they reared one?' he asked Hoppner, a cruel reference to the death of Mary Shelley's two babies, William and Clara. Allegra thrived with her father. She ate well, had plenty of air, drove on the Corso with Teresa each day, she was growing fast and was a great favourite with everyone; in fact, Byron complained, she was being spoiled because her fair skin made her stand out from the dusky Italian children. He was determined that Claire should never have her and that Allegra would leave him only when she went to school either in England or at an Italian convent. Claire's whinings and demands created such aversion in Byron that he could only bring himself to deal with her through intermediaries. However, he agreed that Claire could see Allegra 'whenever there is convenience of vicinity and access – otherwise no'.[61] Byron's phobia, according to Teresa, occasionally extended to Allegra. She said he would sometimes turn away from the little girl in disgust saying, 'Take her away, she looks too much like her mother.'[62]

Count Guiccioli became hostile to Byron and broke into Teresa's writing desk looking for something incriminating. Their affair was common knowledge in Ravenna and Teresa thought her husband might have been influenced by people who disliked Byron's liberal politics. Guiccioli found nothing but demanded Byron never visit his house again and took such unpleasant revenge on Teresa that she asked her father for permission to return to his protection.

The Gambas liked Byron and were convinced of the sincerity of his feelings for Teresa. Count Gamba decided to apply to the Pope for a separation for Teresa from her tyrannical husband. Meanwhile Guiccioli continued to search for evidence of his wife's infidelity and managed to extract statements from eighteen of his servants which he sent to the Pope. In July 1820 Teresa was granted a separation from her husband on the grounds that she could no longer live safely with him. Before Guiccioli had heard of the decision Teresa hurried to meet her father outside the walls of Ravenna and fled to Filetto under his protection.[63]

Byron searched for a house in the country where Allegra could stay during the summer heat and settled on the Villa Bacinetti, 6 miles from Ravenna. Before he could move her, however, she developed a fever and for three days her condition steadily worsened; on the fifth day, 7 August 1820, she had regained sufficient strength to break a toy carriage given to her by Teresa. Byron issued urgent orders to have the Villa Bacinetti made ready as soon as possible and on 12 August Allegra and her nurses moved in.

Claire kept up her unremitting barrage of letters. Byron appealed to

Shelley, who asked for his understanding, pleading that Claire was not well. She had offended Byron again, this time by suggesting that he was not taking proper care of Allegra. He replied through Hoppner that he had hired two maids and a country house for her and he intended to bring her up to be a Christian and a married woman and as far as Claire's right to see her was concerned, she was free to do so under proper restrictions but he would not allow her to throw everything into confusion with Bedlam behaviour. His final comment to Hoppner was, 'to express it delicately – I think Madame Claire is a damned bitch.'[64] Claire's hatred of Byron was now uncontrollable and she took comfort in composing what she called 'caricatures' – fantasy stories showing him indulging in every vice she could think of.

Count Gamba was a liberal and a patriot, and Byron, with his Whig leanings, became friends with the old man and his twenty-year-old son, Pietro, who had just returned from school in Rome and Naples. Both father and son were involved in the secret societies which were springing up all over Italy, aimed at freeing it from Austria; it was a cause which appealed to Byron. Through the friendship of the Gambas he attached himself to the Carbonari, although he was not impressed with the melodrama and bravado which formed a great part of their meetings. He became the chief of the section *Mericani* (Americans) and rashly allowed them to store their weapons in his rooms in the Palazzo Guiccioli. A rising had been planned for the Romagna in September but it was unsuccessful. There were occasional scuffles on the street and one night the commandant of troops fell mortally wounded outside Byron's door; the corpse was placed on Fletcher's bed where it stayed until the following day.

With revolution at his door Byron worried what would become of Allegra, who was now an intelligent, wilful little girl, rapidly becoming uncontrollable, which was not surprising, as he had already noticed with pride how closely she resembled him. He was repeating his mother's mistakes in spoiling her and was rewarded, as she had been, with sulks and temper tantrums. The idea of sending her to a convent had been at the back of his mind for some time, but it was only after he discovered that one of the maids was teaching her to lie that he made the final decision. On the recommendations of Teresa's grandparents and his banker in Ravenna, Pellegrino Ghigi, he arranged for Allegra to enter the nearby school run by Capucine nuns in the Convent of San Giovanni, at Bagnacavallo, 12 miles from Ravenna. It was a popular and fashionable school which had recently opened and specialized in educating girls from the ages of seven to eighteen from the best local families. On 1 March 1821 Ghigi accompanied Allegra to the convent to join his own daughter,

Aspasia. The fees were 70 scudi each half year and at Easter it was the custom for each pupil to present the nuns with a lamb, and at Christmas a capon. Each girl provided her own bed, chest of drawers, two chairs and a washstand and her clothes, at least eighteen chemises and a warm dress made of black wool. In addition to these Allegra took six dresses, three of cotton, one of velvet, one of muslin and another of voile, two pairs of gloves, a little cap, a string of coral, dolls and a silver spoon and fork. Byron later sent her his peer's gown to be cut up and made into warm winter dresses. On arriving at the convent Allegra stretched out her hands to the nuns to be kissed and ordered the two lay sisters who had been told to amuse her in the garden, to stand back, telling them that they were her servants. She was an uncomplicated, cheerful, adaptable child who had already made several friends before she went to bed, to sleep soundly on her first night away from home.

As the youngest she was petted and soon became the favourite of nuns and girls alike. From Suor Felice she learned drawing and geography, from Suor Violante arithmetic and handwriting, from Suor Cecilia singing, from Suor Rosalia Bible stories; Suor Orsola recounted her own visions and Suor Diomira taught her the art of artificial flower making; Suor Edvige specialized in Italian grammar and embroidery. Suor Fedele, whose duty it was to keep an eye on her, was surprised when Allegra, who can have had no religious training from Byron, asked who was this Lord who was greater than she. On being told, with the other girls, to carry a little cross on her shoulder to the refectory as a token of obedience, Allegra said to the astonished nuns she would do it, but only for the love of God – though she did not like the sandals she had been given to wear as they reminded her of the kind which only the poor people wore.

Claire was working in Florence as a governess when she heard that Allegra had been put in a convent. She wrote desperately to Byron,

I represent to you that putting of Allegra at her years, into a convent, is to me a serious and deep affliction. . . . I have been at some pains to inquire into their system, and I find that the state of the children is nothing less than miserable. . . . Every traveller and writer upon Italy joins in condemning them, which would be alone sufficient testimony, without adverting to the state of ignorance and profligacy of the Italian women, all pupils of convents. They are bad wives, most unnatural mothers; licentious and ignorant. They are the dishonour and unhappiness of society. Allegra's misfortune, in being condemned by her father to a life of ignorance and degradation . . . will be received by the world as a perfect fulfilment of all the censures passed upon you. How will Lady Byron – never yet justified for her conduct towards you –

be soothed and rejoice in the honourable safety of herself and child, and all the world be bolder to praise her prudence, my unhappy Allegra furnishing the condemning evidence![65]

Faced with the sideswipe at Teresa who had only recently left a convent school at eighteen, and the sore spot of Lady Byron's implacable silence, Byron's reply to Hoppner was reasoned and unimpassioned.

I by no means intended nor intend to give a *natural* child an *English* education, because with the disadvantages of her birth her settlement would be doubly difficult. Abroad, with a fair foreign education, and a portion of five or six thousand pounds, she might and may marry very respectably, in England such a dowry would be a pittance, while elsewhere it is a fortune. It is besides my wish that she should be a Roman *Catholic*, which I look upon as the best religion as it is assuredly the oldest of the various branches of Christianity. I have not explained my notions as to the *place* where she now is, it is the best I could find for the present, but I have no prejudices in its favour.[66]

He took comfort in the good reports on Allegra's progress, writing to Shelley, 'The child continues doing well, and the accounts are regular and favourable. It is gratifying to me that you and Mrs Shelley do not disapprove of the step which I have taken, which is merely temporary.'[67]

Mary tried to reason with Claire, pointing out that the air in Romagna was healthy and Allegra was safe in the convent. She encouraged her to look on the bright side – after all Byron might be reconciled with Annabella and lose all interest in Allegra. She also emphasized that it had been Claire's decision to pass Allegra into Byron's care, despite Shelley's advice.

At the beginning of July 1821 Pietro and Ruggero Gamba were banished from Ravenna for political intrigue and ordered to leave within twenty-four hours. They fled to Florence. Guiccioli threatened to force Teresa into a convent for violating the terms of her separation. She left Ravenna reluctantly and refused to move any further away from Byron than Bologna, but eventually he persuaded her to join her father and brother in Florence. For a while Byron considered moving to Switzerland and taking the whole Gamba clan with him. When Shelley got wind of his plans he took up a longstanding invitation, arriving in Ravenna at ten o'clock in the evening of 6 August. Byron was delighted to see him and they stayed up talking until five the following morning. Allegra, Byron said, had developed an imperious and violent temper, but she was a beautiful child and whatever happened he would not leave her alone in Italy. He repeated to Shelley an accusation made by Elise, the grumbling nursemaid, and passed on to him by the Hoppners, that Claire had once been Shelley's mistress and had borne him a child which had been put into a foundling hospital at Naples. Shelley hotly denied this but it is doubtful if Byron believed him. Although it is unlikely that Claire or Mary could have been the mother of the baby, there are records of a baby girl, Elena Adelaide Shelley, who was born on 27 February 1819 and died on 9 June 1820, being registered at the orphanage by Shelley.

Shelley persuaded Byron to abandon his Swiss plans and consider moving to Pisa instead. To his surprise Byron agreed, if Shelley undertook to find him somewhere suitable to live. Shelley was also enthusiastic about producing a new literary magazine and to do it properly he suggested that they invite Leigh Hunt and his brother John to Italy to work on it. The *Liberal* would publish his own and Byron's poetry and enable Hunt to get out of debt. Byron was less eager but Shelley nevertheless wrote to Hunt on Byron's behalf, suggesting that he come to Italy to manage the magazine and that all three share the profits. In his usual profligate way Hunt ran out of money before he could leave England and wrote directly to Byron asking him to pay his fare; typically, Byron sent the money.

Life in Ravenna was so pleasant that eight days passed before Shelley went to the convent at Bagnacavallo. Allegra looked paler than he remembered her but charming in a white muslin dress with a black silk apron. She was shy at first but soon recovered after he gave her a little gold chain. She took him on a tour of the convent, running and skipping so fast he could scarcely keep up. She showed him her toy carriage in which she and her friends gave each other rides along the paths in the garden and her bed of which she seemed especially proud. She ran to the refectory to point out her seat and in a moment of high spirits rang the special bell that called all the nuns in the community to assemble together. To his surprise the Mother Superior did not scold Allegra for being naughty. Shelley grudgingly acknowledged she was well treated and that her behaviour had improved almost out of recognition. He was astonished to see her offer his present, a basket of sweetmeats, to the girls and nuns before taking any herself; she had changed from a spoilt little autocrat into a well-mannered girl. 'This is not like the old Allegra,' he told Mary. When asked what she would like from her Mama, Allegra replied that she would like a kiss and a new dress made of silk and gold. And what, Shelley wanted to know, should he say to Papa? She replied that she would like him to visit her and bring Mama with him. The 'Mama' she was thinking about was Teresa.[68]

The Mother Superior, hearing of the Swiss plan, had written to Byron inviting him to visit Allegra before he left; on the back of the same piece of paper Allegra carefully wrote, 'My dear Papa – It being fair-time I should so much like a visit from my Papa, as I have many desires to satisfy; will you not please your Allegrina who loves you so?' In his usual deprecating way he remarked to Hoppner that the letter 'is sincere enough but not very flattering – for she wants to see me because it "is the fair" to get some paternal gingerbread – I suppose.'[69] Although Byron did not accept that invitation Allegra did not lack visitors as Teresa's grandparents went to see her, as did other friends.

By September the Gambas had moved to Pisa and the Shelleys were established in a house at the top of the Tre Palazzi di Chiesa which looked across the countryside to the sea. They had acquired for Byron the Casa Lanfranchi on the Lungarno.

Byron told Augusta of his plans to move to Pisa for the winter on 5 October. He was feeling particularly bitter towards her, having realized she was being manipulated by his wife. 'You will probably never see me again as long as you live. Indeed you don't deserve it – for having behaved so *coldly*.' He continued, describing his feelings for Teresa, 'It is nearly three years that this "liaison" has lasted – I was dreadfully in love – and she blindly so – for she has sacrificed everything to this headlong passion. – That comes of being romantic – I can say that without being so *furiously* in love as at first – I am more attached to her – than I thought it possible to be to any woman after three years.' What Lady Byron thought when she read the next few lines cannot be guessed at. 'If Lady B. would but please to die – and the Countess G's husband – (for Catholics can't marry though divorced) we should probably have to marry – though I would rather *not* – thinking it the way to hate each other – for all people whatsoever – However – you must not calculate upon seeing me again in a hurry, if ever.'[70]

On 29 October Byron swung out of Ravenna in his ageing Napoleonic carriage having left Allegra in the hands of Pellegrino Ghigi together with his zoo, a mongrel, a heron, a badger, a goat with a broken leg and two monkeys. On the road between Imola and Bologna Byron met his old school friend Lord Clare. It was a short but emotional meeting; they were together for only five minutes as Clare was hurrying to Rome. Byron met Rogers at Bologna, they crossed the Apennines together and took a quick trip round some of the more famous sights before Byron's caravan set off again. Thirty miles from Florence, at Empoli, the great green carriage with a convoy of smaller coaches tagging along in its wake forced the public coach to pull off the road. Sitting in the public coach was Claire, returning to Florence.

20 Lady Caroline Lamb was 'the cleverest most agreeable, absurd, amiable, perplexing, dangerous, fascinating little being that lives now or ought to have lived 2,000 years ago.'

21 The Hon. Mrs George Lamb whose beautiful singing voice reminded Byron of his dead friend John Edleston.

22 Lady Charlotte Harley, widely believed to be the daughter of Sir Francis Burdett and Byron's Ianthe: 'Whom I should love forever if she could always be only eleven years old.'

23 Thomas Moore, Byron's friend and biographer. After his visit to Venice, Byron wrote: 'Moore and I did nothing but laugh.'

24 Sir Frederick Burdett, the popular reformer and the friend of the Byrons and Trevanions.

25 Augusta Leigh: '. . . you are *the nearest relation* I have in *the world both by the ties of Blood* and *affection.*'

26 Lady Frances Wedderburn Webster engaged Byron in a dangerous flirtation during the autumn of 1813 at Aston Hall, where his father seduced Augusta's mother, Amelia, Baroness Conyers.

27 Lady Harriet Granville, the spirited letter-writer and commentator.

28 John Cam Hobhouse, Byron's companion during his travels in 1809, stalwart friend and defender after Byron's death.

29 Annabella at about the time of her
marriage: 'I do admire her as a very superior
woman a little encumbered with Virtue.'

30 Byron at about the time of his
marriage: 'I have great hopes that we
shall love each other all our lives as
much as if we had never married at
all.'

31 Halnaby Hall, where Byron and Annabella spent their honeymoon.

32 The Hyde Park Turnpike, showing Piccadilly Terrace where Byron and Annabella spent the only year of their marriage. He compared their house, No. 13, to 'a barrack'.

33 Lady Jersey, society hostess and powerful patroness of Almack's, who publicly stood by Byron during the separation.

34 Margaret Mercer Elphinstone: '. . . defended me in a large company, which *at that time* [during the separation scandal] required more courage and firmness than most women possess.'

35 Madame de Staël: 'Her figure was not bad; her legs tolerable; her arms good. Altogether, I can conceive for her soul, and so forth. She would have made a great man.'

36 Claire Clairmont at twenty. Thomas Medwin wrote that 'she was a brunette with very dark hair and eyes'.

37 Villa Diodati: 'I have taken a very pretty villa in a vineyard – with the Alps behind – and Mt Jura and the Lake before.'

38 Ada: 'I never saw so clever and entertaining a child as little Ada, Lord Byron's child. She is full of fun,' wrote the Hon. Mrs George Lamb when Ada was four and a half.

39 Allegra: 'a pretty little girl enough, and reckoned like papa. . . . She is about twenty months old,' Byron wrote proudly to Thomas Moore.

40 Percy Bysshe Shelley 'is *truth* itself – and *honour* itself – notwithstanding his out-of-the-way notions about religion'.

41 Margarita Cogni was 'very dark – tall – the Venetian face – very fine black eyes – and certain other qualities which need not be mentioned'.

42 Countess Teresa Guiccioli at eighteen: 'She was a kind of Italian Caroline Lamb – but very pretty and gentle.'

43 John Fitzgibbon, 2nd Earl of Clare: 'I have always loved him better than any *male* thing in the world.'

44 Palazzo Guiccioli, Ravenna, where Count Guiccioli allowed Byron to live rent free in the upper floor.

45 Leigh Hunt: 'A man who seems incapable or unwilling to do anything further for himself – at least, to the purpose.'

46 Byron in Genoa in 1823: 'his coat appears to have been many years made, is much too large – and all his garments convey the idea of having been purchased ready-made, so ill do they fit him'.

47 Edward John Trelawny: 'If he will learn to tell the truth and wash his hands we may make a gentleman of him yet.'

48 Lady Blessington: 'Miladi seems high literary. . . . She is also very pretty, even in a morning – a species of beauty on which the sun of Italy does not shine so frequently as the chandelier.'

49 Byron playing with Lyon: '. . . You are no rogue Lyon; thou art an honest fellow; thou art more faithful than man.'

50 Ithaca, where Byron dreamed 'that Greece might still be free'.

51 Missolonghi: Byron's house is in the background.

52 Ada in 1819 aged four: 'Thy face is like thy mother's, my fair child!'

53 Charles Babbage, mathematician, mechanical genius and friend to Ada.

54 The Hon. William King before his marriage, wearing Greek costume.

55 Ada. The portrait by Margaret Carpenter was completed soon after Ada's marriage and considered a good likeness by her mother.

Byron was so delighted by the Casa Lanfranchi and its enclosed garden on the bank of the Arno that he invited Augusta and the Leigh family to join him there at his expense. 'You could bring your drone of a husband with you – it would do him good – and probably save the lives of some of the children, if they are delicate.'[71] The house had a large cool entrance hall with a giant staircase leading to a huge room where Byron's sullen bulldog Moretto ran about. Byron often entertained in a smaller room which contained a billiard table and a small library. He described his new home to Murray: 'I have got here into a famous old feudal palazzo on the Arno – large enough for a garrison – with dungeons below – and cells in the walls – and so full of *ghosts* that the learned Fletcher (my Valet) has begged leave to change his room – and then refused to occupy his *new* room – because there were more Ghosts there than in the other.'[72]

On 10 December 1821 he wrote sadly to Murray, 'This day and this hour (one on the Clock) my daughter is six years old. I wonder when I shall see her again or if ever I shall see her at all. . . . By the way – send me my daughter Ada's miniature. I have only the print – which gives little or no idea of her complexion.' He sent locks of his hair to Augusta and asked to have one of the '*best behaved* curls' set in a gold locket for Ada. 'Round the locket let there be this Italian inscription "Il Sangue non è mai Acqua.' – And do not let the engravers blunder. – It means "Blood is never water" – and alludes merely to relationship – being a common proverb. – I should wish her to wear this – that she may know she has (or had) a father in the world.' On hearing she had a fiery temper he wryly commented, 'My Lady's was a nice little sullen nucleus of concentrated Savageness to mould my daughter upon, – to say nothing of her two grandmothers.'[73] He celebrated Ada's next birthday with a mutton chop and a bottle of ale. Medwin noticed that he was unusually silent and melancholy during their evening ride until he suddenly said, 'This is Ada's birthday, and might have been the happiest day of my life: as it is!' He paused and seemed ashamed of having betrayed his feelings.

The news of the long-awaited death of his mother-in-law on 28 January 1822 did not reach Byron until 15 February. He felt sorry for Annabella, 'for she adored her mother. The world will think I am pleased at this event, but they are much mistaken.' With his extra income from Lady Noel's estate Byron allowed Trelawny, a professional adventurer and friend of Shelley, to persuade him into commissioning a yacht, *The Bolivar*, from his friend Captain Roberts. Shelley had already ordered his own craft, which Byron and Trelawny called *Don Juan* but the Shelleys prefered to call *Ariel*, and they talked of spending many hours sailing on the Bay of Spezia.

Claire, disappointed that Byron had not brought Allegra to Pisa,

induced a friend, Mr Tighe, to visit the Convent at Bagnacavallo in secret
and find out all he could about conditions there. His report, according to
Claire, was distressing. There was fever in the Romagna marshes, the food
at the convent was inadequate and there were no fires. In February Claire
considered joining her brother Charles in Vienna where, he told her,
there was a demand for English governesses, but before she left she
appealed once more to Byron, 'I assure you I can no longer resist the
internal inexplicable feeling which haunts me that I shall never see her
any more. I entreat you to destroy this feeling by allowing me to see
her.'[74] He ignored her. His loathing for her made him uncharac-
teristically callous. 'He positively could not bear her,' Teresa said, 'she was
like a perpetual remorse to his sensitive soul.'[75] When taken to task for
his cruelty by Shelley, Byron shrugged his shoulders with impatience
saying that women could not live without making scenes. It is said that
Shelley had difficulty in not knocking him down.

Claire planned fantastic schemes to rescue Allegra which horrified
Shelley. He reminded her, 'Lord Byron is inflexible and you are in his
power. Remember Claire, when you rejected my earnest advice, and
checked me with that contempt which I have never merited from you, at
Milan, and how vain is now your regret!'[76]

On 13 April Allegra developed a fever severe enough for the nuns to
call in Dr Rasi. He thought she looked consumptive and ordered her to
be bled three times. Faithful Ghigi reported to Byron on 15 April that she
seemed much better and was now out of danger, but, he emphasized, she
had had a very dangerous illness. She was nursed in a comfortable room
with three doctors in attendance and surrounded by nuns. If any fault
was to be found, Ghigi wrote, it would have been that there had been too
much care. Byron became worried when his letter arrived and sent off a
courier to instruct the nuns to call in Professor Tommasini from Bologna
if necessary.

On 19 April Suor Marianne and Suor Fedele helped Allegra drink milk
and water, the only food the doctors would allow her, although she had
asked for some soft cheese. They placed hot compresses on her forehead
and in the evening Suor Marianna still had hope of recovery. As day was
breaking the next morning, Padre Vincenzo Fabbri was seen running to
Allegra's room to christen her, ensuring that when death came she would
go directly to heaven. The nuns gathered kneeling round her bed and it
was during the soft murmur of their prayers Allegra died.[77]

Byron was uneasy at the time the courier had taken to return, but when
he saw Teresa's face there was a moment of suspense before he said, 'I
understand – it is enough, say no more.' He remained immovable in the
same position for an hour and no words of consolation Teresa offered

seemed to reach his ears. The following morning he said to her, 'She is more fortunate than we are. Besides, her position in the world would scarcely have allowed her to be happy. It is God's will – let us mention it no more.' He wrote to Lord Holland that her death had chilled his blood with horror. 'While she lived,' he told Lady Blessington, 'her existence never seemed necessary to my happiness; but no sooner did I lose her, than it appeared to me as if I could not live without her.'

He told Shelley that the 'blow was stunning and unexpected; for I thought the danger over'. Perhaps if he had nursed her himself, as he had done twice before, she might not have died. Both he and Allegra had recovered from similar fevers. 'I do not know that I have anything to reproach in my conduct,' he wrote. 'But it is a moment when we are apt to think that, if this or that had been done, such event might have been prevented, – though every day and hour shows us that they are the most natural and inevitable.' He told Sir Walter Scott, 'I have just lost my natural daughter, Allegra, by a fever. The only consolation, save time, is the reflection that she is either at rest or happy; for her few years (only five) prevented her from having incurred any sin, except what we inherit from Adam.' Teresa noticed his attention to Ada was more intense and he became unsettled if for any reason the usual accounts of her health were delayed.

He asked Murray to take care of the funeral arrangements as, he explained, 'You are aware that protestants are not allowed holy ground in Catholic countries.' Teresa arranged with Henry Dunn, an English merchant working in Leghorn, for the embalmed body, enclosed in a lead coffin, to be shipped back to England. He intended Allegra's remains to be privately buried in Harrow church; he asked for her body to be placed within the church to the left of the door and a marble tablet set on the wall inscribed with the words: 'In memory of Allegra – daughter of G.G. Lord Byron – who died at Bagnacavallo in Italy April 20th. 1822. aged five years and three months. – "I shall go to her, but she shall not return to me. 2nd Samuel 12. – 23."'[78] The funeral took place on 10 September; but she was buried outside the church and her tablet was not put up. To his fury Byron found that there had been a story in the newspapers about the funeral of 'my poor little natural baby' saying she was to be buried with her gravestone opposite Lady Byron's pew. 'I had not the most distant idea that Lady B. was a frequenter of Harrow Church – and to say the truth – though I have no reason to believe her a woman of much feeling – I should have thought it the last place – she should have frequented as every part of Harrow must have reminded her of one whom it had been better she should forget. – However had I known it – the infant would not have been buried there, nor would *I* myself (though it is the spot where I once and long wished to have had my ashes laid) now rest in my grave – if I thought this woman was to trample on it. – It is enough that she has partly dug it.'[79] Annabella's friend from Lowestoft, the Reverend John William Cunningham, Vicar of Harrow, together with members of his congregation had successfully objected to the tablet, feeling it would be an offence against taste and propriety.

The Shelleys had decided to spend the summer on the Gulf of Spezia, inviting Claire to join them, and it was while she was off house-hunting that the news of Allegra's death arrived. Fearing Claire might do something foolish to Byron they took her to the house they had secured at San Terenzo, not far from Lerici, and it was there in the Casa Magni that she learnt of Allegra's death. At first she surrendered herself to an outburst of grief and despair. This was followed by a fearful calmness. She wrote bitterly and accusingly to Byron and he passed the letter to Shelley who responded, 'I had no idea that her letter was written in that temper, and I think I need not assure you that, whatever mine or Mary's ideas might have been respecting the system of education you intended to adopt, we sympathize too much in your loss, and appreciate too well your feelings, to have allowed such a letter to be sent you had we suspected its contents.'[80]

Claire asked to see her child's coffin. Byron sent her a lock of Allegra's hair and a miniature. In September she set off for Vienna to be with her brother but was unable to find employment and moved to Moscow where she worked for the family of a successful lawyer. In 1823, Lady Mountcashell, the common-law wife of George Tighe, approached Byron asking him to allocate to Claire a small part of whatever money he had intended to leave for Allegra. He refused to help directly but intimated he might send her money through Mary Shelley. Mary misunderstood his intentions and Claire received nothing. In 1844 she received Shelley's legacy and returned to England. She declined an offer of marriage with the old rogue Trelawny, converted to Catholicism and spent her last years in Florence where she died on 19 March 1879 aged ninety-one. She provided the inspiration for *The Aspern Papers*, written by Henry James less than ten years after her death.

CHAPTER SIX

Greece

The death of Allegra was followed on 8 July by that of Shelley and his friend Edward Williams who were drowned crossing the Bay of Spezia from Leghorn to Lerici in the *Don Juan*. The bodies were temporarily buried in the sand until August when the authorities gave permission for them to be cremated and prepared for burial. On 14 August the 'shapeless mass of bones and flesh' – all that remained of Williams – was burnt in the presence of his friends and a group of curious spectators, including many well-dressed women. 'Don't repeat this with me,' said Byron, 'let my carcase rot where it falls.' The fierce heat of the flames drove the onlookers into the shade. 'Let us try the strength of these waters that drowned our friends. How far out do you think they were when their boat sank?' Byron asked Trelawny, walking into the sea.[1] Before they had swum a mile Byron was sick and came back to shore. On the following day, in the intense heat of the summer, a pyre was made ready for Shelley and, watched by Byron, Hunt, Captain Shenley, Italian officers and soldiers, the body was burned together with a copy of Keats's poems which had been found on Shelley's body, the pages turned back as though he had been reading. 'You can have no idea,' wrote Byron, 'what an extraordinary effect such a funeral pile has, on a desolate shore, with mountains in the background and the sea before, the singular appearance the salt and frankincense gave to the flame. All of Shelley was consumed, except his *heart*, which would not take the flame, and is now preserved in spirits of wine.' Trelawny had snatched it from the flames and passed it to Byron who passed it to Hunt who eventually gave it to Mary. She wrapped it in silk and carried it about with her until she died.[2] Sickened by the scene and the stench of burning flesh Byron plunged into the sea and swam to the *Bolivar* which was at anchor a mile and a half off shore.[3] The August sun burned down on his unprotected skin and when he came out of the water he had an enormous blister which covered most of his back. (Teresa kept the burned skin in her box of souvenirs.)

Hunt had arrived a few days before, accompanied by his pregnant, shrewish wife, Marianne, and six children. Mrs Hunt still harboured a grudge against Byron because Annabella had not asked to be introduced to her in 1815 when Byron was a regular visitor to the Hunt home. The resentful couple moved into the ground floor of Palazzo Lanfranchi, belittling Byron's generosity and complaining that the accommodation was fit only for servants. Marianne disliked the furniture (chosen by Shelley) and they resented having to listen to Byron's cheerful rendering of Rossini in his bath each morning. Byron thought their children 'dirtier and more mischievous than Yahoos', adding, 'what they can't destroy with their filth they will with their fingers'.[4] He encouraged his bulldog Moretto to patrol the main staircase and repel any children who tried to enter his part of the house.

Forced to flee again in the autumn of 1822 when the Gambas were banished from Tuscan territory, Byron dragged his household and the Hunt tribe from Pisa to Genoa. The Hunts and their 'six little blackguards' travelled separately to the Casa Negreto, the house they shared with Mary Shelley, while Teresa and Byron took possession of an old palazzo, Casa Saluzzo at Albaro, a mile and a half outside Genoa.

Teresa's ability to rouse Byron to passionate heights had waned and he found life at the Casa Saluzzo domestic and dull. He began to think of going to South America or Greece and although he knew Teresa would be delighted to go too, he maintained that 'I do not choose to expose her to a long voyage, and a residence in an unsettled country.'[5]

On 31 March the Blessingtons arrived in Genoa and immediately called on Byron. Lady Blessington thought he looked thin and pale but remarkably 'gentlemanlike', adding, 'He owes nothing of this to his toilet, as his coat appears to have been many years made, is much too large – and all his garments convey the idea of having been purchased ready-made, so ill do they fit him.' Her ladyship continued, 'There is a *gaucherie* in his movement, which evidently proceeds from the perpetual consciousness of his lameness, that appears to haunt him; for he tried to conceal his foot when seated, and when walking, had a nervous rapidity in his manner. He is very slightly lame, and the deformity of his foot is so little remarkable that I am now not aware which foot it is.' The only fault she found in him was 'flippancy and a total want of that natural self-possession and dignity which ought to characterise a man of birth and education'.[6]

Byron was piqued by his wife's refusal to explain her reasons for the separation or answer his letters. He had hoped that Ada might have become a bond between them. Lady Blessington observed that 'His heart yearns to see his child; all children of the same age remind him of her.' Gossip reached him that Annabella was uncertain of his intentions towards Ada and to allay her suspicions he wrote, 'in the event of any accident occurring to the mother, and my remaining the survivor, it would be my wish to have her plans carried into effect, both with regard to the education of the child, and the person or persons under whose care Ly. B. might be desirous that she should be placed. It is not my intention to interfere with her in any way on the subject during her life.'7 Hugh Montgomery who was visiting Genoa, fearful that Byron might soften Annabella's heart, spitefully informed her that he was wearing a brooch which contained Augusta's hair.

In 1821 the Greeks rose in a revolt against their Turkish oppressors and the idea of reviving the glories of Greece and liberating them became a cause in which many idealistic young men wished to be involved. In April 1823 Edward Blaquiere, a founder member of the London Greek Committee, made an appointment to see Byron at the Casa Saluzzo with Andreas Luriottis, a delegate of the Greek government; Hobhouse, another member of the committee, had told them of Byron's interest in Greece. The interview went better than they could have hoped. Not only did Byron commit himself to their cause but he offered to go to Greece in July if the Greek Provisional Government thought he could be of any use. In May he was made a member of the committee in London. He wrote, 'I beg that the Committee will command me in any and every way – if I am favoured with any instructions – I shall endeavour to obey them to the letter – whether conformable to my own private opinion or not.'8

In his enthusiasm Byron wrote to Trelawny in Rome, 'You must have heard that I am going to Greece – why do you not come to me? I can do nothing without you and am exceedingly anxious to see you. Pray come, for I am at last determined to go to Greece: – it is the only place I was ever contented in. I am serious; and did not write before, as I might have given you a journey for nothing. They all say I can be of use to Greece; I do not know how – nor do they; but, at all events, let us go.' To Captain Roberts he said, 'I am determined to go somewhere, and hope we shall all be at sea together by next month, as I am tired of this place, the shore, and all the people on it.'9

Teresa, feeling Byron's love slipping away, became jealous of Lady Blessington, little knowing that her real enemy was the Greek committee. Byron had made up his mind to go but was unable to break the news to her. His mother's violent nature and ability to create emotional storms made him wary of confrontations and the infidelity of Lucy and Susan Vaughan had left him with a distrust of women which led him into cruelty. His treatment of the unstable Caroline Lamb and persistent Claire Clairmont changed their love for him into unremitting hatred. After making several half-hearted attempts his courage failed and he characteristically asked Pietro to tell her of his plans. Teresa was plunged into despair; she begged him in floods of tears to let her come too and spent hours writing him pleading letters, but he had made up his mind and told her that 'a man ought to do something more for society than write verses'.

The Gambas had been recalled from exile with the proviso that Teresa must accompany her father in accordance with the separation agreement. The news could not have come at a more opportune time and Byron encouraged Teresa to be reconciled to Count Guiccioli who had indicated that he was willing to have her back. Her distress irritated Byron and he told Kinnaird, 'She wants to go up to Greece too! forsooth – precious place to go at present! of course the idea is ridiculous,' but he was afraid she would make scenes in public and then 'we shall have another romance – and tale of ill usage and abandonment – and Lady Caroling – and Lady Byroning – and Glenarvoning – all cut and dry; – there never was a man who gave up so much to women – and all I have gained by it – has been the character of treating them harshly.'[10] He continued to advise Teresa to return to her husband and commented to Lady Blessington that 'the difference between love in early youth and in maturity is that like measles, love was most dangerous when it came late in life.' He had recovered from his bout but Teresa, weeping and broken-hearted, went back to Ravenna with her father.

Byron suffered from nostalgia and homesickness. He was convinced he would not come back from Greece alive and day-dreamed of returning to England, asking Annabella to forgive him and being reunited with Ada, but he knew it was a fantasy and comforted himself with the hope that when Ada was older she would cherish his memory and weep over his misfortunes. 'The triumph then will be mine,' he told Lady Blessington, 'and the tears that my child will drop over expressions wrung from me by mental agony, – the various allusions to her and myself in my works – console me in many a gloomy hour. Ada's mother has feasted on the smiles of her infancy and growth, but the tears of her maturity shall be mine.'[11]

After several false starts Byron sailed from Genoa on 16 July on the English brig *Hercules*, captained by its owner, John Scott. He took with him Trelawny, Pietro Gamba, Fletcher, Tita, Benjamin Lewis, a black American groom, formerly employed by Trelawny, two other servants and a young, newly qualified doctor, Francesco Bruno. The ship was battered by a squall just outside the harbour, forcing the *Hercules* back to Genoa. They sailed again the next day arriving at Argostoli, the principal harbour on Cephalonia, on 3 August where they were made welcome by Captain John Kennedy, secretary to the English Resident.

The position of the Greeks was very confused and to get a clear picture of the situation Byron sent messengers to Corfu and Missolonghi.

Meanwhile his party crossed the mountains to Saint Eufina and sailed to Ithaca where they were entertained by Captain Wright Knox, the Resident Governor.[12] At a party given by Captain Knox and his wife, Byron met Thomas Smith, Secretary to the Chief Justice at Corfu. On being asked if he had recently come from England Smith replied he had been at Corfu for two years. 'Then,' said Byron, 'you can bring us no news of the Greek Committee? Here we are all waiting orders, and no orders seem likely to come. Ha ha!' He continued, 'I find but one opinion among all people whom I have met since I came here – that no good is to be done for these rascally Greeks; that I am sure to be deceived, disgusted and all the rest of it. It may be so; but it is chiefly to satisfy myself upon these very points that I am going. I go prepared for anything, expecting a deal of roguery and imposition but hoping to do some good.'[13]

To Smith's surprise he talked freely of Ada and was not embarrassed when the subject of the separation was raised, although Mrs Knox was confused and tried to pass it over, but he persisted saying, 'I dare say it will turn out that I have been terribly in the wrong, *but I always want to know what I did.*' Forty-seven years later on 27 January 1870 Dr Lushington admitted to Mr Bathurst, Registrar of the Admiralty Court and the surviving trustee of Lady Noel Byron's papers, that he considered the real cause of Lady Byron's separation was Byron's conduct towards her, which Dr Lushington described with great emotion as being 'most foul and gross'.[14]

To kill time until the messengers returned an excursion was arranged to the fountain of Arethusa where they drank the waters and ate a picnic of cold chicken. The next day they visited the School of Homer. During the journey Trelawny took the tiller and after an hour or so of rowing in intense heat, which Lewis had compared to that of the West Indies, Byron called to Tita, 'We must have some inspiration. Here Tita, l'hippocrena!' From the bowels of the boat Tita produced a two-gallon jar of English gin, another earthenware one of water and a quart pitcher into which he poured the spirit. Byron uncorked the jar, 'Now, gentlemen, drink deep, or taste not the Pierian spring; it is the true poetic source. I'm a rogue if I have drunk today. Come. This is the way.' He filled half a tumbler with gin and then at arms length poured water from the jar until the tumbler sparkled in the sun and drank it down while it still effervesced. Tita handed each passenger a cool gin-swizzle and a biscuit which Byron took from a huge tin.[15]

In early September he moved from his quarters on the *Hercules* to the little village of Metaxata, 7 miles from Argostoli, where he lived until December when he left for Missolonghi. He was alarmed by the news that

Ada had not been well, suffering severe headaches caused, the doctors said, from the distension of the arteries in her head.[16] Whether he would have approved of Lady Byron's chosen nursing techniques is doubtful, as her preferred treatment for this type of malady was to apply leeches to the scalp and, as one fell off replete with blood, to replace it with another immediately. On receiving news of Ada's illness he suspended writing his journal and it was not until October, when he heard from Augusta that she had recovered, that he resumed it again.

As the presence of the wealthy English lord became known so the begging letters increased. He generously provided £4,000 to enable the Greek fleet to put to sea and while he waited to be called into action he entertained Augusta's half-brother, Lord Sydney Osborne, State Secretary of the Ionian Islands from Corfu, George Finlay, the author of a seven-volume history of Greece, Colonel the Honourable Leicester Stanhope, agent for the London committee, and 23-year-old Julius Millingen, a physician sponsored by the London Greek Committee.

Eventually Byron received the long-awaited invitation from the Legislative Committee and Prince Mavrocordato, the great Greek scholar and patriot, and set sail for Missolonghi on a light, fast-sailing vessel called a *mistico* on 29 December. Colonel Stanhope wrote to the committee in London, 'The Turkish fleet has ventured out, and is at this moment blockading the port. Beyond these again are seen the Greek ships, and among the rest the one that was sent for Lord Byron. Whether he is on board or not is a question.' The people were 'looking forward to Lord Byron's arrival, as they would to the coming of the Messiah'.[17]

No sooner had Byron left port than the wind changed and he was delayed for two days. Once under way the travellers were caught up in a series of adventures and misadventures. Pietro Gamba, Lewis, and the other servants who were travelling with the stores, horses, armaments and 8,000 dollars were captured by the Turks and taken to Patras. Pietro was taken to see the Pasha who treated him kindly and released the vessel and freight. Meanwhile Byron, believing the Turkish fleet to be still in the Bay of Lepanto, was surprised to find himself floating under the stern of a Turkish frigate. By good fortune the Turks mistook them for a Greek *brûlot* and the ship was able to slide away to safety. On 4 January both Byron's ship and his stores arrived safely in Missolonghi.

Troops fired salutes as Byron stepped on shore resplendent in his aide-de-camp's dashing red uniform before an enormous crowd assembled to welcome him. He walked with Prince Mavrocordatos through a din of wild music and discharges of artillery to his lodging. The atmosphere was so emotional that Pietro Gamba was not far from tears and could hardly describe the scene.[18]

Missolonghi was the base for any attack on Patras and Lepanto, the last Turkish strongholds on the mainland and it was essential to defend it against an expected spring offensive. The town was a miserable, damp settlement of five thousand people, partly Greek and partly Turkish, living in dingy, two-storey wooden houses surrounded by salt-marshes and shallows rich in insect life.

Byron created his own bodyguard of fifty-six Suliotes and quartered them in the large outer room of his house. On wet days he would spend most of his time with them or playing with his favourite dog, Lyon, who slept outside his door. Byron made a brave display when he went out accompanied by his bodyguards. They would form a procession with the captain of his guard and Suliotes walking in front, Byron following on horseback flanked by Pietro Gamba on one side and the Greek interpreter on the other. Behind them rode Lewis and Tita dressed as *chasseurs*, followed by yet more Suliotes. The committee in London sent out mechanics and engineers to set up an arsenal under the command of William Parry, Firemaster. He was a frank, honest and practical man and Byron relied on his unvarnished opinions, giving him full rein and inviting him to lodge with him.

Byron took his military duties seriously. He liked to be up at nine o'clock, breakfast on tea, dry toast and watercress at ten and give Parry his orders for the day. At eleven o'clock he inspected the accounts, checking and auditing every item, then he rode, or, if the weather was bad, amused himself target shooting. He was an accomplished shot despite his shaking hand and could hit an egg four times out of five at a distance of 10 or 12 yards. In the afternoon he entertained friends, callers and occasionally Prince Mavrocordatos; during the evening he rode for a few hours before dinner. He was still watching his weight and dinner usually consisted of a small portion of fish, cooked without spices or sauces, or dried toast, vegetables and cheese accompanied by a small amount of wine or cider. He never touched spirits. After dinner he joined in the drilling of his officers or played a game of single-stick, talked with friends or studied military tactics with Parry before returning to his room to read or write. He seldom slept more than five hours a night.[19]

Byron discovered he had a talent for military command and concentrated on a plan to capture Lepanto. He appointed Parry as commander of the artillery brigade but German officers, sent out by the London committee, thought it beneath their dignity to serve under a mere firemaster. A Prussian, Herr Kinderman, gave up his commission in disgust, causing Byron to pack the Germans off home. He provided them with a month's pay each and told them they were at liberty to leave when they pleased. They had been a double annoyance to him, as for the cost of each one of these argumentative officers he could have paid four Greek Suliotes.

Byron believed that the Greeks would fight better if they were trained, disciplined and supplied with the necessary materials of war, money, ammunition and guns and led by their own officers. 'There is an inveterate hatred amongst the Greeks of all these foreigners; and sending them here has done the Greek cause far more mischief, than ever the little and unfortunately misapplied, assistance given by the Germans and English has done good.'[20]

On 15 February 1824, 600 Suliotes threatened to mutiny and plunder the town unless they were paid. Byron took charge and agreed he would take them on to his payroll on condition they acted under his orders.

In the evening Parry noticed Byron looked agitated and flushed. He complained of thirst and ordered a glass of cider. Within minutes of drinking it he became dizzy, struggled up from the settee, staggered and fell into Parry's arms. Parry forced a drop of brandy between his lips then Byron clamped his teeth together, became speechless, blacked out, his body was wracked with strong convulsions and his face became distorted. He gradually recovered enough to be carried up to his rooms and put to bed. He seemed better in the morning but he was still very weak and his face haggard and pale. Dr Bruno recommended bleeding and despite Parry's objections Byron allowed Bruno to place eight leeches on his temples. The inexperienced doctor was unable to stop the blood and Byron fainted. Parry tore off strips of his clothing and Tita burned them under Byron's nose, while Parry rubbed his temples and lips with brandy and the blood was eventually staunched. Byron made light of the affair, saying he had behaved like a fine lady fainting at the sight of blood. Parry thought it was far more serious and told him to take care of himself and eat a more nourishing diet. Byron disagreed saying 'he was sure he ought to live low'. 'Not too low, my Lord,' pleaded Parry, 'in this swampy place some stimulus is necessary; but your physician should know best.' Byron agreed saying, 'Yes, Parry, he is an excellent young man, and well acquainted with his profession; I shall therefore be guided entirely by him.'[21]

On 21 February the Suliotes rose up again and Prince Mavrocordatos appealed once more to Byron who advanced 4,800 dollars for the soldiers' back pay, telling him firmly that from now on he must not consider him personally responsible. An earthquake shook Missolonghi that evening and all the inhabitants and Suliotes took to the streets, firing their carbines in the air, superstitiously hoping to stop the earthquake or check its progress. A few days later the house shook again; the Suliotes ran into the street with their carbines blazing while Byron laughed heartily. He had ordered a number of his soldiers to jump up and down on the upper floor with all their weight to simulate an earthquake.[22]

Byron suffered from violent headaches in April but he was temporarily cheered by a letter from Augusta giving him news of Ada. The thought of being unable to see and cuddle her made him melancholy. 'I often, in imagination, pass over a long lapse of years,' Byron once told Lady Blessington, 'and console myself for present privations, in anticipating the time when my daughter will know me by reading my works.'

On 9 April he came back from his morning ride feverish, soaked with rain and in some pain. Dr Bruno immediately proposed bleeding but Byron refused. A couple of days later he felt unwell, suffering shivering fits all day and developing pains in every part of his body. Parry was convinced that he would not recover unless he left Missolonghi, its mists and dampness. Byron reluctantly agreed but next day had a relapse, refused to eat and stayed in bed. The preparations to leave were complete but before they could embark on a ship a fierce gale rocked Missolonghi, making it impossible for vessels to leave the harbour. It rained all day, flooding the countryside and leaving the town marooned.

Byron took to his bed on 14 April; the only people allowed to see him were Pietro Gamba, the two doctors, Tita, Fletcher and Parry. He became delirious and for two days talked wildly in a mixture of English and Italian. Outside the maddening sirocco grew in strength, slamming doors and swirling round the house while torrential rain pounded and drummed on the roof and at the windows. Byron and his servants were isolated. Even if they had wanted to send for another doctor from Zante it would have been impossible to get through the storm.

Parry spent the evening of the next day with Byron, who was by now sitting up in bed quite calmly, and they talked until ten o'clock. 'Parry,' he said,

> I am perfectly collected, I am sure I am in my senses, but a melancholy will creep over me at times. – My wife! My Ada! My country! The situation of this place, my removal impossible, and perhaps death, all combine to make me sad. Since I have been ill I have given to all my plans such serious consideration. You shall go on at your leisure preparing for building the schooner, and when other things are done, we will put the last hand to this work, by a visit to America. To reflect on this has been a pleasure to me, and has turned my mind from ungrateful thoughts. When I left Italy I had time on board the brig to give full scope to memory and reflection. It was then I came to that resolution I have already informed you of. I am convinced on the happiness of domestic life. No man on earth respects a virtuous woman

more than I do, and the prospect of retirement in England with my wife and Ada gives me an idea of happiness I have never experienced before. [He continued,] I have closely observed today the conduct of all around me. Tita is an admirable fellow; he has not been out of the house for several days. Bruno is an excellent young man and very skilful, but I am afraid he is too agitated. I wish you to be as much about me as possible, you may prevent me being jaded to death, and when I recover I assure you I shall adopt a different mode of living.[23]

He yearned for domesticity and believed that if he could perform some heroic act it would redeem his reputation and that the Greek enterprise offered him the opportunity he needed. He told Lady Blessington that 'If I leave, and return from Greece with something *better* and *higher* than the reputation or glory of a poet, opinions may change, as the successful are always judged favourably in our country; my laurels may cover my faults better than the bays have done, and give a totally different reading to my thoughts, words and deeds.'[24]

Parry complained that the sickroom was in chaos: 'there was neither method, order, nor quiet,' in Byron's room. 'A clever skillful English surgeon possessing the confidence of his employer would have put all this in train; but Dr Bruno had no idea of doing such thing. There was also a want of many comforts.' Dr Bruno knew very little English, Fletcher spoke almost no Italian, Tita spoke only Italian, Parry spoke only English and no one understood what the Greek servants were saying. 'In all the attendants there was the officiousness of zeal; but owing to their ignorance of each other's language, their zeal only added to the confusion. This circumstance, and the want of common necessaries, made Lord Byron's apartment such a picture of distress and even anguish during the two or three last days of his life, as I never before beheld and wish never again to witness.'[25]

Parry urged the doctors not to physic and bleed Byron but to keep his hands and feet warm. They ignored his advice. Dr Julius Millingen was summoned in his official capacity as the physician sent by the Greek committee; he, like Bruno, believed in the efficacy of profuse bleeding. Mrs Byron had had a great fear of it and asked Byron to promise her he would never allow himself to be bled. Hitherto Byron had said his aversion to the custom was stronger than any doctor's arguments and he had steadfastly refused to submit, until Millingen threatened him with the prospect of a life of insanity. He then threw out his arm saying angrily, 'There, – you are I see, a d—d set of butchers, – take away as much blood as you like, but have done with it.' The next day he was bled twice, fainting each time.[26]

Easter Day fell on 18 April and to avoid disturbing Byron, and to please the townspeople, Parry marched the artillery brigade and the Suliotes outside the town to exercise them. It was almost midday when he first saw Byron, whose condition had deteriorated. 'Such was the confusion amongst people about him on my return that I could learn little or nothing of what had passed, except that a consultation had taken place.' It was after this consultation that Pietro, Millingen, Fletcher and Tita realized Byron was near to death. Millingen and Fletcher, unable to stop weeping left the room but Tita stayed, holding Byron's hand, his face turned away from him. 'Oh questa è una bella scena!' said Byron. 'Call Parry.' Almost immediately he was seized by delirium and talked wildly as though in the heat of a battle calling out in a mixture of Italian and English, 'Forwards – forwards – courage – follow my example.' After gaining control of himself Fletcher came back into the room and Byron having regained his senses turned to him, 'I am afraid you and Tita will be ill with sitting up night and day.' It was obvious to them that he knew he was dying and wanted to make his last wishes known. Fletcher asked if he should fetch a pen and paper but Byron said, 'Oh no. There is no time. It is now nearly over. Go to my sister, tell her, go to Lady Byron, you will see her and say —.' His voice sank away and he muttered to himself for another twenty minutes in such a low tone that only a few words could be understood – 'Augusta', 'Ada', 'Hobhouse', 'Kinnaird'.

'Now,' he ended, 'I have told you all.'

Puzzled, Fletcher said, 'My lord, I have not understood a word your Lordship has been saying.'

'Not understand me?' A look of distress crossed Byron's face, 'What a pity! – then it is too late; all is over.'

'I hope not,' answered Fletcher, 'but the Lord's will be done!'

'Yes, not mine,' replied Byron.

The only other words he utttered were 'my sister – my child'.[27]

The consultation between the doctors earlier that day had ended in a heated argument. Millingen wanted to apply leeches to the temples, behind the ears and along the course of the jugular vein with a large blister between the shoulder, and sinapisms (mustard plasters) to his feet.[28] Bruno, as Byron's doctor, had the last word and ordered an antispasmodic potion containing, among other things, bark, valarian and ether. Aware of Byron's confidence in Parry he was chosen to administer the liquid. 'My Lord, take the bark, it will do you good, it will recover your lordship.' Taking Parry's hand he said, 'Give it me.' He swallowed four mouthfuls. Parry and Tita tried to warm his ice cold hands. Seeing the distress the bandage round his head was causing, Parry loosened it. Byron, in great pain, clenched his hands and gnashed his teeth. '*Ah*

Christi,' he moaned. As soon as the bandage was loose tears ran down his cheeks. Parry said, 'My Lord, I thank God, I hope you will now be better; shed as many tears as you can, you will sleep and find ease.' Byron said faintly, 'Yes, the pain is gone, I shall sleep now.' He took Parry's hand and said a quiet goodnight. Parry hoped his sufferings were over.

But an hour later he woke in a stupor induced by Bruno's concoction – more was given to him. His eyes stayed open for a short while and he muttered incoherently then he closed them again saying, 'Now I shall go to sleep,' turned over and fell into a twenty-four hour coma. The only sound in the room was the rattling in his throat. On Monday, 19 April at six o'clock in the evening, a terrifying storm broke over Missolonghi with vivid flashes of lightning and deafening thunder-claps. At the same time the death rattle in Byron's throat stopped.[29]

Dr Bruno conducted an autopsy removing Byron's heart, brain and intestines which were enclosed in separate containers, one of which remained in Greece. The hacked body was placed into a chest lined with tin and covered with a black cloak with his helmet, a sword and a crown of laurel placed on top of that. The funeral was held on 22 April at the church of St Nicholas. The coffin was closed on 26 April. Colonel Stanhope at first thought the body should be sent to Athens for burial, but it was later decided to ship it back to England – much to Parry's relief. The latter had been prepared to fight against a Greek burial because Byron had once asked him, 'Well, old boy, should you kick the bucket in Greece, have you any wish that your body should be sent to England?'

'No, my Lord, no particular wish.'

'Well, I have then; and mind this shall be an agreement betwixt us – If I should die in Greece, and you survive me, *do you see that my body is sent to England*.'[30]

On 25 May, Colonel Stanhope, Bruno, Fletcher, Lewis and Byron's faithful Newfoundland dog, Lyon, embarked on the brig *Florida* to accompany Byron on the long voyage home.

The *Florida* arrived at Rochester on 1 July and Hobhouse was there to receive the body and escort it to London. 'I was the last person who shook hands with Byron when he left England in 1816. I recollected his waving his cap to me as the packet bounded off on a curling wave from the pier-head at Dover, and here I was now coming back to England with his corpse.' The coffin was taken to the large drawing room on the first storey of Sir Edward Knatchbull's house at 25 Great George Street, Westminster, where it lay in state, hung with a black cloth and illuminated by candles. So many people wanted to pay their respects that it became necessary to issue tickets. Fletcher was in a talkative mood when Mary Shelley arrived, telling her that Lady Byron had asked to see him and when he arrived she had been in a state of passionate grief, recovering sufficiently to tell him that even if Byron had lived she would never have lived with him again. She seemed to him to be as implacable as she was when she first signed the separation. He also said that in a moment of consciousness Byron had spoken of Claire and his wish to do something for her. However, it is possible that Fletcher confused the name Claire with Lord Clare, Byron's school friend.

Before the funeral the body, still inside its temporary Greek container, was placed into a more substantial one of lead which in turn was placed in the final ornamental wooden coffin draped with a purple velvet pall surmounted by a silver coronet. Samuel Rogers, Hobhouse, John Hanson, Newton Hanson, Dr John Bowring, Fletcher and an American visitor were present during the ceremony. The body was wrapped in a blue cloth cloak leaving the throat and head uncovered. The American thought the face well preserved with 'nothing of death about it', but Augusta, who had seen it earlier, and Hobhouse both thought Byron was almost unrecognizable with hardly a trace of his identity left. The face was puffy, the eyebrows shaggy, the teeth discoloured, the eyelids sunken where his eyes had been removed by the embalmers, and his red mustachios took away any resemblance to the man they remembered.

The news of his friend's death had reached Hobhouse on 14 May when he was woken just after eight by a loud tapping on his bedroom door and a packet of letters was put into his hand. The outer one was signed 'Sidney Osborne' and the words 'By Express'. Fearing the worst, Hobhouse opened it and found himself 'In an agony of grief such as I have experienced only twice before in my life. . . . I opened the despatches from Corfu, and there saw the details of the fatal event.'[31]

He hurried to find Sir Francis Burdett and Kinnaird. Burdett agreed to inform Augusta and Kinnaird alerted the newspaper offices while Captain George Anson, the new Lord Byron, rode out to Beckenham to tell Annabella. Thomas Moore was told by an assistant in Colborn's library.

On 15 May Hobhouse called to see Augusta and they were joined by George Byron who said he had left Annabella in a distressed state. She had told him that 'she had no right to be considered by Lord Byron's friends, but she had her feelings. She wished to see any accounts that had come of his last moments. I agreed.'

The news arrived when Augusta was exhausted with nursing her children – the two eldest were recovering from a serious illness and the rest affected. Augusta asked Hobhouse to visit her and they read

Fletcher's letter describing Byron's last hours and wept together. Now Byron was dead the cautious Hobhouse wanted to preserve his posthumous reputation and insisted that the memoirs Byron had given to Moore should be destroyed. His view was supported by Kinnaird and together they persuaded the timid Augusta to agree. Only two days after the news of her brother's death, Augusta wrote, 'It is *my* very decided opinion that the Memoirs *ought* to be burnt, and I think the sooner the better.'[32] The following day the pages were torn up and burned in John Murray's fireplace. Opinions varied on what harmful details the memoirs may have contained, but Mary Shelley, who had read the manuscript in Venice, thought it harmless.

On being asked by Augusta if she had any instruction or wishes for the disposal of her husband's body Annabella replied that the matter could be left to Hobhouse. She added a postcript, 'If you like you may show this.' Astounded, he remarked that the 'coldness and calculation of so young a woman on such an occasion are quite unaccountable'.[33] 'If Lady Byron has a heart, it is deeper seated and harder to get at then anybody else's heart whom I've known,' one of her friends commented to Byron's old school friend Harness.[34] The Dean of Westminster refused to allow Byron to be buried in Westminster Abbey so arrangements were made for him to be placed in the family vault at Hucknall Torkard.

The funeral procession left Great George Street for the journey to Nottinghamshire on 12 July followed by forty-five empty carriages sent as marks of respect, among them those of Lord Carlisle, Lord Morpeth, and Lord Aberdeen. There were huge crowds along the route and many people watched from their windows. The empty carriages followed the hearse until it reached the outskirts of London where the paved road ended near St Pancras church. They then turned for home. 'Mr George Leigh, Captain Richard Byron, Mr Hanson, and myself were in the first carriage;' wrote Hobhouse, 'Sir Francis Burdett, Mr Kinnaird, Mr Ellice and Mr Michael Bruce, Colonel Leicester Stanhope and Mr Trevanion, were in the second and third; Mr Moore, Mr Rogers, Mr Campbell and Orlando the Greek Deputy, were in the last mourning-coach.'[35] Mary Shelley watched the procession as it passed her house in rural Kentish Town and made its way slowly up Highgate Hill. The cortège was three days on the road before reaching the Blackamoore's Head in Nottingham where the body lay in state over night.

The next morning the procession was joined by Francis Hodgson, Colonel Wildman, the new owner of Newstead, the Mayor and Corporation of Nottingham and many tenants from Newstead. The procession took five hours to reach Hucknall. The church and churchyard were so crowded it was difficult for the mourners to follow the coffin up the aisle. After the service the church was left open late into the night for people to pay their respects, and it was not until the next day that Byron's coffin was placed in the vault to rest close to that of the Wicked Lord's and next to that of his indulgent, passionate mother.[36]

CHAPTER SEVEN

Medora

Ada was an obedient cheerful little girl and, to her mother's delight, showed an early aptitude for mathematics. At two she enjoyed drawing large Bs, playing with billiard balls, running, trying on her mother's jewellery and carriage rides. She was a gregarious child and joined in whatever was going on, laughing when her companions laughed and chatting away to herself. Augusta told Hodgson, 'The little girl is always well and represented as the finest and most intelligent child it is possible to meet with. I hear different reports as to her beauty, some say there is a strong resemblance to her father.'[1]

'I never saw so clever and entertaining child as little Ada, Lord Byron's child,' observed Mrs George Lamb after seeing Annabella and three-year-old Ada on holiday in Tunbridge Wells. 'She is full of fun, but very good-tempered and good, and I hope she will inherit none of his faults. Poor little thing! She is early celebrated in verse, and I have no doubt he will be always trying to work on her mind by his writings.'[2]

Byron asked Augusta when Ada was five to 'inform Lady Byron that I am obliged by her readiness to have Ada taught Music and Italian, according to my wish (when she arrives at the proper period) and that in return I will give her as little trouble as can be avoided upon the subject of her education – tutelage – and guardianship. A girl is in all cases better with the mother, unless there is some unusual objection, and I shall not allow my own private feelings to interfere with what is for the advantage of the child; She may bring her up in her own way.'[3]

After Allegra's recent death Byron was more than ever concerned about Ada and wanted to know as much about her as possible. 'Is she social or solitary, taciturn or talkative, fond of reading or otherwise? – and what is her *tic* I mean her foible, is she passionate? I hope that the Gods have made her anything save *poetical* it is enough to have one such fool in a family.'[4] Augusta relayed Annabella's answers. 'Her prevailing characteristic is cheerfulness and good-temper. Observation. Not devoid of imagination, but it is chiefly exercised in connection with her mechanical ingenuity – the manufacture of ships and boats, etc. Prefers prose to verse, because puzzled by poetical diction. Not very persevering. Draws well. Open and ingenuous temper, now under control. Tall and robust.'[5]

He was delighted with the report and the silhouette of Ada included with the letter. He proudly showed them to Colonel Stanhope 'who was struck with the resemblance of *parts* of it to the *paternal* line'. He described his recent seizure to Augusta urging her to warn Annabella in case his condition was hereditary. Two months later he was dead and the unfinished letter was found lying on the floor of the room together with a bloodstained handkerchief, a ringlet, a ribbon and the profile of Ada.

Within four days of the news of Byron's death arriving in England Annabella told the seven-year-old child, who wept. Anxious to dispel any idea that Ada might feel anything for Byron, Annabella told Mrs Villiers that the tears were 'I believe more from the sight of my agitation, and from the thought that she might have lost *me* than from any other cause, for what could an unseen being be to a child like her?'[6]

When she was eleven, Ada accompanied her invalid mother on a tour to Holland, Germany, Italy, Switzerland and France which lasted for over a year. On their return Annabella rented a large house called Bifrons outside Canterbury where she left Ada for long periods in the care of servants while she took health cures. Ada occupied herself studying the flight of birds and dreamt of the possibilities of flying machines. She told her mother with great glee of the pleasure she enjoyed studying the wing of a dead crow. Annabella disapproved of her activities and suggested she use her time more productively, so Ada amiably searched for a new interest and discovered geometry, which pleased her mathematical mother.[7]

Annabella's habits were nomadic and by the time Ada was thirteen they had left Bifrons and were established in a large villa at Hanger Hill in Ealing. Ada caught measles and, immediately she recovered, was struck down by a mysterious complaint which deprived her of the use of her legs. The disability was so severe that she refused a treat, a visit to London to stay with Lady Gosford, telling her mother that the carriage was too small to take her air-mattress which she would need on a long journey. Lady Holland was saddened when she saw Ada in Brighton in May 1829 'deprived of the use of her limbs'. She was told by Lord Melbourne that Ada had been examined by Sir Benjamin Brodie, President of the Royal College of Surgeons, but his report had not been hopeful.[8]

One of Annabella's special interests was charitable loan societies and it was to discuss these that Francis Trench, later Rector of Islip, was invited to dinner. He was very impressed with Lady Byron, 'one of the cleverest and most benevolent persons' he had ever met and described Ada as having 'a fine form of countenance, large expressive eyes and dark curling hair. Her features bear a likeness to her father's, but require some observation before it appears strongly. Then, I think, it does. At present her health is delicate, and she is obliged to use crutches.'[9] Ada's recovery was long and slow. She may, of course, have been less seriously incapacitated than she appeared as she had lived all her life with a compulsive hypochondriac and saw ill-health as a way to gain attention. Whatever her affliction was, it left no lasting damage as she grew to become an enthusiastic horsewoman and skilful dancer.

Ada was not allowed to mix with her Leigh cousins and when she was young Annabella had ensured she was never left alone in the same room as her aunt. However, Augusta could not resist sending Ada a present for her fifteenth birthday. She chose a prayer book and ordered it to be specially bound with 'ADA' in Old English characters engraved on the back. She dedicated it 'To the Hon. Miss Byron, with every kind and affectionate wish' and sent it to her niece in an envelope addressed to Lady Byron. The present was never acknowledged.

At the end of 1832 Lady Byron left Hanger Hill for another large house, Fordhook, close to Ealing Common, formerly the home of Henry Fielding. There she entertained Miss Selina Doyle and her brother, Colonel Francis Doyle, allies through the separation, and Miss Mary Millicent Montgomery, a childhood friend and another professional invalid. It had been Miss Montgomery's brother Hugh, as well as George Eden, whom Annabella had allowed Byron to believe she was seriously considering as a husband. Miss Carr, Dr Lushington's sister-in-law, was another visitor. The women were busy-bodies and although Lady Byron did not object to their overbearing interference, Ada did, nicknaming them the Three Furies.

When Miss Lawrence, Ada's governess, left to get married, Ada's education was placed in the hands of a series of tutors. William Turner, the young and handsome son of friends, was hired to teach her Latin and, as might have been expected, it was not long before they were chattering happily together. On one occasion when Miss Doyle took exception to their happiness she smartly reprimanded Ada, sending her from the room. Furious and humiliated she came back under the pretext of collecting her books and passed a note to Turner, right under the nose of the disapproving maiden lady, suggesting they meet at midnight in one of the outhouses. That night Ada crept out of the sleeping house to meet Turner who introduced her to extensive amorous exploration which intensified her affection for him. During the next few days she could not hide her feelings as she endured the acute pleasures and agonies of calf love. Her loving glances were intercepted and understood by her mother and the Furies. Turner was instantly dismissed. Undeterred, Ada followed him home. His astonished parents welcomed her but sent her back as quickly as they could before her absence was noticed, and the whole incident was hushed up. Ada confided in Woronzow Grieg many years later that she had fallen in love with Turner and that 'matters went as far as they possibly could without the connection being actually completed'.[10] Sophia De Morgan, daughter of William Frend, the mathematics tutor of both mother and daughter, wrote, 'There was I hope, no real misconduct at that time and an open scandal was prevented but it was very evident that the daughter who inherited many of her father's peculiarities also inherited his tendencies.'

Lady Byron took up phrenology and cultivated the acknowleged experts, Dr André Combe and his brother Mr George Combe.[11] She insensitively subjected Ada to the ordeal of having her bumps read and her character dissected by the Furies. Ada resented the attention and, like her father, felt self-conscious because she was plump. She was clumsy and pale after her long illness; as well as being reserved and lacking social graces, she had become shy and monosyllabic in company. She resented being the centre of attention and discussion and, most of all, she resented her mother and her coven of friends. She was going through the difficult period many girls experience before they blossom into adults. She became sullen, rebellious, and refused to perform on cue, behaving with almost as much bad grace as her father had at the same age. Mrs De Morgan, who disliked Ada, let it be known that she disapproved of her being allowed to sleep on a sofa wrapped in a rug at night instead of going to bed. She observed that Ada kissed her mother coldly and only on sufferance, that Ada had no taste for poetry and that she was vain and not to be trusted. Mrs De Morgan allowed she had an appreciation of music and a gift for mathematics, throwing in as an afterthought that she was good-natured and had a few kind feelings but, worst of all, saying she had the same love of startling and surprising people that her father had.[12]

In 1833 Ada was presented at court. The glittering occasion took place on 10 May and was attended by the Duke of Orleans, the Duke of Brunswick, Talleyrand and his niece, the Duchess of Dino, the Duke of Wellington, Lord Melbourne and the Dowager Duchess of Leeds, stepmother of the 6th duke, Augusta's half brother. Ada, in her new dress of white satin and tulle, waited a quarter of an hour and suffered a few nervous moments before being presented, but even though she was still delicate she did not feel at all tired. She liked the Duke of Wellington's straightforward manner, Talleyrand reminded her of 'an old monkey' and the Duke of Orleans was very pleasant company.[13]

On 5 June Ada met the mathematician and inventor Charles Babbage, who was to become her friend, teacher and confidant. Babbage was forty-two years old, good-looking, a widower and famous for his Difference Machine and for the entertaining Saturday evening assemblies which he held at his home in Dorset Street, off Manchester Square. He had successfully obtained £1,500 from the recently formed Astronomical Society to be used in developing the calculating machine and then obtained £17,000 from the government to fund his research, becoming the envy of less successful pioneers. However, the payments from the government were erratic and uncertain and he was frequently driven to subsidize the work out of his own pocket. The project could not continue without regular funds and John Clement, the foreman, was eventually forced to dismiss the workers, keeping all Babbage's drawings and specialized tools, as was his due. However, the calculating machine was sufficiently advanced for its potential to be appreciated. Babbage kept it in a building behind his house, using it as the centrepiece of attention at his Saturday night parties.

Babbage invited Ada and her mother to see the Difference Machine and, after they had examined it, he told them how he had tried to impress the Duke of Wellington, in an attempt to raise more money for research. Knowing the duke liked to dance, he said the engine could do everything except compose dances. The joke fell flat. Lady Byron thought Babbage was far too lighthearted when he was not talking mathematics. She was not favourably impressed by his new machine either, but Ada found it very exciting. She enjoyed mathematics and hoped to study science and technology. Lady Byron understood her daughter's ambitions and encouraged her by allowing her to attend the popular lectures on the Difference Machine that were being given at the Mechanics Institute by Dr Dionysius Lardner. As well as having a deep interest in mathematics Ada was a musical girl, asking for instruction on the harp in addition to her guitar lessons. It was about this time that she first attended an opera, *Anna Bolena* and laughed at the operatic conventions which expected the audience to believe that a woman could get up after fainting and burst into song.

William IV and Queen Adelaide invited Ada and her mother to a Drawing Room at the Brighton Pavilion in November. Annabella wore a deep-red figured satin gown cut low in the front with a peak and long sleeves. Her neck was completely covered with white satin and fine undyed silk lace called *blonde*. Her outfit was completed by a white hat, more silk lace and feathers. Beneath her dress she wore flannel and under that she 'had a blister on, which saved my chests'. According to her generous daughter, who did not describe her own dress, Annabella looked very pretty indeed. It was a highly successful evening for Annabella, who was invited to sit with the queen and was predictably disappointed at the banal conversation.[14]

In February 1834 Hobhouse met Ada at yet another Drawing Room. 'She is a large, coarse-skinned young woman,' he wrote, 'but with something of my friend's features, particularly the mouth. I was exceedingly disappointed.'[15] Lady Holland cattily remarked to her son in May, 'The *beauty* at the Queen's Ball was Miss Louisa Pagent, Sir Arthur's daughter. Miss Byron is reckoned a very ordinary young lady: none of the paternal sparkle.'[16]

In the autumn the spritely invalid took Ada on an educational tour of the factories in the midlands and the north. They watched ribbons being made in Coventry, looked at spar at Ashby-de-la-Zouch, saw potters working at their wheels and china being painted at Derby and, surprisingly, Annabella took Ada to a race meeting at Doncaster. Although she disapproved of gambling she wanted Ada to see first-hand how it was done as part of her education.[17]

Ada's ambition to be considered as a scientist and mathematician was advanced in March 1834 when she wrote to her former tutor, William Frend, asking him how rainbows were constructed and what were his opinions on Mrs Somerville's recently published book *The Connection of the Physical Sciences.* Frend introduced Ada to Mrs Somerville and encouraged their friendship and, to Ada's delight, Mrs Somerville (described by Hobhouse as 'a most pleasing, unaffected person, not handsome, but agreeable in her looks') sympathized and encouraged her ambition and hopes by taking her to lectures and concerts in London. After many of these excursions Ada spent the night at the Somerville house in Chelsea. Mary Somerville, a highly respected member of the scientific world, had translated Laplace's *Mécanique Céleste* into the popular English version *Celestial Mechanism of the Heavens* in 1831. She married twice, once to Samuel Greig, an officer in the Russian Navy, by whom she had had a son Woronzow, and, after his death, to her cousin, William Somerville, by whom she had two daughters.

Ada spent a great deal of time with the Somerville family, attending lectures or riding in rural Chelsea. On the occasions when Annabella, because of her delicate health, could not accompany Ada to dinner parties given in London's scientifically minded society, Mary Somerville would take her place and chaperone her eager protégée.

Ada was still a rather plain, plump girl at seventeen but that did not deter fortune hunters. She was approached by the Reverend Charles Murray, Treasurer of the Ecclesiastical Commission, but, before Ada could do anything stupid, Annabella sent the clergyman packing and his attempt ended in tears and confusion. This was just as well since the Reverend Charles subsequently vanished taking £9,000 of the commission's money and leaving debts amounting to £25,000.[18]

During the spring of 1835 Ada was invited to a house party given by Sir George Philips, the Member of Parliament for South Warwickshire and an acquaintance of her father. One of the other guests was William, Lord King. He was eleven years her senior and had recently served as Secretary to the Commission of the Ionian Islands under his cousin Lord Nugent, the governor. He was familiar with the Middle East and an accomplished linguist, speaking Greek, French, Italian and Spanish. He owned a town house in London and two estates, Ockham in Surrey and Ashley Lodge at Porlock in Somerset. This handsome, highly eligible man was an admirer of Byron whom he had never met, though Thomas Medwin introduced him to Teresa Guiccioli at a ball given by Prince Borghese in Florence.[19] He was at first fascinated by Ada because she was his hero's daughter then rapidly fell in love with her.

In early June Lady Byron recognized that Lord King's attentions to her daughter were becoming serious. She spoke to Ada, warning her to be on her guard, but before she finished the sentence Ada laughed saying, 'Oh, Mama, I know what you mean – you think Lord King intends to propose to me. I think so too, and if he does I have made up my mind to accept him.'[20] King was elated by his success and returned to Ashley Lodge to await Lady Byron's decision. He released his pent-up emotions by attacking trees. He hacked off huge branches from the arbutus trees, bay and myrtle bushes and opened up the sea view to the house.

After several meetings at Fordhook with Lady Byron, Lord King officially asked her permission to tell his family of his intentions. He had to be tactful as he was not on good terms with his mother. Long engagements were considered to be unhealthy and, where there were no obstacles, unnecessary. Ada's settlement was immediately drawn up and King was allotted £3,000 annual income and Ada was given £300 a year pin money. Lady Byron's stern sense of justice could not allow King to marry Ada without revealing her earlier infatuation with her tutor. It is unlikely that Ada had told her all the sensual details and certainly Lord King found nothing in the revelations to alter his intention.

Many letters of congratulation were sent and Ada received gratuitous advice from the Furies, none of whom had ever been married. Friends of her mother were anxious she should show sufficient gratitude to King and sent instructions on how to be a proper wife. William IV congratulated Lady Byron and on 29 June the announcement appeared in the *Morning Post* and *Morning Herald*.

It would appear that Ada did not want to be married in a church but chose to follow her mother's example and be married at home. If it was her choice it was an odd one considering the less than happy marriage her mother had made. A special licence was obtained from the Archbishop of Canterbury and the couple were married by the Reverend Samuel Gamlen in the drawing room at Fordhook on 8 July 1835. The thirty-year-old bridegroom took his nineteen-year-old bride to Ockham, his Surrey estate, for their honeymoon.

The following day Lady Byron provided a dinner for the servants and their friends at Fordhook and they cheered the new Lord and Lady King until the walls of the house trembled.

The World of Fashion reported the marriage in its 'Marriages and Deaths in High Life' column: 'The fair Augusta Ada Byron, "Ada, sole daughter of my house and heart", has become the wife of Lord King.'

Lady Byron was more than content with her new son-in-law and formed an informal pact with him to watch over Ada. She wrote to him almost daily, beginning on the day after the wedding. They gave each other pet names – Ada became Bird, Avis or Thrush, Annabella was Hen while William was Crow, Cock or Mate. With Ada off her hands Lady Byron began to busy herself with good works and urged King to follow suit. He founded an industrial school for poor boys at Ockham in 1836 along the same lines as the one she had established not far from Fordhook at Ealing Grove. She enjoyed visiting prisons and lunatic asylums in this country and in France, became a leading light in the Co-operative Society and in developing schools for the poor (one of which sent ten girls to South Africa), was active in founding labour schools and financed an agricultural school out of her own money.[21] She argued for the establishment of a Prison Discipline Society and the Children's Friend Society.

Ada continued her studies after her marriage, still harbouring the desire to be a mathematician of note. The discovery that she was to have a child did not come as a surprise but was a setback to her ambitions. The Kings spent their first Christmas together at Ockham and it was there that she first saw the picture of her father in Albanian dress painted by Phillips. It used to hang over the fireplace at Kirkby Mallory but had been covered by a green curtain for many years; under the terms of her will Lady Noel had forbidden Ada to see it until she was twenty-one – and then only with the permission of her mother. Early in May the following year she moved into the town house at 10 St James's Square to await the birth of her child. She continued her work and had been studying with her old tutor, William Frend, on the afternoon of the day that Byron Noel King was born, 12 May 1836. Ada and William were playful parents, sending for Baby Byron while they were still in bed naked and spinning him across the bed until he almost touched the ceiling. Byron was followed in September the following year by Anne Isabella. Ada was a little disappointed as she did not like girls and Byron always remained her favourite child. Not long after the birth she contracted a debilitating illness which from its symptoms could have been cholera. She recovered slowly and lost a considerable amount of weight. William admired her new shape but Annabella was worried about her daughter's health.

Ada had now become a pretty, dark-haired woman with a graceful figure who enjoyed dancing but, like her mother, had little interest in clothes or children. Soon after her marriage she caused a sensation at a ball given by the young Queen Victoria by dressing as one of her father's heroines in a semi-oriental costume with her waist-length hair drawn into long dark plaits through which she had woven ropes of pearls. Descriptions of her exotic costume spread through the assembly and before the evening had ended everyone had managed to file past her, pretending to talk to each other while darting side-long glances at the picturesque woman sitting on the sofa.[22]

Ada was an enthusiast and when she became interested in something she took it up single-mindedly. While learning to play the violin she ignored everything else and walked for hours on end round and round a billiard table practising and playing. Her liking and talent for music continued. In addition to the violin, piano and guitar she played the harp, her favourite instrument at musical evenings and during her pregnancies.

In June 1837 young Queen Victoria came to the throne and her most trusted adviser was Annabella's cousin William Lamb. Annabella courted and deferred to him and it may have been only coincidence that in the following June King was elevated to the Earldom of Lovelace in the Coronation Honours while George Byron had been an extra Lord-in-waiting to the queen for some time. Such good fortune did not smile on the Leighs. George lost the pension from the Crown which both he and his father had enjoyed and Augusta lost the pension which had been granted to her on the death of Queen Charlotte. Fortunately she was still allowed to keep the flat in St James's Palace.

The Lovelace family continued to grow and prosper. Ada's second son, Ralph, was born at St James's Square on 2 July 1839 and on 10 August the following year Lord Lovelace was sworn in as Lord-Lieutenant of Surrey. Hobhouse was at the palace attending a council and saw Lovelace for the first time.

Convinced that it was her destiny to become a mathematical genius, Ada began to study, mostly by correspondence, with Augustus De Morgan, the logician and mathematician, professor at University College London. Soon after her marriage she had written to Babbage asking for advice and hinting that she would like to work closely with him, saying that she believed she was intellectually capable of making a contribution to science. However, it was not until several years later that her ambition was achieved.

Lovelace held advanced views on women and disagreed with the widely held belief that the overtaxing of a woman's intellect would harm her body. He supported Ada in her ambitions and joined with her in inviting Babbage to Ockham. They hoped to be able to use their influential position in society to attract sufficient funds to allow the work on the Difference Machine to be completed or to cover the cost of Babbage's new project, the Analytical Engine. In January 1840 Babbage accepted their invitation. Ada, in her pleasure and excitement, told him dictatorially to come prepared to join in their new passion, skating, and to bring lots of warm clothes as she was sending an open carriage to meet him at Weybridge. It was a convivial and productive time and Ada happily made plans to set aside a couple of hours each day to work.

Meanwhile Annabella had been travelling on the continent for some time visiting prisons and lunatic asylums, when in the summer of 1840 Sir George Stephen, a solicitor to the Reversionary Interest Society passed on to her a letter written to him by her niece, Elizabeth Medora Leigh. Augusta, in a rare moment of prudence, had executed a deed which ensured £3,000 would be paid to her daughter on the deaths of Lady Byron and herself. Reduced to living in penury with a young daughter in Pontivy, France, Medora had decided to sell her reversionary interest in the deed. Sir George Stephen was willing to provide the money but only in exchange for the deed itself, which Augusta wisely refused to release. Medora told Sir George that her aunt, 'Lady Noel Byron, would use any influence she might possess with my mother, to induce her to give up to me that which was my right.' Annabella immediately saw an opportunity to meddle in Augusta's affairs and wrote what her niece described as 'a most kind letter, with money and offers of protection for me and Marie'.[23]

As soon as her travelling expenses arrived in August 1840, Medora and her daughter set out for Tours to meet their benefactress. Annabella was shocked to see how ill she looked and although she had intended to leave Medora with friends in Tours, she changed her mind in view of her niece's physical condition and her mentally confused state. They had travelled as far as Fontainbleau when Annabella succumbed to another of her mysterious illnesses; and it was during the period of her recovery that the two women enjoyed the honeymoon period of their relationship as they discussed the circumstances of Medora's birth. Annabella encouraged her to press ahead with an appeal to the Court of Chancery to force Augusta to hand over the deed, offering her the use of Byron's letters written at the time of the separation to help the suit along. In a rush of emotion Annabella asked to be called by Byron's old nick-name, 'Pip' and, according to her niece, said it was 'her only wish to provide for me, according to Lord Byron's intentions respecting me, and according to my rank in life'.[24]

In the New Year Ada received a present of a red and gold pin-cushion from her mother's new protégée. All at once the mutterings, hints, innuendoes and whisperings of the Furies fell into place when Ada received a startling letter from her mother in which she told Ada that Medora was the result of an incestuous relationship between her father and her aunt. Ada had already come to suspect what her father's crime had been and realized why she was not allowed to see her aunt, but she had not guessed there had been a child. However, she replied to her mother with scientific aplomb, 'I am not in the least *astonished* in fact you merely *confirm* what I have for *years and years* felt scarcely a doubt about, but should have considered it most improper in me to hint to you that I in any way suspected.' But she commented later, 'I should tell you that I did not suspect the daughter as being the *result* of it. In fact the notion would not naturally occur, because Mrs L., being married at the time, it might not have been easy to prove this, or even to feel any degree of certainty about it.' She continued, on thin ice, 'I should like sometime to know how you came ever to suspect anything so monstrous. The natural intimacy and familiarity of a Brother and Sister certainly could not suggest it to any but a very depraved and vicious mind, which *yours* assuredly was not.'[25] Annabella could not say she developed the story having first had her own vague suspicions confirmed by the well-known congenital liar and trouble-maker Caroline Lamb, so she said she had come to the conclusion that there had been 'criminal intercourse' between Augusta and Byron before her marriage during her only visit to Six Mile Bottom in March 1815. Both she and Lushington knew that when she left Piccadilly ten months afterwards, she was not sure incest had ever taken place.[26] Ada accepted her mother's version but William did not, keeping his opinions to himself.

In compliance with her mother's wishes Ada reluctantly put her lessons aside and set off alone for Paris on 6 April, leaving William at home nursing an attack of influenza. Within two days Medora had told Ada her extraordinary story. She accused Augusta and Georgiana of conspiring to cause her downfall with Henry Trevanion. She claimed he had drugged and ravished her on two separate occasions, but fortunately she had remained unconscious through both episodes. The two women listened fascinated as she told them that Augusta had suppressed Annabella's letters to Byron, that she had been Trevanion's mistress, that she had entered into a pact to pass on to him her daughters in chronological order to be debauched and had just recently signalled that Emily, the youngest, was ready for his attentions. Medora also accused her foolish but devout mother of trying to force her to destroy the second Trevanion child before it was born. Ada remarked to William that she had never seen her mother look so well.

Annabella had been involved in Medora's story from the day in December 1825 when Augusta had written excitedly to tell her that Georgiana had received a proposal of marriage from a Cornish cousin, Henry Trevanion. Augusta was most surprised that Georgiana could attract any young man. 'She is such a *quiet* being – with very sound and excellent sense and good judgement, but not brilliant in any way and I should have said too *awkwardly* shy to be admired.'[27] George Leigh and Henry Trevanion's father, John, disapproved of the match as neither bride nor groom had enough money to live on, but Augusta strenuously fought for 'the thing being brought to pass as soon as possible. They are young – but they are both very steady, and have anything but extravagant notions.' The stress of waiting pressed heavily on Henry and prevented him continuing with his law studies. Annabella, either out of kindness or mischief, provided financial support and the wedding took place on 4 February 1826, at St James's Piccadilly. Georgiana, Byron's favourite niece, was given away by Colonel Henry Wyndham, a family friend, as George Leigh refused to attend the wedding. The only witnesses were Augusta and eleven-year-old Medora.

It was an unhappy marriage from the beginning, marked by bickering and poverty. Henry's health became so delicate that he was forced to abandon any hope of succeeding in a legal career; though it was not damaged to the degree that it prevented him from providing extra mouths. Within the first year of her marriage Georgiana gave birth to Bertha, swiftly followed by Agnes. Unable to support his family, Henry was furthur embarrassed when his father reneged on his marriage settlement of £100. Augusta scraped up £2,000 on the expectation of Byron's legacy and supported her children, son-in-law, grandchildren and husband. Through all these financial doldrums George Leigh employed a manservant and continued to move freely in sporting circles, though frequently in danger of being arrested for debt. While maintaining her large household Augusta paid out £200 annually to a home in Kensington where her autistic daughter, Augusta Charlotte, lived. Despite these desperate circumstances Augusta's affection for her son-in-law Henry did not flag, 'He has been *quite* what I expected of him, and my greatest comfort.'[28]

In March 1829 Annabella offered Bifrons to the Trevanions and it was in the gloomy house near Canterbury that Georgiana had her third baby.

The Trevanions moved to Kent taking with them Georgiana's younger sister Medora. The girl had often acted as a buffer between the unhappy pair during their short, stormy marriage and her assigned role at Bifrons was to be peacemaker. She accompanied them under protest, Augusta insisting she should be nearby to help Georgey, who was growing to hate Henry. Medora later claimed to dislike him as intensely as the rest of the family but Augusta remained blind to his faults; she told the disgruntled girl to have compassion and not to make fun of him because he was ill and finding it difficult to accept her charity.

As soon as they reached Bifrons, Georgiana took to her bed, preferring to spend her time upstairs alone, leaving Medora to amuse and cope with Henry. The young girl kept him company inside and outside the house during the day and in the evenings and sometimes at night. Georgiana had such a loathing of her husband that she used to send Medora into Henry's bedroom on errands instead of going herself even at dead of night when all the servants were asleep. This was foolhardy since Henry, like Byron, was a sexual opportunist. Medora soon fell victim to Henry's advances and before long she told him she was expecting a child. Henry refused to tell Georgiana himself but urged Medora to confess and implore forgiveness for them both. Georgiana was appalled and took much of the blame upon herself, saying she should have been more careful of Medora. Surprisingly she did not condemn Henry. After discussion they asked the unsuspecting Augusta for permission to take Medora to France.

The widow of Byron's loathed tenant, Lord Grey de Ruthyn, was living in the Canterbury area with her new husband, the Revd William Eden, and, well aware of what was going on at Bifrons, they informed Annabella. In January 1830, George Byron, the 7th Lord, organized and Annabella paid for Medora and the two Trevanions to travel to Calais where, in February 1830, Medora gave birth to a baby boy. The child was taken from her immediately to be brought up in France but died of convulsions three months later. As soon as Medora was fit enough to travel, which was about the same time the child died, she returned to live with her mother at St James's Palace and the Trevanions lodged with an aunt in Cadogan Place. Augusta had no inkling of what had happened.[29]

It is unlikely that either Annabella or George Byron helped the Trevanions out of the goodness of their hearts. George was beholden to Annabella for an annuity of £2,000 as Byron had cut him out of his will for supporting her during the separation and had left his estate to the Leighs. Annabella's charitable action is also suspect as she was locked in a tussle with Augusta over the replacement of one of the trustees to her marriage settlement. Kinnaird, who was dying of cancer, resigned in 1829 as the trustee appointed to represent Augusta; Annabella high-handedly selected Stephen Lushington as his replacement and Augusta objected. Lushington told Annabella, 'A trustee of Mrs Leigh's nomination might injure you and Ada to her advantage.' He continued, 'A trustee of your selection could not injure Mrs Leigh for your interest. You have already extended your forgiveness to Mrs Leigh to so unparalleled an extent that I must in candour say that all she can feel, write, or say in this transaction is comparatively of no importance. Any personal contact with her is, I think, a degradation to you.' Annabella instructed her solicitors to inform Augusta that her decision was final. Although momentarily stunned and 'dreadfully hurt' Augusta freely offered her forgiveness to Annabella.[30] The thought of receiving forgiveness from such a sinner was unbearable and she did not reply but redoubled her efforts to blacken Augusta's reputation in the hope that her remaining pension of £300 a year and the apartment in St James's Palace would be withdrawn.

In January 1830 the first volume of Thomas Moore's '*Life, Letters and Journals of Lord Byron* was published and Annabella took offence at the implication that her mother had had a hand in the separation. She wrote a carefully edited account of the event calling it *Remarks on Mr Moore's Life of Lord Byron by Lady Byron*.[31] It was, she claimed, a private report but it was bound and sent to everyone she could think of, including the king. Lady Holland commented to her son, 'Lady Byron is getting into a silly controversy with Moore upon some passages in his book. She will be the loser as many suppressed passages will be disclosed and she will not like it. Your Papa is doing his utmost to quell her restlessness, but in vain. I am afraid she is a cold obstinate woman.'[32] Hobhouse first saw the *Remarks* in a bookseller's window on the day of Kinnaird's funeral and wanted to spring to Augusta's defence, but she was reluctant to give him permission and Lord Holland advised silence, saying that Lady Byron would feel more if no notice were taken of her and she were treated with contempt by Byron's friends than if she were to figure in a controversy. 'This is true,' noted Hobhouse adding that he had seen enough to convince himself that the woman was either crazy or totally indifferent to truth. Augusta wrote to Hodgson, 'What has she to gain now that he is powerless to injure or oppress her in any way? I do think nothing, were it ever so bad, could possibly justify anyone defaming the dead.'[33] To Benjamin Haydon, the painter, Hobhouse said 'he agreed with me that she [Annabella] was totally unfit for him, was a fool and an old maid by anticipation, that there was nothing between 'em but pecuniary necessity.'[34]

The second volume of Moore's life was published in 1831 and was a best seller. 'I long to hear what you think of this book,' Augusta wrote to

Hodgson. 'What will Lady B. do or say? What can she? And yet if she is quiet she must *writhe* under the torture!'[35]

All through the summer and autumn of 1830 Augusta tried without success to encourage Medora to be young, take advantage of her position, enjoy herself, go out in society and attend balls. Her behaviour puzzled her mother as 'hitherto she had much enjoyed the public amusements and children's dances to which she had been taken from a very early age.' Medora refused to enter into society saying sanctimoniously, 'I endeavoured to excuse myself on account of my extreme youth, and by the fact that I was in mourning for another sister whom we had recently lost' (Augusta Charlotte had died). She ignored her mother and spent her time shut in the apartment at St James's Palace. When Augusta was on duty at court she was out two or three days a week and often could not return until well after midnight and on many of those occasions she left Medora and Trevanion in the drawing room. By January 1831 Medora was pregnant again and, as before, Trevanion insisted that she should be the one to confess. He dictated a letter for her to give her mother in which Augusta found herself blamed for both the babies. The letter was so devastating that Augusta burnt it and then wrote long, confused and agonized letters to each of them. Surprisingly, like Georgiana, she did not blame Henry. She wrote to him, 'Now Dearest – let me implore of you to be comforted – to do your utmost to make the best of circumstances – to trust in my affection. That you are tried, SEVERELY tried, I feel – and I pray God to support you and comfort you and guide you! and I feel confident he will never abandon you if you trust in Him! Do not accuse yourself, dearest, and make yourself out *what you are NOT!*' It is difficult to see how he was 'tried' unless Augusta was admitting her daughter was a nymphomaniac.

Her letter to Medora was severe, 'You have committed *two* of the most deadly crimes! recollect who you have injured! – and whom you are injuring – not only your own Soul, but that of another, you think *more* dear than yourself. Think *whom* you have deprived of *his* affection! . . . I implore my dearest child therefore, as regards these fears, to be prudent and circumspect to the last degree.' She continued, rather unrealistically, to hope Medora would be confirmed at Easter. 'I hoped to be able to prepare you sufficiently myself with the help of reading – but now I feel it would be a great satisfaction to me if some clergyman were to assist in this.'[36] In Medora's case an entire college of cardinals might not have been able to prepare her. Georgiana came to Medora's assistance by claiming some of the blame again while Trevanion emotionally confessed to having taken laudanum.

Georgiana and Augusta approached Henry's family and in March a house at Colerne, near Bath, was made available to them but Georgiana would only agree to go if Medora came to protect her from Trevanion's violence. Medora was so eager to stay near Henry that she threatened to poison herself if she was not allowed to accompany them. In the end Augusta agreed to the scheme but only because she wanted them out of London as she was terrified Colonel Leigh would find out what had been going on.

Such a household could not live in peace and in June Georgiana appealed to Augusta to help her leave Trevanion and his cruelty. Augusta, unable to cope, asked Colonel Wyndham to speak to her husband. Leigh immediately drove to Wiltshire, taking with him an attorney, a constable and a woman who passed as a lady's maid. Under the pretext of bringing Medora home he took her to a 'safe' house in Lisson Grove owned by a Mrs Pollen. The house was run like a prison, the windows were nailed down and there were secure chains and locks on the door. Before leaving Colerne, Medora had been allowed ten minutes alone with Henry when he made her promise that she would escape from her mother and run away with him at the first opportunity. When Medora returned to her room to take her things to the coach she found Georgiana lying in wait and in great distress. She asked to be forgiven and assured her that she would try to get a divorce so Medora could marry Trevanion.

Leigh was particularly upset by these events as Medora was his favourite daughter and the one who looked most like him. He visited her at Lisson Grove, but after the third visit she told him not to come again. Augusta was even less welcome and only visited Medora once. The only other contact Medora had with the outside world was when one of her aunts sent her some religious books and tracts. These were received without comment.

The Leighs took Hobhouse into their confidence, telling him that, far from wanting to leave Trevanion, Georgiana was so attached to him she was willing to follow him to prison. Augusta's attitude was even more surprising to Hobhouse as she seemed to be afraid of speaking against Trevanion. He was startled to learn that the unrepentant lovers read the Bible together each morning and that Trevanion was now wandering the streets of London looking for Medora with a pistol in his pocket.

Medora had been at Lisson Grove for about two weeks when she saw Trevanion and Georgiana drive past. Trevanion spotted her at the window and for the next two weeks passed the house daily. It was then that Medora found notes from him neatly sewn into her clean underclothes when they came back from the laundry. The notes, which Georgiana had sewn into the clothes, contained a code by which Medora could decipher the signs Trevanion made to her from the street. One day Mrs Pollen told her she was free to walk about the house and showed her how to undo the chains on the door. 'I did not hesitate,' Medora wrote in her account, 'but at once put on my bonnet, followed her instructions, and found Trevanion outside waiting to receive me. We left the street with all possible haste and secrecy, which we might have spared ourselves, as nobody attempted to follow us. We made our way to the Continent, and for two years after this time lived together as man and wife on the coast of Normandy, under the assumed name of Monsieur and Madame Aubin.'[37]

In December 1831 Medora entered the Roman Catholic Church and Georgiana applied for a divorce which, according to Trevanion, could not be obtained. During their life together in Normandy Medora had several miscarriages and in June 1833 she expressed a desire to take the religious life. She asked Augusta to send her £60, which would cover her fees for a year as a boarder in a convent. Augusta riffled through her small funds but, although willing to help, she could not afford to send all the money at once. In the meantime Medora submitted to Trevanion's pleas in spite of knowing that each time she gave in to his importunings she was, in the eyes of her new faith, committing a mortal sin. She had enough money in July to enter a convent at Carhaix in Lower Brittany, only to leave it a month later when she discovered she was pregnant again. The compassionate abbess allowed her to use the convent as a mailing address and Medora lodged nearby using Augusta's money for subsistence. 'I did not feel that I was doing wrong. Trevanion was not under the same roof with me, and from the time I entered the convent I never was but as a sister to him'. Her daughter was born on 19 May 1834.[38] Medora and Henry passed locally as brother and sister. The baptismal certificate shows that Anne Violette Leigh was born to Elizabeth Leigh (née Trevanion) and her husband Henry Leigh; the deceitful document was signed by Henry Trevanion acting for the baby's absent father.

The Trevanions moved to Morlaix in Brittany where they lived in an old damp manor house infested with rats. Trevanion developed his hobbies of religion and shooting, while Medora busied herself with Anne Violette whom she called Marie. 'We never met alone, and seldom met at all,' she said.

Trevanion returned briefly to England, managed to raise some money and tried to mortgage Georgiana's marriage settlement, the money due to come to her and his children after Annabella's death, which was their portion of the £60,000 that Byron had put in trust. Byron's co-executor, John Hanson, refused to have anything to do with him, telling Hobhouse, 'I really think poor Mrs Leigh and all connected with her are mad.'

On returning to the tumbledown manor house, Trevanion attempted to renew sexual relations with Medora. 'But,' she said, 'I was no longer a child – I was twenty-one; and two years' experience had enabled me to know how to resist.' His advances rebuffed, Trevanion took a mistress and forced Medora to act as a servant. For the next three years she lived in poverty and illness, confiding all her troubles to the local physician, Dr Victor Carrel. Believing her to be consumptive he helped her in 1838 to write to her mother and Lady Chichester asking them for money to enable her to leave Trevanion. Lady Chichester sent her £5, which Medora used to move to the nearby town of Pontivy where she relapsed into ill health.

Medora had persuaded Augusta to allow her the unrealistic sum of £120 a year – which was much more than she could afford; although Augusta continued to write loving letters she was quite unable to provide her with the money she needed. It was when this became clear that Medora first thought of selling her interest in the deed, contacted Sir George Stephen and swung into Lady Byron's orbit again. On arriving in Paris from Tours Lady Byron and Medora settled into lodgings at 24 rue de Rivoli, later moving to 22 Place Vendôme.

Neither Annabella nor Medora told Augusta what had happened and it was left to Doctor Carrel to inform her that Medora was now living with her aunt in Paris. Unable to restrain herself any longer, Augusta wrote to the silent Annabella in January 1841 asking for news of Medora. Annabella rebuffed her, replying sanctimoniously that if she had truly loved her daughter she would not need to ask for information:

Your affectionate letters to her must appear a cruel mockery to those who know that you left her, for so long a time, only the alternatives of vice or starvation. Her malady, the effect of physical and mental suffering combined, can be retarded . . . only by extreme care and by her avoiding all distressing excitement. The former I can secure, but not the latter – I would save you, if it be not too late, from adding the guilt of her death to that of her birth. Leave her in peace! This advice is given in no hostile spirit, but with the firm determination to protect her to the utmost of my power.[39]

In her confusion and deep sorrow Augusta turned to her former ally and confidante, Therese Villiers, who rushed across London from her home in Knightsbridge to St James's Palace to help. She organized Augusta, reviewed her finances and told Annabella,

Her income is £800 per annum. Out of this she has to board her husband when at home, and her son Henry always, to maintain herself, Emily, and her servants entirely. She gives her eldest son George £100 per annum – her son Frederick has never cost her less (if so little) as £200 per ann: and she has *entirely* to provide (as far as she can) for the wants and really necessaries of Georgiana Trevanion and her three growing-up daughters! As may be supposed, however, the supply has been quite unequal to the demand, and Georgiana is deeply in debt for the bare means of subsistence.

Mrs Villiers verified that Augusta had made a 'perfectly correct' statement of what had happened between her and Medora since she ran away with Trevanion. The papers were endorsed by Augusta's half-sister Mary, now the dowager Countess of Chichester, and her son the 3rd earl and sent to Paris on 12 February. They were returned unopened to Augusta's solicitors the following day together with a message from Annabella, 'I wrote in the envelope to Mrs Leigh that I considered the correspondence terminated by my answer to her inquiry.'[40]

In an attempt to clear Augusta of any complicity with Trevanion, Mrs Villiers copied and sent Annabella a letter written by Medora to Augusta in 1838:

My own dearest dear Mamma, never think that you have ever pained me by even a harsh word or thought. If, when under the influence of other feelings, my conduct towards you may have led you to suppose you seemed harsh, or anything but what you are, and always were – the best, the kindest and most devoted of mothers, forgive me this amongst my other faults – believe the fault was not on your side – no – no – indeed – I well feel and know *that*. God Almighty be merciful to those who betrayed my confidence in you, my own dear Moé – *that* confidence existing, my ruin could not have been effected – but no – you are right – we must not look on what can only pain us.

'I could scarcely believe,' Mrs Villiers told Annabella, 'this is the same daughter who is now engaged in a law-suit against the same mother . . . and all because she *could not* do what she only promised to do IF SHE COULD.' Annabella replied, 'Let Mrs Leigh have the benefit of her daughter's affection . . . [the letter] was very natural from one who believed herself dying, and was worked upon by such a letter as that to which this is obviously a reply.'[41]

Medora had been living under Annabella's wing for almost nine months when Ada arrived in April 1841 and for much of that time had been feeding her with fresh titbits of gossip and receiving small amounts of money. When not discussing her distressing past Medora was kept in the background. She had her own room in a separate wing of the house in the Place Vendôme to ensure she was not in the way of any guests Lady Byron chose to entertain. Ada was able to visit her when she wished, but Medora was not allowed to walk freely about the house. She was not invited to accompany the family to the theatre and did not share in the shopping trips organized by Annabella to equip Ada for her presentation to Louis Philippe. When William, recovered from influenza, joined them in Paris he was polite to Medora but not effusive. Although Ada was suitably horrified at Medora's revelations and the story of Annabella's unhappy marriage, now revealed to her in minute detail, she was looking forward to returning to her scientific activities. The Lovelaces returned home in May after their presentation at the French court.

Later that month Annabella brought Medora and Marie to England and insisted that Medora resume the name Madame Aubin for appearance sake. She placed them in lodgings run by relations of Mrs De Morgan in Bedford Street until she had found a suitable house to rent. Ada and William visited them in London and Mrs De Morgan thought Ada seemed delighted at having a sister and appeared to be quite affectionate towards her. Medora said she 'received kindness and promises from both, and was made to feel that I was to be Ada's sister in all things, as I was really'.[42]

In July Annabella leased Moore Place in Esher, not far from the Lovelaces' home at Ockham, and invited Medora to look on it as her home. Meanwhile she paid for Marie to attend a school at Notting Hill run by a relative of Mrs Jameson. Annabella had been friends with Mrs Jameson, an essayist and art critic, since her charity school days and she left Medora in her care at Esher during her frequent absences. Annabella rapidly became disenchanted with Medora who was beginning to reveal her true colours. She complained that she was bored, disliked country life, missed the attentions of men and began to amuse herself by spreading stories and causing disquiet among Annabella's friends. She even floated a rumour that Sir George Stephen, who had gone out of his way to help her, was committing adultery with his sister-in-law. She appreciated the power she had in posing as Byron's daughter and the embarrassment she could cause her relatives. However, a ray of sunshine appeared for Annabella in October when Colonel Leigh was imprisoned for debt following a fairly public arrest made on the race course at Newmarket.[43]

In May 1842 Medora's Chancery suit against her mother was postponed, though everyone still feared the revelations that might come from it.[44] Then, to the relief of both sides, the case was withdrawn the day before it was due to be heard when Augusta surrendered the deed to Annabella's solicitors.[45] Lady Byron met all the costs of the case including Augusta's share and was quick to tell her friends of her generosity, but Augusta was well aware of who had encouraged her daughter to bring the case. Medora's reaction was unexpected. Furious that she had not been able publicly to ruin her mother, she wrote, 'The suit was concluded in a way, without consultation with me, that showed me that all that had been promised me, unsolicited and unsought, was not sincere, and that I had been in a manner sacrificed in my mother's interest. I openly expressed to Lady Byron all I felt, and my determination of leaving England immediately, and solicited from her (Lady Byron) the means to do so.' Medora's dislike of the treatment she had received was matched by Lady Byron's desire to get rid of her. In a character sketch of Medora written on 6 June Lady Byron wrote, 'There are in my opinion but two holds on this character. Love of approbation and of money. . . . In attempting to hurt those who oppose her, she will hurt herself; but this will be not from recklessness but miscalculation. She expects to make people serve her better by bullying.'[46]

Lady Byron was temporarily forced to leave Moore Place by Medora's temper tantrums, during which she threatened revenge on her saying she was her worst enemy. Eventually arrangements were made for Medora to return to France. On a visit to London and still hoping to squeeze more money out of her benefactress, she described her mother crossing St James's Square outside the Lovelace town house 'dressed in a dark brown kind of muslin gown with white pattern, a black silk shawl with long fringe and gathered round her as if she was afraid of losing it & a straw leghorn bonnet trimmed with white satin ribbons. Her large eyes are ever & indeed *unchanged*, her walk is most altered – she shuffles along as if she tried to carry the ground she walks on with her & looks WICKED. . . . Oh how horrible she looked – so wicked – so hyena-like.'[47] Mrs Jameson noticed Medora appeared to be agitated when she returned to Moore Place that night and she confessed to Annabella that she had 'drunk quantities of wine'.

Annabella agreed to provide £150 a year for Medora and Marie and to pay her maid's wages and travelling expenses. The money would be paid quarterly and begin as soon as they had settled at Hyères, the town Medora had chosen as suitable because of her delicate health. While staying in Paris Lady Byron and Ada had engaged Nathalie Beaurepaire as a lady's maid for Medora and Nathalie, her husband Victor and their daughter Victorine had accompanied Medora to England. Nathalie was unwilling to return to France without her husband and it was only after a heated argument that Ada persuaded her mother to allow Victor to accompany them as a courier. For an extra £10 Nathalie agreed to spy on Medora and report to Lady Byron who would continue to pay Victorine's school fees.

Ada went to Moore Place to say goodbye to Medora and was met with half an hour of screaming and abuse. Medora howled that she had been ill-used and she had not been given enough money. She threatened she would find a husband even if it meant throwing herself down the throat of the first man she met. She had nothing good to say of anyone, especially Augusta, Mrs Jameson and Annabella. Eventually, to everyone's relief she set off for France on the evening of Friday 22 July 1842.

Medora left her strong-box, in which she stored all her papers and the 'proof' that she was Byron's daughter, in the care of Lady Byron at Moore Place, but she placed the precious deed in Ada's care to be locked away with the Lovelace papers at Ockham.

Medora got no further than Lyons before she had spent the whole of her first quarter's allowance and appealed to Lady Byron for more money, claiming she had developed consumption. During the journey through France Medora and Nathalie ceased to be mistress and maid and became friends. Nathalie told Medora she wanted to serve a 'lady whose conduct had ever been irreproachable' and Medora confessed she was the child of incest and that she had run off with her sister's husband and so fell far short of Nathalie's expectations. She suggested Nathalie should leave her as 'my life and past history were not such as she would wish', but Nathalie refused, assuring her mistress of her 'devotion under all circumstances',[48] filing the information for future use.

Despite the lower cost of living in France Medora was unable to live within her income at Hyères and wrote again asking for money. Annabella lost patience and told her to move to somewhere cheaper if she could not manage. Victor tried to justify the expenses by asking the Mayor of Hyères and an expatriate Englishman to certify that their expenditure was not excessive. They were forced to move to a cheaper house not far from Toulon but by this time Lady Byron was not prepared to continue to support Victor, whose function as courier had now ceased, although he was managing the household finances. She instructed Medora to dismiss him saying she would not pay his wages after 1 January 1843. 'He laughed,' reported Medora and said he would not desert her. The lure of Paris was strong and in March Medora deliberately disobeyed Lady Byron's instructions and took rooms at the Hotel du Rhin, Paris, knowing she could not pay the bill and using Annabella's name as security. Selina and Adelaide Doyle were in Paris and Medora told them a pathetic tale and Adelaide, believing she was completely destitute, paid the hotel bill. Lady Byron was most annoyed and surprised that Adelaide should have been so easily deceived and still withheld money from Medora. Just as she had had no qualms about taking her mother to court so Medora decided to see if she could obtain help from the French courts. On the advice of the Beaurepaires she consulted one of the most successful advocates in France, Antoine Berryer, who was amazed to learn that she was Byron's daughter and offered to help her in any way he could.

Annabella was genuinely disturbed at Medora's irrational behaviour, and believing she might be mad, asked Dr King, a physician at Brighton Hospital and the proprietor of a lunatic asylum in Sussex, to examine her. He first called on Medora one Sunday afternoon in late May, but she sent him away with the instruction to see Berryer. King furiously threatened to leave Paris within forty-eight hours but on Wednesday, following instructions from Berryer, Medora agreed to see him. She showed him Lady Byron's letters in which she had made promises and offered financial help. Fearing Medora might have solid grounds for a case against Lady Byron, King offered her £300 a year, double the amount she was receiving, on condition that she agree to place herself and Marie in Lady Byron's hands. She refused the terms. Dr King urged her to reconsider and think of the alternative, possible starvation, but she was adamant. Driven to desperation by what he considered her foolishness he exclaimed in exasperation, 'Sign, sign, you great fool!'[49]

Having rejected Annabella's offer Medora was forced to borrow on the deed which was now held by Lady Byron's solicitors, Wharton and Ford. Sir George Stephen still refused to advance any money until he had the deed and Wharton and Ford refused to trust such a valuable document to the post. They informed Berryer that Medora must collect it herself or send a responsible person to receive it for her.

This last blow was almost too much for Medora and she retired to bed. While her guard was down Nathalie persuaded her to write a letter authorizing her to collect the deed from Wharton and Ford and to retrieve her strong-box from Lady Byron. Although Medora had a few qualms about the plan they were calmed when Nathalie assured her it had Berryer's blessing. It soon became clear from a letter she received from Nathalie that she was not fulfilling her commission and Medora consulted Berryer who sent her to Lytton Bulwer at the British Embassy who 'instantly said it was of the greatest importance to prevent her [Nathalie] getting possession of the Deed'. Both Bulwer and Berryer distrusted the Beaurepaires and urged her to countermand her instructions and to 'conciliate Lady Byron'.[50]

Curious to know at first-hand what her ungrateful niece was saying,

Lady Byron agreed to meet Nathalie. She was not pleased when Nathalie slyly indicated that she knew Medora's secret and she pretended unconvincingly that she did not understand her. Lovelace wrote to Sir George Stephen for advice and was taken aback to learn that he believed Medora quite capable of blackmailing her family and extorting money. In order to protect Ada and Lady Byron, Lovelace suggested Nathalie should be directed to Augusta's family who would be concerned about any harmful gossip. Lady Byron was annoyed at his interference and refused to have anything to do with Augusta or Lady Chichester, but it was too late. The Beaurepaires had already visited the Chichesters who were alarmed but willing to contribute something towards Medora's support. The Earl of Chichester wrote to Medora twice telling her not to 'reject Lady Byron's kindness, liberality and generosity, [of] all of which,' sneered Medora in her memoir, 'I am ignorant'.

A near neighbour from Hyères, 57-year-old Captain Joseph Barrallier, a veteran of the Peninsular War, had recently arrived in Paris on his way to England; after he heard about Medora's situation he chivalrously accompanied her to London, paid her fare and settled her into lodgings at 8 Church Row, Old St Pancras. Captain Barrallier had no idea of the depth of bitterness that existed between Medora and Lady Byron and probably thought Medora would soon be taken off his hands.

Captain Barrallier called at Wharton and Ford, Lady Byron's solicitors, and told them that he was willing to help Miss Leigh in any way he could, but he could not continue to support her financially. He then went on to Banon and Smith in Westminster to conduct his own business and spoke to Mr Thomas Smith, the same Smith who had taken part in Byron's picnic at the School of Homer and had dined with him at the home of Captain and Mrs Wright Knox in 1823. Although eager to help, Smith cautiously described Medora as a lady who 'represented herself as the fourth child of the Hon. Augusta Leigh, the sister of Lord Byron. She was born, she said, in 1814, and was consequently in her twenty-eighth year. She was good-looking rather than eminently handsome, had dark eyes and hair, and a dark complexion, and was altogether a very lively and agreeable person.' She was accompanied by her daughter, 'the little girl Marie to whom she was passionately attached'. Smith asked Medora to write an account of her complicated life.[51] The document was long and became more incoherent and self-pitying as it progressed. However, Smith was touched by the hardships she described and told her he intended to try and make peace between her and Lady Byron. He made an appointment to meet Stephen Lushington on the afternoon of 21 July 1843 and kept careful minutes of their meeting. Lushington read out a letter from Lady Byron in which she said she 'was not to be moved, by arguments used in behalf of Miss Leigh, from her determination to have no further intercourse with her' and that Mr Smith 'was very imperfectly informed as to Miss Leigh's conduct towards her and she (Lady Byron) did not mean to make it more known. She deeply commiserated with Miss Leigh, but she could not consent to renew communication with her.' Smith was dismayed, noting in his minutes that 'the case became one of simple starvation for Miss Leigh and her child; that Captain Barrallier was not only unable to continue to pay for her living but he must return to France immediately and the girl would be utterly destitute.' He continued, 'I urged everything that I could think of to induce Dr Lushington to view the matter as of infinite importance to Lady Byron's and to Lady Lovelace's peace of mind.'[52]

Smith mentioned that the French servants were in London and that Beaurepaire had boasted he was looking for an opportunity to insult or assault Lord Lovelace so that he would be arrested and taken to Bow Street where he could ensure Medora's disreputable history would be highlighted in the police reports. Lushington was not surprised as Beaurepaire had already brought an action against Lady Byron. Neither of the Beaurepaires had believed Annabella's wide-eyed protests of innocence and were quite sure she knew the status of her niece when they were employed. Their lawyer, Mr Dod, was preparing a case of fraud, accusing Lady Byron of misrepresenting Medora's status as, far from being a 'respectable' widow, Madame Aubin was an unmarried woman with a bastard. If the case was successful the Beaurepaires stood to gain considerable damages but even if the case was dismissed the 'horrid secret' that Lady Byron had restricted and rationed to her familiars would be public and Ada, Miss Doyle, Dr King and herself would have to give evidence.

Dod refused to settle without 'characters' for his clients and a great deal of time was spent coaxing Annabella to write something suitable. She had earlier foolishly refused to write a reference for Nathalie when she applied for a post with Lady Howard, just as she had spitefully refused to write one for Mrs Fletcher in 1819. The case was eventually settled out of court; Annabella met the costs of all the solicitors, Beaurepaire received £100 and Nathalie entered the service of Lady Howard.[53] Smith was distressed to hear of the action, but pointed out to Lushington that most of the mischief had been caused by the unscrupulous French couple and surely some consideration should be given to Medora's youth and inexperience.

On Lushington's advice Smith approached Sir George Stephen who told Smith the only way Medora could extricate herself from her painful situation was to 'surrender the Deed of Appointment, as a sacred provision, to trustees – for her child. She must write an expression of her sincere contrition for her conduct to Lady Byron and lastly, return to seclusion in France.' He continued, 'On these terms, I will exert myself to the utmost, to obtain for her from her friends a permanent and comfortable domicile in France, and I am convinced that I shall succeed.'[54] Lady Byron was firm that the deed should remain in her hands and Medora was equally firm that she should have it.

Barrallier's slim funds could not bear the extra expense of providing for Medora for much longer and Smith appealed to Lord Lovelace who declined to help, saying 'Captain Barrallier's intervention in the matter was wholly uninitiated by Lady Noel Byron and by himself (Lord Lovelace).' It was not until many weeks later and with outstanding bad grace that Lady Byron refunded Barrallier a small portion of the money he had spent feeding and housing Medora and Marie.[55]

Medora knew her mother was forgiving and sentimental and on 12 August she went to St James's Palace intending to call on her. Augusta, now fifty-nine, with a weak heart and plagued with debts, felt unable to cope and instructed her footman to say she was 'Not at home.' Medora took the snub to heart and the following day wrote her mother a letter which Smith described as 'haughty, unfilial, and cruel'. Augusta did not reply nor did she change her mind and five weeks later Medora was still unsuccessfully trying to see her. Medora spent 14 August writing begging letters to her relations and Byron's friends. Hobhouse commented the following day that 'I have a letter from a person signing herself Elizabeth Medora Leigh stating herself *to be child of Lord Byron* & asking *for charity.*' The only member of her family to reply was the Duke of Leeds who sent £10. This encouraged Medora to send him nine days later a long whining letter setting out all her grievances. Barrallier forwarded a copy to Smith with the note, 'It is entirely her own composition. *I* did not like it.' Neither did the duke. He never replied.[56]

Lushington and Stephen both advised Annabella to surrender the deed which she did unwillingly and Medora marched triumphantly to the offices of Wharton and Ford to collect it. Both Smith and Barrallier strongly advised her not to borrow on it but to accept Lady Byron's conditions.

In October Medora moved to 18 Aldenham Terrace, Old St Pancras Road and wrote to Barrallier to tell him she intended to terminate her affairs with Smith. She transferred her business to Sir John Hughes, who suggested contacting Trevanion and asking for help. It was not until Christmas Day that she could bring herself to give him permission to do so, but Trevanion was not interested in helping his former mistress or his child. Medora finally realized that she had no friends in England; she

had abused most of them, lied about others and not even her mother
would help her. On 27 May 1844 she used the deed to borrow £500 from
Captain Hugh Cossart Baker, paid her debts and left for France.

She settled in a pension at St Germain-en-Laye, a small town on the
outskirts of Paris, and placed Marie in the Convent of the Nativity
nearby. Towards the end of 1845, when she was swamped with debts, she
was fortunate enough to be hired as a servant in the same pension
where she had been a guest. One of the lodgers, Colonel Jacques-
Philippe Delmas de Gramont, the Commandant of the 8th Hussars had
brought his own servant, Jean-Louis Taillefer, a sturdy man from a
peasant background, thirty-four years old, with two more years of
military service to complete. Medora and Taillefer frequently came
across each other in the course of their working day and Taillefer fell in
love. True to her prediction, Medora threw herself down the throat of
the first available man and by May 1846 found herself pregnant. She
continued to work until November when Taillefer arranged for her to
live in St Affrique, a town only a few miles from where he was born in
the village of Lapaeyre in southern France.[57]

Marie and Medora lodged with the local apothecary, later moving to an
inn where on 27 January 1847 her son Jean-Louis Elie was born. Taillefer
acknowledged his bastard and the child was christened with Marie acting
as his godmother. As soon as they could travel Taillefer established them
in his own village as Madame Aubin and her children.

Taillefer was not allowed to marry until he had completed his military
service but he was true to his word and returned to Medora in July 1848
still eager to marry her. After a slight delay in getting the correct papers
the civil ceremony took place on 23 August 1848 with the religious
marriage on the following day, celebrated with dancing, drinking and
feasting until midnight.[58]

Madame Aubin, as she was still called, often helped her illiterate
neighbours with writing or reading letters. She acquired a piano and was
often heard singing to herself. She began to sneak out hints of her past
but she was well liked and Taillefer loved her and both the children. Her
pleasant life was disturbed a few days before her first wedding anniversary
when she woke feeling very ill. She suffered chills and fevers, thirst,
nausea, headaches and dreadful pains in her back. She endured all this
until on the third day she broke out into a rash which covered her entire
body. It was smallpox. On her wedding anniversary, fearing death,
Medora wrote to Sir John Hughes instructing him to ensure that all her
possessions should pass to her husband, including the Deed of
Appointment and the box containing her papers which he held. She
magnanimously forgave her mother and signed the document. She

lingered for another six days before a coma and death claimed her at four in the afternoon of 29 August 1849.[59]

Hughes was puzzled as to why Medora had signed her will with her maiden name, he was unable to read the names of the other witnesses and did not submit the will for probate. Three years later Colonel G. de Waroquier formerly of the 8th Hussars, Taillefer's former regiment, unsuccessfuly took up the case, but it was not until May 1863 that Hughes opened the strong-box in the presence of Monsieur Roux from the French Embassy. Roux declared that he was satisfied there was evidence to suggest that Medora was Byron's child. However, Hughes, following the English custom of burning immoral papers, cast all the documents into the fire with the exception of two letters, the one he had written to Trevanion asking for financial help for Medora and Trevanion's reply, neither of which proved or disproved Medora's case.

CHAPTER EIGHT

Ada

After attending a lecture on the Analytical Engine given by Babbage in Turin in 1840, Luigi Federigo Menabrea, a young military engineer, wrote a description of the engine attempting to explain how it would work. This was submitted to the *Bibliothèque Universelle de Genève* and was published in October 1842. Ada translated it and gave it to Babbage as a present and was highly flattered when he expressed surprise that she had not written a similar paper herself. He suggested that she should add her own notes to her translation and have them published together. She set to work enthusiastically supplying notes to material Babbage produced. Her knowledge of the machine was so extensive that she was able to pick out and correct a mathematical error. Ada hoped that her notes would influence the government and scientists by showing them the potential value of the revolutionary machine. She also hoped to stimulate funds for research and gain public recognition for her friend. Both Lovelaces were anxious that the machine should succeed, but they feared that Babbage's fertile imagination would drive him on to a new invention before the machine was complete.

Babbage was so impressed with Ada's work that he thought it was sufficiently important to stand on its own. This view was shared by Charles Wheatstone, a Fellow of the Royal Society and inventor of the 'electric telegraph'. Ada's work was published in August 1843 and achieved posthumous fame in 1979 when Commander John D. Cooper of the U.S. Naval Materiel suggested that the United States Department of Defense call their newly developed computer language 'Ada', as many people regarded her as the first computer programmer.[1]

When Ada left Medora and her mother in Paris in May 1842 she had hoped to be able to devote herself to her scientific studies and in August William had taken her and the children to the peace of Ashley Combe. However, she was troubled by bad health and although they enjoyed a visit from Babbage, it was clear she was in no condition for concentrated study. Moreover, as she had feared, he turned his attention from the Analytical Machine to other projects. During the next two years Ada loyally supported her mother in her troubles with Medora but still found time to translate Menabrea's paper.

Not long after their return from Paris the Lovelaces attended a dinner given by Lord Zetland. Among the guests was Byron's old friend Hobhouse and during the evening Ada was pointed out to him. 'I went up to her, and introduced myself, and had a very singular conversation with her during which she told me more than once that she "did not like me." However she ended by saying that she should be glad to see me any day between one and two in the afternoon.' She asked him if he thought she looked like her father. Hobhouse told her, 'I did think the lower part of her face like'. He recalled, she said she lived very little in the world, and certainly her manners and her talk are not those of a woman of the world. 'Not that they are free from affectation, nor simple – quite the contrary. However, I saw her at a disadvantage. I ventured to tell her what I know to be true – that I was the best friend her father ever had.'[2] Ada knew Hobhouse was the leader of the 'Piccadilly Crew' and therefore anathema to her mother, but it did not stop her taking and reading a pamphlet written by Hobhouse in an attempt to persuade the Dean and Chapter of Westminster Abbey to allow Thorwaldsen's statue of Byron in Poet's Corner.

'I had a party to dine with me,' Hobhouse noted in May 1845, 'amongst whom were Lord and Lady Lovelace. Lady Lovelace, though rather fantastic, was amiable and interesting in manner, as several of my guests observed. She certainly reminded me much of her father's expression, especially the upper part of her face.' The likeness must have been more obvious when Ada was animated since earlier he had thought it was the lower half of her face which reminded him most strongly of his friend. On another occasion he thought she looked 'ill and thoughtful, and with a sort of constrained manner, far from pleasant. She weighs her words and speaks deliberately, as if repeating.' On 3 June 1846 Hobhouse sat next to her at dinner. 'Poor thing!' he wrote. 'She is looking very ill indeed, and from what she told me I should fear the worst consequences.' He continued, 'Lady Lovelace and her husband seem much attached to each other but I fear their happiness, if happy they are will soon be at an end.'[3]

Ada had been bothered for several years by attacks of indigestion and gastritis which had been treated by their family physician, Dr Locock. He prescribed copious bleeding and laudanum. In Ada's case the drug produced delusions of grandeur, destroying her sense of perspective and causing her to believe she was a genius deserving of tribute. She enthusiastically took up poetry, the theatre and singing and pursued them with the same fervour she had shown in learning to play the violin and harp. She developed a passionate affection for her father's memory and told Francis Trench that, 'I play as much (on the harp) perhaps more than ever, and I really do get on gloriously. I believe no creature ever could will things like a Byron. And perhaps that is at the bottom of the genius-like tendencies in my family. We can throw our *whole life and existence* for the time being into whatever we *will* to do and accomplish.'[4] She was as involved with her singing as with the harp and sang for several hours each day, claiming the exercise to be good for her health, expanding her lungs and easing her asthma. Lady Byron and Lovelace were alarmed at such excesses and tried to lead her back to the study of mathematics, but she persisted in singing. She was basically unhappy and felt thwarted in her ambitions and hemmed in by her family.

William had not been a great help to her, spending most of his time landscaping the garden at Ashley Combe. He was a self-taught architect and although he spent lavishly building towers and digging tunnels to protect the servants in bad weather, he refused to have a bathroom fitted at Ockham despite Dr Locock's recommendation that it would be good for Ada to take hot baths. Ada longed to be the centre of William's attention but could not compete with his mania for architecture, eventually drifting into a pleasant flirtation with Frederick Knight, a near neighbour and publisher. When well-meaning friends warned her that she was being indiscreet she made a point of riding more frequently with Knight. She had also captivated Dr James Phillip Kay, who had been introduced to her by her mother.[5] Like Lady Byron who had always blamed Harrow for Byron's idiosyncrasies, he was an opponent of public schools. Phillip Kay took Ada to the opera and was on the brink of falling in love, telling Lady Byron when he eventually decided to marry, that he felt the friendship he had with Ada would have to end.[6] Ada's relationship with Babbage remained close and playful.

Lady Byron felt the time was right to appoint a tutor for her grandchildren and it was while she was suffering a period of ill health at Clifton that she met Dr William Benjamin Carpenter. He seemed the ideal choice to teach the children. He was thirty years old, a Unitarian, a published author of physiology and a kind but completely humourless man. She suggested to Lovelace that he hire Carpenter and he agreed, as he usually did to anything that Lady Byron proposed, and informed Carpenter that he would be considered as a tutor for a trial period of one year. Carpenter was discontented with the offer and made an appointment to see Ada alone after dinner one evening to discuss the terms of his employment. Ada was suffering from one of her periodic bout of digestive illness and could eat only small amounts of food but she was drinking, on her doctor's orders, considerable amounts of claret as well as taking laudanum to ease the pain. When Carpenter called at eight o'clock she was both tipsy and drugged. He must have been most surprised at the turn of the conversation. Ada confided that not only did she dislike her children's company but she was growing apart from William. Her flirtatious manner led Dr Carpenter to believe he was on terms of great familiarity with her. On regaining her senses Ada wrote him a gentle warning letter pointing out that there were 'impassable barriers' beyond which they must not stray.[7] Although Carpenter claimed to be offended, it did not stop him taking the offered position at £400 a year together with a rent-free house. Later Ockham was let to Stephen Lushington, the Lovelaces moved to their new property in Surrey, East Horsley Towers, and Carpenter lost the use of the house. This caused great bitterness and after a period of bickering Carpenter resigned and soon afterwards was observed spreading vicious stories of his unfair treatment at the hands of the Lovelaces to their friends and acquaintances. In December Ada was disturbed by a rumour which originated at Ockham and involved gossip about her rides with Frederick Knight. Ada believed she knew the identity of the rumour-monger and called him a 'traitor'.[8] It seems likely that she was thinking of the discontented Carpenter. Her health continued to deteriorate and after an examination carried out by Locock Ada was found to be in a 'sad state'.[9] He continued to prescribe laudanum which induced fantasies in which Ada created her own universe with comets and planets. She confided to Woronzow Grieg, probably under the influence of the drugs, that she felt nothing for William and saw him only as the person who had given her social position. She took an interest in mesmerism believing it could cure diseases of mind and body, but it could not cure the swelling in her hands nor the weight gains of up to eight pounds a week.

Meanwhile she had become interested in the new scientific approach to electricity and its potentials. Lovelace, who was extremely proud of his wife's achievements, gave a copy of the Menabrea translation to Andrew Crosse, a specialist in that field. Andrew Crosse and his son John were invited to Ashley Combe for a few days in November 1844 and they got on so splendidly that it was agreed that both Lovelaces would accompany them back to their home, Fyne Court, Broomfield, about 20 miles away. When it came time to leave, Lovelace was unable to accompany them but he provided the carriage for the journey. Fyne Court was in chaos when Ada arrived and the disorganized rooms were far too cold for someone as delicate as she was; she concluded that the best thing to do was to return to the warmth of her own home and bring 23-year-old John Crosse with her. Still hoping to make her name in scientific circles she was pleased when Crosse and Wheatstone independently gave her the same advice: she should write scientific treatises in German. Wheatstone added that if she could obtain a reputation for serious work she might be chosen to advise Prince Albert who was known for his progressive thinking. Ada day-dreamed of becoming Prince Albert's scientific adviser and influencing him, in a way no man could, to help the cause of science. Her hopes in this direction suffered a blow when she heard that Queen Victoria was 'selfish' about her husband.[10]

Lady Byron had taken Ralph to live with her at Moore Place and hired a Mr Hertford to tutor him; he was soon followed to Esher by his unwilling sister, Annabella. Ralph was not allowed to go to school, isolated from children of his own age and educated by a string of tutors. His elder brother, Byron, was placed in the hands of Dr King and his wife in Brighton but was soon moved to the care of Lady Byron's land agent in Leicestershire, where he was encouraged to take an interest in agriculture as preparation for running the Lovelace estate. He hated the life and proved to be intractable; in the autumn of 1849 he was packed off into the navy as a midshipman and shipped to Australia.[11]

In September 1848 Lady Byron became genuinely ill and the Lovelaces, believing she was dying, paid formal visits to her death-bed. Miraculously she recovered only to falter again a year later. Ada, as a dutiful daughter, lived at Moore Place and nursed her mother, but for the first time showed signs of rebellion. She longed to return to her own home and she had many things on her mind. Without telling William and with the help of Woronzow Greig, she had borrowed £500 from a banker, Henry Currie. She had been reluctant to ask William for money as she knew he was beggaring himself, indulging his architectural mania by doubling the size of the mansion at East Horsley. She had gradually fallen into debt over the last couple of years but until recently, after Lady Byron's recovery, had every reason to believe she would be able to repay everything she owed after her mother's apparently imminent death. Under the terms of the will William would have become the life tenant of the Wentworth estates and Ada had no reason to believe he would not be generous to her. Eventually she was forced to reveal her debts to William, explaining them away as money she had overspent on books and music. She asked him to raise her income to £500, but he refused, offering to pay only for the elaborate dresses she needed when she was invited to court. This particular piece of meanness enraged her and she told him she was being blackmailed.[12] Within two weeks he sent her £100.

In 1850 young Annabella came back from her grandmother to live with her parents again, but no inducement would persuade Lady Byron to return Ralph and he remained in her care until she died. The Lovelaces could not afford to fall out with Lady Byron because she had bought the lease of their new house at 6 Great Cumberland Place and had allowed William to borrow money from her at a low interest for repairs and furniture. In return she had the run of the house and Lovelace had to insure his life to the value of the loan. They had moved out of the house in St James's Square in 1846[13] and since then had been forced to hire temporary furnished rooms near Hyde Park for the London season.

Ada enjoyed good health during the spring and summer of 1850. She took a great interest in horse racing and supported two horses in the Derby, *Voltigeur*, owned by Lord Zetland, and *Bolingbroke* owned by Lady Albemarle. On 10 June the Lovelaces gave a large party, inviting a mixture of fashionable and scientific friends, but Ada's happiness was clouded a few days later when Grieg reported that the old rumours about her flirtations were flying around again. This time the names quoted included John Crosse as well as Carpenter, Knight and Phillip Kay. She brushed them aside and on 21 June attended a Drawing Room and the opera. At a ball the following day Queen Victoria honoured them with one of her rare smiles and invited them to another ball in July.[14] The highlight of the year was still to come, the tour they had planned to visit friends ending with a day at the races at Doncaster to see *Voltigeur* run in the St Leger.

The Lovelaces left London on 22 August after Ada had made a flying visit to Moore Place to say goodbye to her mother, who generously gave her £30 travelling money. They halted first at Knebworth in Hertfordshire to see Bulwer Lytton, then moved on to see George Byron at Thrumpton in Nottinghamshire, and the Nightingales (Lady Byron was a friend of Mrs Faunce de Laune, sister to the more famous Florence) in Derbyshire. They were pleased to see the Reverend Samuel Gamlen, Rector of Bossal, Yorkshire, who had married them fifteen years before and the Zetlands at Aske. The tour was crowned by a short visit to the Cumberland lakes and across country for a day or two at Newstead Abbey.

Ada had enjoyed herself enormously until, walking in the Zetlands' garden, she suffered a sudden attack of palpitations. Lady Zetland's doctor, Mr Malcome, thought it had been brought on as the result of over-excitement and Ada was soon back on her feet. It was evening when they arrived at Newstead on 7 September. They ate that night in the Great Hall and slept in rooms over the cloister. The following day Ada wrote a careful letter to Lady Byron, not wanting to disturb too many ghosts. They explored the grounds, admired the lake, its depth and coldness and walked in the woods. They were entertained at Annesley by Mary Chaworth's daughter; her mother, Byron's 'Morning Star', had died in 1833. Ada left no record of her feelings as she stood in Hucknall church so close to the remains of her father, but he was greatly in her mind and she resolved to return. Her first impression of Newstead had been melancholy, but when the time came to depart she felt at home and regretted leaving, telling her mother that she must go back before the year was over. She praised Colonel Wildman for the way he had restored the abbey and cherished Byron's memory. On 11 September the Lovelaces slept at Bolsover Castle having spent the day seeing the beauties of Derbyshire, Castleton, the Peak Cavern, the Old Castle (Peverils) and Haddon Hall.

Ada's careful letter about Newstead and her father produced a tirade from her mother in which she suggested the children would be better off if they did not associate with her if they were to be allowed to believe the notion that their grandmother had abandoned Byron with cold and unforgiving feelings.[15] Ada's innocent comments had touched a raw nerve and Lady Byron could not bear the thought that people had said favourable things about Byron. Ada now knew from Hobhouse that the picture her mother had drawn was not accurate and from Colonel Wildman, a school friend and one of the last people to see Byron before he left England, she learned about his schooldays. Living in her father's house and seeing his bedroom left as if 'he might have walked in' and meeting servants who had known him gave her a completely new picture of Byron.

Lovelace continued on his sightseeing tour while Ada joined the Zetlands. He made his way slowly from Lincoln to Doncaster in time to join the Zetland party on the last day of the race meeting and see the Zetlands' horse *Flying Dutchman* beaten by *Voltigeur* in the Doncaster Cup. Ada described the race as 'like single combat between two heroes'.[16] Lovelace thought the spectacle of the race course magnificent but he was distressed to lose £3 or £4 to a pickpocket as he escorted Lady Zetland round the course. Ada enjoyed herself so much and became so enthusiastic that she tried to interest Lovelace in breeding race horses.

The excitement of the course, the powerful sound of the thudding hooves, the jockeys' brilliant silks, the fever of betting all lured Ada to believe that with her amazing ability with figures, she could beat the system. She hazarded more money than was sensible. In January 1851 she arranged to meet Malcolm, an agent she had used for making bets, promising him that she would explain how she intended to make £3,000. She invited Nightingale, Richard Ford and Fleming, all racing gentlemen, to dinner and dazzled them with her enthusiasm and science to the extent that they really believed she could work out a system to improve their chances at the race course.[17]

There are no notes to suggest how she hoped her system would work but in 1820 Babbage had written *An Examination of some Questions connected with Games of Chance* in which he described in algebraic terms the formulae for placing stakes in a system. The book was intended to amuse and not even Lady Byron ever accused Babbage of contributing to the causes of Ada's downfall. Babbage's only sins in her eyes were in keeping Ada's secrets and occasionally placing bets for her. He had also introduced Ada to her new lady's maid, Mary Wilson, who had formerly worked in his household. Mary became Ada's confidante and placed bets for her under the name of Wilson.

The Lovelaces went to the races at York in May 1851 and attended the Royal Society dinner with Sir David Brewster, Dr Locock, Wheatstone, Babbage and Quêtel, the Belgian statistician and astronomer. On 18 May Ada introduced Sir David Brewster, the Scottish physicist, to her mother who urged her to begin another scientific project and suggested the mesmerist works of Mr Rutter and Dr Léger. Lady Byron had been interested in this branch of science for some time and took part in experiments which were held in her hotel rooms in Dover Street.[18]

On 19 May the Lovelaces together with the Zetlands and two thousand other guests attended the Gala Ball given by Queen Victoria at Buckingham Palace to celebrate Prince Albert's achievement, the Great Exhibition. Dinner was served at midnight and the dancing went on till dawn. Ada's scientific friends were delighted with the exhibition and Ada was proud of William, who had won an award for his brick-making.

Things turned black for Ada on Derby Day, 21 May, when she heard that she had lost £3,200. A meeting was called between the members of the betting syndicate, Ada, Ford, Fleming, Crosse and Malcolm. Ada paid off Malcolm for the bets he had placed on her behalf. He in his turn borrowed £1,800 from Lovelace to cover his own losses. Ada still owed Ford £600 but it was not until after her death that the full extent of her debts was revealed.

To add to her misery Ada had not felt comfortable on her horse for some time and even walking had become painful. Shortly after the Derby she suddenly suffered several severe haemorrhages and a Dr Lee was consulted; he made his diagnosis based on a description of her symptoms but on those alone he told William that he believed Ada had cancer. A fashionable doctor, Sir James Clark, was called in for a second opinion. He had a long list of buried mistakes; he had diagnosed the dying Keats as having stomach trouble and the virginal Lady Flora Hastings of being pregnant. Keats died within months of consumption and Lady Flora died, a disgraced woman, of an abdominal tumour. However, Clark was well known for his bedside manner and the care he took in disguising the taste of unpalatable medicine. On this occasion he authorized a full examination by Dr Locock which resulted in a diagnosis of advanced cancer of the cervix and uterus; Locock believed the condition could be cured with the right treatment.[19]

Lovelace was downcast but felt it was kinder not to tell Ada; however, he was sure he must tell Lady Byron and immediately went to Leamington where she was taking treatment. He arrived just as she was about to go to bed, which she found annoying. She listened to him, coldly belittling Locock's report, but was roused to anger on hearing of Ada's gambling debts.[20] She spoke bitterly to him and on 1 July she filed a statement with Lushington outlining her reasons for quarrelling with her dutiful son-in-law, who had always deferred to her wishes. She began by accusing Lovelace of deserting Ada, leaving her exposed to unprincipled and low people, of allowing her to go to Doncaster alone knowing she was overconfident in her powers on the race course. She was also furious with Ada because she had not told her the full extent of her debts. Annabella made her hostility towards William very clear but Ada took William's part and although she continued to write to her mother the letters became strained. Lady Byron claimed he had alienated Ada's affections.

When Annabella fell out with anyone it was forever as she found it impossible to apologize without admitting being in the wrong. Her treatment of Byron and Augusta should have been a warning to Lovelace but he was taken by surprise and distressed at her reaction. He had not been on good terms with his own mother for many years and Lady Byron had taken her place. His overtures of friendship were firmly rejected and when she found out that he had given Ada a letter authorizing her betting at the Derby she felt justified in despising him for the rest of her life. She no longer needed Lovelace's devotion but he found her rejection and coldness painful.

Lovelace's place in Lady Byron's affections was taken by the Reverend Frederick Robertson of Trinity Chapel, Brighton. He was a popular preacher and she found it easy to confide in him, revealing the most intimate details of her married life. It was with Robertson that in April 1851 Annabella made one last attempt to humiliate Augusta. George Leigh had died in May the previous year taking with him his yearly pension of £300, leaving the small sum of £700 a year to provide for his large family. The following January Augusta became ill and poverty drove Emily to write to Lushington asking him to appeal to her godmother for help. After gloating over Augusta's circumstances with George Byron's wife, Lady Byron agreed to meet Augusta. She did not intend to help her financially but to wring the confession from her that she had deliberately connived to prevent a reconciliation between Byron and herself.

Robertson began his account of the last meeting between the two old antagonists: 'On a certain Tuesday morning, of April, 1851, an aged lady, having the appearance of an extreme invalid came to the London Bridge Station, and seated herself in a first-class carriage of the next train for Reigate.' Annabella had arranged for Augusta to be met at the station and to be taken to the White Hart Hotel where she had reserved two private sitting rooms where she and Robertson waited. On Augusta's arrival 'Lady Byron directly charged Mrs Leigh with aggravating Byron's bitterness to her, and encouraging him to remain in enmity towards her. Mrs Leigh repelled the accusation warmly, and in support of her assertions that she had consistently and invariably done her best to be a peace-maker, quoted certain words spoken by Hobhouse – words which agitated Lady Byron profoundly, causing her to start and change colour.'[21] Hobhouse had told Augusta that 'You not only risked the loss of property, but what was much dearer to you, his affection.' Enraged at her failure, 'Lady Byron returned to Brighton with a determination never again to see or hold communication with her sister-in-law. And Mrs Leigh went back to London in grief at Lady Byron's perplexing treatment of her.'

It seems Lady Byron had not read William Parry's 1825 account of Byron's last days in Greece in which he records Byron's hopes of returning home to his family, nor Lady Blessington's 'Conversations of Lord Byron' in which she says 'I do not recollect ever having met Byron that he did not, in some way or another, introduce the subject of Lady Byron. The impression left on my mind was, that she continually occupied his thoughts, and that he most anxiously desired a reconciliation with her.' He explained that

had his pecuniary affairs been in a less ruinous state, his temper would not have been excited, as it daily, hourly was, during the brief period of their union, but the demands of insolent creditors whom he was unable to satisfy, and who drove him nearly out of his senses, until he lost all command of himself, and so forfeited Lady Byron's affection. 'I must admit,' said he, 'that I could not have left a very agreeable impression on her mind. With my irascible temper, worked upon by the constant attack of duns, no wonder that I became gloomy, violent, and I fear, personally uncivil, if not worse and so disgusted her, though, had she really loved me, she would have borne with my infirmities and made allowance for my provocations.'[22]

The meeting between the two old ladies had been strained. Lady Byron tensing every nerve to extract a confession from Augusta that she had stood in the way of a reconciliation and Augusta trying to hide her emotions towards Annabella. She had described them to Hodgson once before:

> I am always afraid of the impetuosity of my feelings on such occasions (of which I am fully aware) making me uncharitable. God forgive her if she had made me what I never was before, or believed I could be; but I will not dwell on my own feelings; you can guess them. If it was not my own dear brother whom it concerned, I do think I should still feel disgusted at such unfeeling conduct. . . . I have always thought that there was nothing in the whole world but the welfare of one's children which could induce one to leave one's husband.[23]

Augusta was frustrated and disappointed that Annabella, who had been her closest friend and who had shared the darkest secrets of her marriage, could now remain so cold and forbidding when she was close to death. She wrote to Robertson asking if she could show him proof that she was telling the truth. He replied,

> I regret to say that I feel it impossible to accede to the proposal which you have made. . . . The proofs which you desire to give me could only be given in Lady Byron's presence, and she will never consent to another meeting. The last was final. . . . If your own conscience is free and clear, and Lady Byron is in no way injured by you, the sense of innocence in God's sight will make the opinion of any human being a matter of small importance. If on the contrary, there was anything for the sorrowful acknowledgement of which that meeting was the last and final opportunity which you can ever have in this world, then, of course, no opinion of Sir John Hobhouse, written or expressed, nor of Lord Byron himself, can reverse the solemn judgement upon the whole matter which must be heard very, very soon, when you meet God face to face. P.S. I ought, perhaps, to add that I did not transmit your letter to Lady Byron and therefore return it. She is resolved that the communication was ended with the last letter she wrote; and, indeed the result of that interview had been a dangerous illness.[24]

Augusta's heart disease worsened and by June she knew she was dying. She was nursed by Emily as she could not afford a professional nurse and Lady Chichester regularly brought the invalid food. Driven by the desperation of grinding poverty Emily sold a box of Byron's letters to John Murray, but it was not enough and on 22 August one of the Leigh sons appeared on Ada's doorstep offering to sell her a rifle and pair of pistols which he said had once belonged to Byron. He told her he was in great distress and having to sell everything he had. Ada placed the matter into Babbage's hands.

Quite suddenly Lady Byron had an uncharacteristic change of heart and asked Emily if there was anything she could do to add to Augusta's comfort. Emily politely refused her help, but two weeks later she admitted there was a debt so urgent she could not keep it from her mother any longer. Lady Byron paid it and began to ask for news regularly, on one occasion calling and asking a servant how Augusta was. In early October the urge to send one last message to 'Dearest Guss' was overwhelming. She asked Emily to whisper 'two words of affection long disused' into the dying woman's ear. On hearing the message, 'Dearest Augusta!' she wept. Augusta died on 12 October aged sixty-seven 'with her hands in those of her youngest daughter Emily who, she said, had always been such a comfort to her'.[25]

The miserable year of illnesses continued. Ada was suffering and weak; to fight the pain she took ten drops of laudanum every four hours and her need for medical attention had grown so great that she was unable to leave Great Cumberland Place. Despite the pain-killing drug she still found it almost impossible to walk and spent most of her days either on the sofa or in her new wheelchair. William was frequently in Surrey performing his duties as Lord Lieutenant of the county and young Annabella stood in for her mother at many of the formal functions.

Lovelace's finances were going from bad to worse and to add to his worries Lady Byron had reneged on the payment of a note he had signed to cover the repairs he was completing on the house. However, she had instructed Lushington to pay off all Ada's debts on condition that she was supplied with a complete list of everything Ada owed. In March 1852 Lushington reported that he had paid the pressing demands but expected more to come. Ada dreaded having to justify her debts to her mother, but the evil day was postponed as Lady Byron was still in Brighton indulging in an illness of her own.

Ada's condition deteriorated to the degree that she needed professional nursing day and night and in April, when she could no longer climb the stairs, two ground-floor rooms were prepared for her. The increasingly intense pain was relieved by opium but her scientific mind was still curious and she developed an interest in cannabis and its effect on pain. She closely questioned Sir Gardener Wilkinson, a family friend and expert on the subject.[26] Her appearance was skeleton-like and shocked Lushington but Locock said he still had hope she would recover; Lushington doubted him.

Mother and daughter met again in May 1852 soon after Lady Byron had paid many of Ada's debts. She had made it her business to find out a great deal about Ada's affairs but said nothing, playing a cat and mouse game, waiting for Ada to confess of her own accord, insisting such an action would purify her soul and release her from the burden of remorse. Lady Byron also banished the painkilling drugs from the sickroom and demanded that Ada submit to the care of her recommended mesmerists, Mrs Cooper and Mr Symes. Their treatment against rampant cancer was unsuccessful. Throughout the treatment Lady Byron watched her daughter daily racked with pain, telling her that pain was an expression of God's will. On 11 June Lady Byron found out that Ada had secretly authorized a copy of the Lovelace diamonds to be made and pawned the originals for £800 to pay off some of her debts. She immediately arranged for Lushington to redeem them from a silversmith in the Strand. Ada begged her not to tell Lovelace.

In July Ada developed a new hard swelling and Dr Locock called in a colleague, Dr West, who gave Ada a full examination on 28 July. He found the cancer so advanced that he was forced to tell the anxious family to expect her to die within a couple of months. The intense pain would not allow Ada to sleep through the night and bouts of nausea were preventing her from eating. Dr Locock gave her strong camphor pills to quell the sickness and Dr West prescribed morphine.[27]

Lovelace returned from Surrey on hearing the sad news. In his sorrow he seemed unable to leave Ada's side but his constant presence and concern wearied her. She told her mother that each time she sent him away he returned to her side like a dog to his master.[28] She was not a naturally cruel person but she was frightened that her mother might tell William about the pawning of his family jewels and hoped to keep the secret safe by humouring her, even if it meant mocking and belittling her husband. The tension in the house was dreadful as Lady Byron now not only blamed William for Ada's indiscretions but for keeping them apart. Ada tried to live as normal a life as possible and sat for her portrait by Henry Phillips, the son of Thomas who had painted the two most popular pictures of her father, but not even his artistic skill could disguise the fact that his sitter was close to death. He portrayed her seated at the piano, her claw-like hands spread over the keys.

On 3 August John Crosse visited her in the evening for an hour. During that time she managed to pass him the Lovelace diamonds and the next day he returned them to Vaughans, the pawnbrokers in the Strand, receiving the same terms as before. There they remained until October when Ada confessed what she had done and Lady Byron sent Grieg to redeem them for the second time and placed them in her own bank.

Ada and Crosse had a lot to hide, for as well as conducting a playful flirtation with him, he had pawned the diamonds – twice. He possessed packets of her imprudent letters which, after her death, Lady Byron redeemed for £600 and had burned. He also held Lovelace's note which had allowed Ada to place the bets at the Derby which had ruined them. Lovelace also discovered that despite passing himself off as a bachelor, Crosse had a wife and children in Reigate.

Dr West prepared a full prognosis on Ada's condition for Woronzow Grieg. He confirmed she had cancer, adding that the first signs should have been noticed some eighteen months to three years before. He outlined in dreadful detail the course the disease was taking, explaining that the whole of Ada's slim body would be invaded by the growth, causing enormous pain. He ended by saying that in cases like this it was the duty of the physician not to hope for recovery but for euthanasia.

Ada knew time was running out and she still wanted to clear her debts and ensure her secrets would be kept after her death. On 12 August she pressed a letter into Babbage's hand. It was a request that should she die he would become her executor.[29] She was frantically trying to cover her tracks. Babbage, for legal reasons, asked her for more precise instructions, but all she did was assure him that her mother and husband would comply with her last wishes.

On 14 August Ada asked Lovelace to write to Colonel Wildman at Newstead to see if it would be possible to be buried next to her father. Ada was determined that the world should know it was her choice to be placed by Byron's side and not a noble whim of her mother's. Lovelace promised that the inscription would make that point clearly. Lady Byron defiantly told Mrs Villiers that although Ada would rest with her father, her love would remain with her mother.[30]

On 18 August Ada wrote a farewell note to Mary Wilson asking her to keep the house quiet and comfortable during the few weeks she had left of life. The following day Charles Dickens accepted her longstanding invitation. They talked about *Dombey and Son* and at her request he read to her the description of young Paul Dombey's peaceful death. He left impressed by the calmness and courage with which she was facing her bleak future. He was to be the last person other than her family that Ada ever saw. On 20 August Lady Byron moved into Great Cumberland Place and dismissed all her daughter's servants.

Ada's eldest son, Byron, now using his courtesy title of Ockham, returned from sea and together with his sister, Annabella, helped to care for their mother. Ada yearned to have all her children near her and sent for Ralph, who was in Switzerland. One day while young Annabella and Ockham were sponging her face Ada fell into a reverie and the splashing of the water in the basin brought back memories of the happy days she had spent with Lovelace at the lakes the year before. It was a cruel shock to return to reality and she was immediately plunged into despair. The cancer's exquisite torture gave her no rest day or night and it became almost impossible for her to find a comfortable position; she was driven to throw herself frantically round the room, its floor now covered with thick mattresses. She was seized by sudden fears and hallucinations – frightened to die in case she was buried alive and believing someone was lurking outside who intended to harm her. It seemed to her doctors that the desire to see Ralph was the only thing that was keeping her alive. Ockham tenderly bathed her face and she sipped port with a beaten egg but nothing, not even morphine, could rid her of pain now. On 26 August Ralph arrived and Ada was happy. In an attempt to amuse her, Mrs Sartoris, formerly Adelaide Kemble, came to sing. As she stood in the hallway she was horrified to see round the door, which was left ajar, Ada crouching on all fours on the mattresses. It was the only position left that she could bear.[31]

On the night of 30 August Ada had a fit, her pulse dropped but her heart continued to beat. To the surprise of the onlookers she gradually recovered consciousness. When Lovelace came in she put her arms around his neck and kissed him, placing one hand in that of her mother and the other in that of her husband and asked them to pray to God to have mercy on her. Lady Byron had forbidden Babbage or Crosse to enter the house, but she brought in the Reverend Robertson and Dr King who tried to prepare the dying woman for death and hope of heaven. Under the stress of their religious exhortations, morphine and pain Ada told her mother that she had committed other sins apart from gambling. Lady Byron insisted she tell Lovelace herself and prepared him for a momentous announcement by saying Ada had something to tell him which he must hear calmly. Afterwards Lovelace left Ada's room with tears in his eyes refusing to discuss what she had said.[32] Lady Byron claimed that she confessed to him that she had committed adultery with Crosse. Ada had not been entirely lucid since her fit two days before and just as Lady Byron had accepted her husband's drunken ravings as truth so she treated her drugged and dying daughter's confessions.

Ockham, who had been staying with Sir Gardener and Lady Wilkinson for a few days, returned to London to say goodbye to his mother before being forced back to sea. Lady Byron was touched by the expression of deep distress on his face as he saw his emaciated mother through the half-open door. He left the house, put his midshipman's uniform in a carpet bag, sent it to his father and ran away to Bristol. He was found in Liverpool a week or so later after failing to be taken on as an able seaman. When he was questioned by the police he gave a false name but eventually agreed to return to London. Lovelace would not allow him to stay with his dying mother and arranged for him to be returned to sea.[33] As she sat next to her daughter, waiting for the end which could only bring freedom to Ada and relief to her friends, Lady Byron was coldly polite to Lovelace showing him no understanding or sympathy. Lovelace had been a loving husband, if a little severe at times, and Ada had lived in fear that she might somehow lose his love. Perhaps she was haunted by her adolescent involvement with her tutor or believed her mother's friends when they said that she must make herself worthy of him; but he was devoted to her and wrote affectionately and regularly whenever he left her, if only for a few days. Lady Byron watched her daughter fight her way to death, annoyed that Ada called only for relief from pain, finally telling the dying woman that she should put her trust in God as her support. Alone in the room next to Ada's, listening for the strained breathing to cease she wrote, 'I write in the hearing of her groans, and of the little Bull-finch singing carelessly his wonted airs. In the next room one whose feelings are far from being in harmony with mine. . . .'[34]

The end came quietly just before ten on the evening of 27 November 1852. Lady Byron immediately moved out of her son-in-law's house and into a hotel in Dover Street.

Lovelace wrote a few weeks later asking for mutual sympathy, affection and reconciliation. Lady Byron replied in her familiar way, asking for a confession of guilt. There followed a short period in which snappish letters passed between the two until Lady Byron ended the correspondence, saying she was ill. Lovelace wrote, 'I hold you in respect and admiration more than ever – but your want of sympathy (in spite of all your gentleness) with those who do not feel exactly as you do, has cruelly destroyed what certainty, hope and comfort remained to me.'[35]

On 3 December Lovelace accompanied Ada to the vault at Hucknall Torkard church and ensured that her violet velvet-covered coffin was lowered into the tomb next to and touching that of her father. The tablet reads: 'In the Byron vault below lie the remains of AUGUSTA ADA, only daughter of George Gordon Noel, 6th Lord Byron and the wife of William, Earl of Lovelace, Born 10th Dec. 1815, died 27 Nov. 1852 R.I.P.' It was as though Lady Byron had never existed.

Byron's prophecy of 1817 had come true.

> Yet, though dull Hate as duty should be
>   taught,
> I know that thou wilt love me; though
>   my name
> Should be shut from thee, as a spell still
>   fraught

With desolation, and a broken claim:
Though the grave closed between us, –
　　'twere the same,
I know that thou wilt love me; though
　　to drain
My blood from out thy being were an
　　aim,
And an attainment, – all would be in
　　vain, –
Still thou wouldst love me, still that more
　　than life retain.

However, the following year Lady Byron erected a memorial in the church at Kirkby Mallory on which was written: 'Inscribed by the express direction of Ada Augusta Lovelace. Born Dec. 10th 1816 died Nov. 17th 1852. To recall her memory. Erected by her mother A.I. Noel Byron. MDCCCLIII'.

Within two days of the harrowing scenes in Great Cumberland Place the Reverend Robertson told Crabb Robinson, the diarist and friend, that Lady Byron was 'the noblest woman he ever knew'. She had intended Robertson to be her literary executor and passed him a mass of documents which she believed would lay the blame of the separation at Byron's feet. During her sessions of soul-baring and confession she had spoken of Byron in such a way that Robertson wrote, 'Lord Byron made her a bad husband, he was a bad man, and under any circumstances would have made a bad husband to any woman doomed to intrust her wifely happiness to him. So abnormally evil was his conduct that the wife soon had reason to suspect that her husband was mad.'[36] Robertson died of consumption in 1853 before he could begin work. The papers were 'handed over to another clergyman, [the Reverend Alexander Ross] who was then the minister of the Presbyterian Hanover Place Chapel', wrote the Reverend Frederick Arnold in 1886, continuing, 'It is remarkable although many years have elapsed, and the interest of the papers continues unabated, that this gentleman has not seen his way to make any literary use of them.'[37]

Five months after Ada's death Lady Byron had met Mrs Harriet Beecher Stowe. They had much in common, as one of Lady Byron's interests was the anti-slavery campaign in the United States and she had, in fact, sponsored two runaway slaves. When Mrs Stowe returned to England three years later Lady Byron invited her to spend the day with her at her house at Ham Common near Richmond, saying she wanted to have a private and confidential conversation on important subjects. She

56 Lady Noel Byron in 1832 aged about forty.

57 Ada at about twenty-seven, from a sketch by A.E. Chalon.

58 Medora Leigh, from a daguerrotype taken on 19 July 1842 and intended as a parting present to Lady Noel Byron.

59 Ada, from a daguerrotype taken in 1850, the year of her visit to Newstead Abbey.

60 Byron in Albanian dress, painted at the height of his popularity in March 1814 and hidden from his daughter until after her marriage.

61 Lady Noel Byron, from a daguerrotype taken in the 1840s.

62 Lady Noel Byron. Her cousin Robert Noel wrote: 'her views relating to the characters of others . . . always impressed me as if they had been spoken by an oracle'.

63 The grandstand at Epsom. On Derby Day 1851 Ada lost £3,200.

64 Voltigeur (left), the Zetland's horse, was beaten in the Doncaster Cup in 1850 by the Flying Dutchman (right), after a race which Ada described as 'single combat between two horses'.

65 A ball given by Queen Victoria at Buckingham Palace.

66 Ada, from a portrait painted by Henry Phillips five months before she died.

67 Byron, Viscount Ockham, aged thirteen, from a daguerrotype. He is wearing his midshipman's uniform.

68 Hannah Burgess, daughter of William Marshall.

69 'His complexion was transparent, his teeth like pearls; his hair curling; his nails roseate as the shells of the ocean.' . . . 'Mon dieu qu'il était beau!'

hoped that Mrs Stowe, as a foreigner, would hold an unbiased view on the proposed publication of a new, cheap, popular edition of Byron's work which would include a brief description of his life. Lady Byron said she was concerned about the harmful effect this might have on public morals. She told the successful authoress that her friends had asked '*whether she had not a responsibility to society for the truth*; whether *she did right* to allow these writings to gain influence over the popular mind, by giving a silent consent to what she knew to be utter falsehoods'.[38]

When Mrs Stowe arrived at Ham Common she found Lady Byron up and fortunately experiencing one of her '*well*' days since 'She suffered from ossifications of the lungs, from which she might die at any moment.' She described her hostess as slim with 'silvery-white hair on which she wore a plain widow's cap'. After lunch Mrs Stowe plunged straight in by asking if Byron was guilty of incest with Augusta. 'He was guilty of incest with his sister,' Lady Byron replied, turning so pale that Mrs Stowe thought she was about to faint. After a few more questions Lady Byron said, 'I will tell you.' She described how at first she had been stirred by Byron's poetry, feeling a 'deep interest in him personally, as one that had the germs of all that is glorious and noble', and how, when he saw her, she 'perceived his admiration of herself'. Although she was deeply moved by his first offer of marriage she had refused as 'she doubted her own power to be to him all that a wife should be', but she continued to be his friend and kept up a correspondence on moral and literary subjects.

'At last,' she said, 'he sent a very beautiful letter offering himself again. I thought that it was sincere, and that I might now show him all I felt. I wrote what was in my heart. Afterwards I found in one of his journals this notice of my letter "A letter from Bell, – never rains but it pours."'

'And did he not love you then?' Mrs Stowe asked.

'No, my dear, he did not love me.'

'Why then did he wish to marry you?' Lady Byron placed her hand on her new friend's and said in a low voice, 'You will see.' She described the scene at Seaham when she offered to break the engagement and Byron fainted. '*Then*,' she paused, 'I was *sure* he must love me.'

'And did he not? What other cause could have led to this emotion?' Lady Byron looked sad, saying, '*Fear of detection.*'

'What,' said Mrs Stowe, 'did *that cause* then exist?'

'Yes. It did.' During a pause in this fascinating conversation Mrs Stowe asked whether Mrs Leigh was a particularly beautiful or attractive woman.

'No, my dear: she was plain.'

'Was she, then, distinguished for genius or talent of any kind?'

'Oh, no! Poor woman! She was weak, relatively to him, and wholly under his control.'

'And what became of her?' asked Mrs Stowe.

'She afterward repented, and became a truly good woman.'

'Was there a child? I have been told by Mrs— that there was a daughter who had lived some years.' Lady Byron agreed there had been one, 'a daughter, who made her friends much trouble, being of a very difficult nature to manage'.[39]

Mrs Stowe described the interview as having 'almost the solemnity of a death-bed avowal'. She left for Paris with her memoranda, dates and an outline of the story promising to return Lady Byron's papers as soon as she had marshalled all the facts and formed an opinion. Lady Byron, 'this delicate creature – so frail in body that she seemed always hovering on the brink of the eternal world, yet so strong in spirit, and so unceasing in her various ministries of mercy',[40] had only to wait two weeks for Mrs Stowe's advice. Her first reaction had been to publish all the details, but on reflection she decided that Lady Byron would be entirely justifed 'in leaving the truth to be disclosed after her death; and recommended that all the facts necessary should be put in the hands of some person, to be published.' 'I trust,' Lady Byron said, 'that the spirit of self-vindication will neither be found in my pages nor imputed to me.'

In 1858 Lady Byron caught a debilitating illness which she was unable to throw off and on the day before her sixty-eighth birthday at about four o'clock in the morning of 16 May 1860 she died in her sleep, attended by her granddaughter Annabella and an old friend, Mrs Barwell. She was buried in Kensal Green Cemetery next to a memorial to Stephen Lushington's sisters.[41]

Ten years later Teresa Guiccioli published anonymously *Lord Byron jugé par les témoins de sa vie* which was translated by Hubert Jerningham and published in England soon after as *My Recollections of Lord Byron*. She had kind words for Augusta but strongly condemned Lady Byron saying that the cause of the separation was her refusal to identify the crime she claimed Byron had committed and her cold, unforgiving nature. Springing to rebut the criticism, Mrs Stowe published her record of the conversation at Ham Common, simultaneously in *Macmillan's Magazine* in England and *Atlantic Monthly* in America. She explained her actions by saying that she had waited to see if an English memoir would be written 'of the person whom she considered the most remarkable woman that England has produced in the century'. When this did not seem forthcoming she was driven to protect Lady Byron and her good name in America and felt 'the public should have this refutation of the slanders of the Countess Guiccioli's book'.

Mrs Stowe was under the mistaken impression that she was one of the few people to whom Lady Byron had spoken, not knowing, as Francis

Trench pointed out in a letter to the *Times*, that there were hardly any relatives or friends of Lady Byron who were not aware of her version of events.[42] Very few people then remembered the stir Thomas Moore's *Life* had caused in 1830 or that Lady Byron had published her *Remarks* in a pamphlet ostensibly to clear her mother's name but by implication blackening Augusta's. It is significant that neither Colonel Leigh nor Lord Lovelace believed her accusations, but the world took sides and even Queen Victoria, well versed in earlier scandals by Lord Melbourne, told the Crown Princess of Prussia that she thought the Byron scandal was too shameful, saying she had not read Mrs Stowe's account as she had a particular horror of scandal and gossip, and she knew it was quite untrue.[43]

Ralph Lovelace, in *Astarte*, written to justify his grandmother, said, 'It may be noted that Mrs Stowe did not claim to have had permission or direction from Lady Byron to make the story public.'[44] However, Mrs Stowe recorded that at the Ham Common interview Lady Byron 'began to speak of her grounds for thinking it might be her duty fully to publish this story before she left the world'.

Lord Macaulay, reviewing Moore's *Life* of Byron in 1830, said,

We know no spectacle so ridiculous as the British Public in one of its periodical fits of morality. In general, elopements, divorces, and family quarrels pass with little notice. We read the scandal, talk about it for a day, and forget it. But once in six or seven years our virtue becomes outrageous. We cannot suffer the laws of religion and decency to be violated. We must make a stand against vice. We must teach libertines that the English people appreciate the importance of domestic ties. Accordingly some unfortunate man, in no respect more depraved than hundreds whose offences have been treated with lenity, is singled out as an expiatory sacrifice.

In 1869 Hubert Jerningham called on Teresa, now nearly seventy years old but with her enthusiasm for Byron unaltered. She analysed for him Byron's attitudes to the women who had influenced him, saying, 'He was not like other men. He loved his mother, he loved Ada, and he loved me – three different loves which he endeavoured to relish, but which, poor dear man, he was never permitted to enjoy. His mother was taken early from him; Ada was not allowed to be near him; and circumstances prevented my being more than his friend.' (Surely said tongue in cheek; even her new husband, the Marquis de Boissey, when asked if his wife had had her name linked with Lord Byron's replied proudly, 'Mais c'est elle-même, c'est elle!') She continued, 'In Ada's way stood Allegra, in mine was Lady Byron; and giant-like rose above all his love for Augusta.'

'How often has he not spoken of her to me! and, much as I loved him, how often was I irritated by his tender affection for his sister! Augusta. C'était un refrain perpétuel.'[45] She added breathlessly, 'Mon Dieu, qu'il était beau!'

Epilogue

Byron had four children by four mothers. Two by servants, one by his wife and another by a girl who today would be called a 'groupie'. He is also credited with a child from an incestuous union with his half-sister and a son by a Spanish beauty from Cadiz.

The fates of his legitimate daughter Ada and his illegitimate daughter Allegra are well known. The unhappy life of his niece and goddaughter, Medora Leigh, has stimulated books and speculation and the evidence is still considered ambiguous, though in 1824 Caroline Lamb told her young lover, Bulwer Lytton, that she had hoped her lies would end Byron's marriage and drive him back to her; Lytton wrote, '. . . of the hideous calumny concerning himself [Lord Byron] and Mrs Leigh (indeed, of all calumnies involving the charge of crime) she certainly acquitted him.'[1]

During the 1840s a man calling himself Major George Gordon Byron arrived in London. He claimed to be Byron's son by the Countess De Luna, the result of a Roman Catholic marriage performed in Cadiz in 1809. Major Byron, or De Gibler, as he sometimes called himself, accused Byron of deliberately seducing the countess with the intention of repudiating the marriage on his return to England and the countess, deserted and deeply ashamed, arranged for her son to be secretly brought up in Switzerland. In 1844 Major Byron launched a campaign of begging letters to Byron's friends. He asked each of them to lend him £900, but when his appeal was ignored he reduced the amount he wished to borrow to £9. Hobhouse told Lady Holland that Byron had not conducted an affair in Cadiz and that Major Byron was an imposter.[2] However, Major Byron was a gifted forger, concocting and publishing letters of his reputed father as *The Unedited Works of Lord Byron* in America until they were revealed as forgeries. He later turned his attention to Keats and Shelley and the standard of his work was high enough to deceive Mary Shelley, who bought many faked letters believing them to have been written by her husband.[3]

Almost nothing is known of the lives of the two children borne by the servants but, if Byron's poem 'To My Son' is to be believed, William, his first child, was born in 1805 to a serving-girl called either Helen or Ellen,

187

who died soon afterwards.[4] This baby was followed by a child born to
Lucy, a housemaid at Newstead, in 1809. Mrs Byron had agreed to look
after William and when Byron left for his tour of the East in July of that
year he left Lucy in her care. On returning to Newstead in 1811 he
recalled Lucy from her home in Warwickshire to be the chief 'of all the
makers and unmakers of beds in the household', but made no mention
of his child.[5] In January 1812 his new favourite, Susan Vaughan, tactlessly
reminded him of 'the night you come up to our room, when I was in bed
– the time you locked the door. You woked the boys and ask'd George if
he knew you.'[6] Susan does not say how many boys there were in the room
with George, Fletcher's son. If Lucy's son were there it is strange he was
not mentioned as leaving Newstead with his mother when she and Susan
were dismissed in disgrace later that month.[7]

Unwanted aristocratic bastards were often placed in families which
were found for the purpose by lawyers or friends and great care was taken
to make it almost impossible for the child to even guess at its origins
unless one of the parents deliberately arranged to be found, but it is not
out of keeping with Byron's character to expect he would leave clues; he
was proud of his prowess and boasted to his friends at the advent of each
of his children.

One family friend who had the opportunity to help find a home for a
Byron baby was Sir Francis Burdett. He had been elected to Parliament in
the same year as John Trevanion, a friend and cousin of Augusta and
Byron from Cornwall. In 1800 Burdett had inherited from his aunt a
large country house, Ramsbury Manor in the village of Ramsbury,
Wiltshire, but he and his wealthy wife Sophia, daughter of the banker
Thomas Coutts, preferred to live either in London or fashionable Bath.
They kept a small staff at the manor house and were on very good terms
with the tradesmen in the village. In 1807 Byron wrote affectionately
about his toddler son William; it would be nice to think that through Sir
Francis Burdett Byron had arranged for him to be placed with a couple
on his estate at Ramsbury. What is certain is that a boy called William was
baptized in Ramsbury in August 1807, the son of John and Sarah
Marshall. There are no further local records of this William Marshall,
suggesting that he probably left the area.

On 7 June 1825 a young man from Wiltshire, William Marshall,
claiming to be Byron's son, married Hannah Ayre at St Bride's Fleet
Street and took his bride to live at 5 Darlington Place in the Borough,
London. The couple had at least three children, George, Isabella and
Mary Anne before Hannah died. William married his second wife, Ann
Ayre on 22 January 1835 at the Parish Church of St John in Waterloo
Road.

William was literate which was unusual for a cow keeper and milkman but life was hard for the family. Hannah, the first child of his second marriage, used to tell her fascinated grandchildren how she led her father's cows through the streets of south London to graze on Camberwell Green. She was unhappy at home and married Benjamin Burgess, an iron plate worker, on Christmas Day 1852 when she was only sixteen, later admitting that one of the reasons for her early marriage was to escape from her drunken father. Hannah died in 1934 when she was ninety-nine but her family remember her telling them that her father confessed proudly to being Lord Byron's son born to a serving girl. To prove his point he showed Hannah a lock of hair which he claimed belonged to his father. Far from feeling proud of her aristocratic blood Hannah was ashamed of her father's illegitimacy, regretted mentioning it and became upset if anyone ever alluded to it.

In 1851, Marshall was a widower once more and for the first time declared his place of birth on the census form to be Wiltshire. To this day the family maintain their claim to be descended from Byron.[8]

The Burdetts and the Trevanions remained friends and Trevanion, at the age of fifty, married Burdett's daughter Susanna while his son, Henry, born of an earlier union, married Georgiana Leigh. It was to a house at Colerne near Bath, Wiltshire, that the young couple took Medora to wait for the birth of the second of her children sired by her brother-in-law.

GENEALOGICAL TABLE

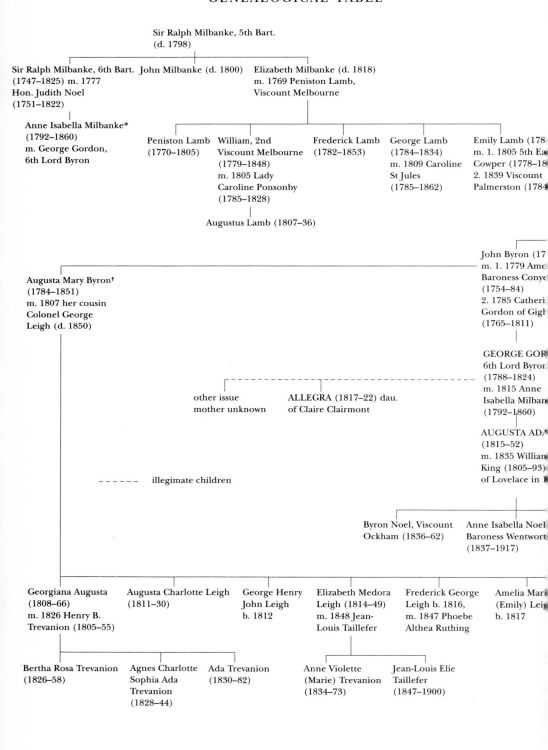

Sir Ralph Milbanke, 5th Bart.
(d. 1798)

Sir Ralph Milbanke, 6th Bart.
(1747–1825) m. 1777
Hon. Judith Noel
(1751–1822)

John Milbanke (d. 1800)

Elizabeth Milbanke (d. 1818)
m. 1769 Peniston Lamb,
Viscount Melbourne

Anne Isabella Milbanke*
(1792–1860)
m. George Gordon,
6th Lord Byron

Peniston Lamb
(1770–1805)

William, 2nd
Viscount Melbourne
(1779–1848)
m. 1805 Lady
Caroline Ponsonby
(1785–1828)

Frederick Lamb
(1782–1853)

George Lamb
(1784–1834)
m. 1809 Caroline
St Jules
(1785–1862)

Emily Lamb (178
m. 1. 1805 5th Ea
Cowper (1778–18
2. 1839 Viscount
Palmerston (1784

Augustus Lamb (1807–36)

John Byron (17
m. 1. 1779 Ame
Baroness Conye
(1754–84)
2. 1785 Catheri
Gordon of Gigh
(1765–1811)

Augusta Mary Byron†
(1784–1851)
m. 1807 her cousin
Colonel George
Leigh (d. 1850)

GEORGE GOR
6th Lord Byron
(1788–1824)
m. 1815 Anne
Isabella Milban
(1792–1860)

other issue
mother unknown

ALLEGRA (1817–22) dau.
of Claire Clairmont

AUGUSTA ADA
(1815–52)
m. 1835 William
King (1805–93)
of Lovelace in 1

illegimate children

Byron Noel, Viscount
Ockham (1836–62)

Anne Isabella Noel
Baroness Wentwort
(1837–1917)

Georgiana Augusta
(1808–66)
m. 1826 Henry B.
Trevanion (1805–55)

Augusta Charlotte Leigh
(1811–30)

George Henry
John Leigh
b. 1812

Elizabeth Medora
Leigh (1814–49)
m. 1848 Jean-
Louis Taillefer

Frederick George
Leigh b. 1816,
m. 1847 Phoebe
Althea Ruthing

Amelia Mari
(Emily) Lei
b. 1817

Bertha Rosa Trevanion
(1826–58)

Agnes Charlotte
Sophia Ada
Trevanion
(1828–44)

Ada Trevanion
(1830–82)

Anne Violette
(Marie) Trevanion
(1834–73)

Jean-Louis Elie
Taillefer
(1847–1900)

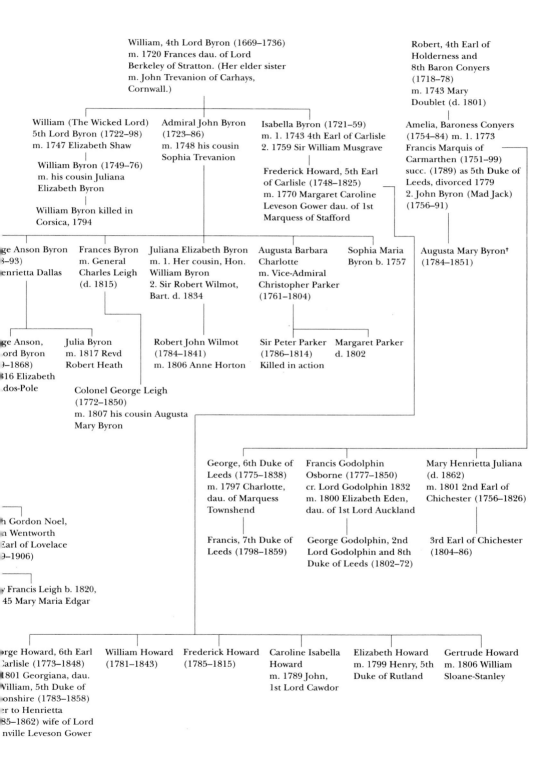

William, 4th Lord Byron (1669–1736)
m. 1720 Frances dau. of Lord
Berkeley of Stratton. (Her elder sister
m. John Trevanion of Carhays,
Cornwall.)

Robert, 4th Earl of
Holderness and
8th Baron Conyers
(1718–78)
m. 1743 Mary
Doublet (d. 1801)

William (The Wicked Lord)
5th Lord Byron (1722–98)
m. 1747 Elizabeth Shaw

Admiral John Byron
(1723–86)
m. 1748 his cousin
Sophia Trevanion

Isabella Byron (1721–59)
m. 1. 1743 4th Earl of Carlisle
2. 1759 Sir William Musgrave

Amelia, Baroness Conyers
(1754–84) m. 1. 1773
Francis Marquis of
Carmarthen (1751–99)
succ. (1789) as 5th Duke of
Leeds, divorced 1779
2. John Byron (Mad Jack)
(1756–91)

William Byron (1749–76)
m. his cousin Juliana
Elizabeth Byron

William Byron killed in
Corsica, 1794

Frederick Howard, 5th Earl
of Carlisle (1748–1825)
m. 1770 Margaret Caroline
Leveson Gower dau. of 1st
Marquess of Stafford

ge Anson Byron
3–93)
enrietta Dallas

Frances Byron
m. General
Charles Leigh
(d. 1815)

Juliana Elizabeth Byron
m. 1. Her cousin, Hon.
William Byron
2. Sir Robert Wilmot,
Bart. d. 1834

Augusta Barbara
Charlotte
m. Vice-Admiral
Christopher Parker
(1761–1804)

Sophia Maria
Byron b. 1757

Augusta Mary Byron†
(1784–1851)

ge Anson,
ord Byron
9–1868)
16 Elizabeth
.dos-Pole

Julia Byron
m. 1817 Revd
Robert Heath

Robert John Wilmot
(1784–1841)
m. 1806 Anne Horton

Sir Peter Parker
(1786–1814)
Killed in action

Margaret Parker
d. 1802

Colonel George Leigh
(1772–1850)
m. 1807 his cousin Augusta
Mary Byron

George, 6th Duke of
Leeds (1775–1838)
m. 1797 Charlotte,
dau. of Marquess
Townshend

Francis Godolphin
Osborne (1777–1850)
cr. Lord Godolphin 1832
m. 1800 Elizabeth Eden,
dau. of 1st Lord Auckland

Mary Henrietta Juliana
(d. 1862)
m. 1801 2nd Earl of
Chichester (1756–1826)

h Gordon Noel,
n Wentworth
Earl of Lovelace
9–1906)

Francis, 7th Duke of
Leeds (1798–1859)

George Godolphin, 2nd
Lord Godolphin and 8th
Duke of Leeds (1802–72)

3rd Earl of Chichester
(1804–86)

y Francis Leigh b. 1820,
45 Mary Maria Edgar

rge Howard, 6th Earl
arlisle (1773–1848)
1801 Georgiana, dau.
Villiam, 5th Duke of
onshire (1783–1858)
r to Henrietta
85–1862) wife of Lord
nville Leveson Gower

William Howard
(1781–1843)

Frederick Howard
(1785–1815)

Caroline Isabella
Howard
m. 1789 John,
1st Lord Cawdor

Elizabeth Howard
m. 1799 Henry, 5th
Duke of Rutland

Gertrude Howard
m. 1806 William
Sloane-Stanley

Notes

CHAPTER ONE (pp. 1–24)

1. Doris Langley Moore, *Ada, Countess of Lovelace* (John Murray, 1977), p. 18.
2. Roland E. Prothero, ed., *The Works of Lord Byron. A New Revised and Enlarged Edition, with Illustrations* (6 vols, London, John Murray, 1901), vol. 1, p. 5.
3. Ethel Colburn Mayne, *Byron* (London, Methuen, 1912), pp. 1–4.
4. Thomas Moore, *The Life, Letters and Journals of Lord Byron* (London, John Murray, 1838), p. 5.
5. Ibid., p. 501.
6. Ibid., p. 5.
7. Ibid., p. 9.
8 Ibid., pp. 1–11.
9. Ibid., p. 13.
10. Violet W. Walker, *The House of Byron. A History of the Family from the Norman Conquest 1066–1988,* revised and completed by Margaret J. Howell (Quiller Press, 1988), pp. 130–1.
11. Mrs Rebeka Heath, *Memoirs* (Nottingham City Archives Ref. DD1251/20/59).
12. Moore, *Life*, p.14.
13. Ibid., p. 15.
14. Ibid., p. 13.
15. Ibid., pp. 15–16.
16. Ibid., p. 15.
17. Prothero, *Works*, vol. 1, p. 10.
18. Moore, *Life*, p. 18.
19. Ibid., p. 19.
20. Prothero, *Works*, vol. 1, p. 318.
21. Moore, *Life*, p. 22.
22. Hubert Cole, *Beau Brummell* (New York, Mason/Charter, 1977), pp. 70–1.
23. Moore, *Life*, p. 26.
24. Prothero, *Works*, vol. 1, p. 16.
25. Moore, *Life*, p. 17.
26. Prothero, *Works*, vol. 1, p. 39.
27. Sir George Leveson-Gower and Iris Palmer, eds, *Hary-o, The Letters of Lady Harriet Cavendish, 1796–1809* (London, John Murray, 1940), p. 165.
28. Ibid., p. 250.

29. Prothero, *Works*, vol. 1, p. 76.
30. Ibid., vol. 1, p. 95.
31. Ibid.
32. Moore, *Life*, p. 30.
33. Ibid., pp. 30–1, 53–4.
34. Ibid., pp. 28–9.
35. Ibid., p. 34.
36. Ibid., pp. 37–8.
37. Ibid., pp. 38–9.
38. Ibid., p. 129.
39. Ibid., p. 35.
40. Ibid., pp. 39–40.
41. Ibid., pp. 50–1 and note.
42. Prothero, *Works*, vol. 1, pp. 113–15.
43. Moore, *Life*, p. 53.
44. Prothero, *Works*, vol. 1, p. 129.
45. Ibid., vol. 1, p. 39.
46. Moore *Life*, p. 57.
47. Ibid., pp. 67, 69.
48. Ibid., p. 70.
49. Ibid., p. 73.
50. Prothero, *Works*, vol. 1, p. 205.
51. Washington Irving, *Abbotsford and Newstead Abbey* (London, Henry G. Bohn, 1850), p. 177.
52. Moore, *Life*, p. 75.
53. Prothero, *Works*, vol. 1, p. 205.
54. Moore, *Life*, p. 63.
55. Ibid., pp. 75–6.
56. R.C. Dallas, *Recollections of the Life of Lord Byron from the Year 1808 to the end of 1814* (Philadelphia, 1824), pp. 33–6.
57. Moore, *Life*, pp. 80–3.
58. Ibid., p. 88.

CHAPTER TWO (pp. 25–39)

1. Moore, *Life*, p. 91.
2. Prothero, *Works*, vol. 1, pp. 244–5.
3. Moore, *Life*, pp. 97–8.
4. Prothero, *Works*, vol. 1, p. 270.
5. Moore, *Life*, p.107.
6. Ibid., p. 178.
7. Joan Haslip, *Lady Hester Stanhope* (Penguin Books, 1934), pp. 84–5.
8. Moore, *Life*, p. 116.
9. Ibid., p.121.
10. Prothero, *Works*, vol. 1, pp. 311–12.

11. Moore, *Life*, pp. 127–8.
12. Ibid., p. 129.
13. Ibid.
14. Ibid., p. 130.
15. Ibid., p. 128.
16. Prothero, *Works*, vol. 2, p. 45.
17. Moore, *Life*, p. 54.
18. Ibid., p. 145.
19. Ibid., p. 150.
20. Vere Foster, ed., *The Two Duchesses – Family Correspondence of and relating to Georgiana Duchess of Devonshire, Elizabeth Duchess of Devonshire, Earl of Bristol (Bishop of Derry), the Countess of Bristol, Lord and Lady Byron, The Earl of Aberdeen, Sir Augustus Foster Bart and others 1777–1859* (Blackie & Son, 1898), p. 352.
21. Leslie A. Marchand, ed., *Byron's Letters and Journals* (12 vols, John Murray, 1973–82), vol. 2, p. 131.
22. Rev. James T. Hodgson, *The Reverend Francis Hodgson, B.D. – A Memoir by his son the Reverend James T. Hodgson, M.A.* (2 vols, 1878), vol. 1, p. 219.
23. Moore, *Life*, p. 153.
24. Ibid., p. 155.
25. Marchand, *Letters and Journals*, vol. 2, p. 159.
26. Alfred Howard, ed., *The Beauties of Byron consisting of selections from his works* (Thomas Tegg, 1826), pp. 211–12.
27. Moore, *Life*, p. 161.
28. Ibid., p. 651.
29. Ibid., p. 12.
30. Malcolm Elwin, *Lord Byron's Wife* (New York, Harcourt Brace & World Inc., 1963), p. 105.
31. Ibid., pp. 111–16.
32. Ethel Colburn Mayne, *The Life of Lady Byron* (Constable & Co., 1929), pp. 35–6.
33. Ibid., p. 23.
34. Foster, *Two Duchesses*, pp. 353–4.
35. Ibid., p. 358.
36. Mayne, *Lady Byron*, p. 24.

CHAPTER THREE (pp. 40–57)

1. Mayne, *Lady Byron*, p. 4.
2. Foster, *Two Duchesses*, pp. 367–8.
3. Ibid., pp. 369–70.
4. Ibid., p. 365.
5. Moore, *Life*, p. 163.
6. Foster, *Two Duchesses*, p. 364.
7. Georgiana Blakiston, *Lord William Russell and his Wife 1815–1846* (London, John Murray, 1972), pp. 4–5.

8. Mayne, *Lady Byron*, p. 32.

9. Foster, *Two Duchesses*, p. 374.

10. Ibid., pp. 360–2.

11. Frederick Locker-Lampson, *My Confidences. An autobiographical Sketch addressed to my descendants* (Smith, Elder & Co., 1896), p. 371.

12. Foster, *Two Duchesses,* p. 165.

13. Moore, *Life*, p. 165.

14. Elwin, *Lord Byron's Wife*, pp. 146, 493.

15. Moore, *Life,* pp. 165–6.

16. Marchand, *Letters and Journals*, vol. 3, p. 40.

17. Moore, *Life*, p. 184.

18. J.E. Morpurgo, ed., *The Autobiography of Leigh Hunt* (The Cresset Press, 1949), pp. 242–4.

19. Moore, *Life*, pp. 183–4.

20. Marchand, *Letters and Journals*, vol. 3, p. 72.

21. Prothero, *Works,* vol. 2, p. 10.

22. Ibid., p. 10.

23. Cole, *Brummell*, p. 106.

24. Moore, *Life*, p. 187.

25. Mary Countess of Lovelace, ed., *Astarte: A Fragment of Truth concerning George Gordon Byron, Sixth Lord Byron. Recorded by his Grandson, Ralph Milbanke, Earl of Lovelace. New Edition, with many additional letters* (1921), pp. 33–4.

26. Ibid., p. 263.

27. Mayne, *Lady Byron*, p. 58.

28. Marchand, *Letters and Journals*, vol. 3, p. 103.

29. Moore, *Life*, vol. 3, p. 227.

30. Prothero, *Works*, vol. 1, p. 20.

31. Ibid., vol. 2, p. 380.

32. Lovelace, *Astarte*, p. 34.

33. Lady Dorchester, ed., *Recollections of a Long Life by Lord Broughton (John Cam Hobhouse) with additional extracts from his private diaries* (John Murray, 1910), p. 83.

34. Moore, *Life*, p. 230.

35. Ibid., p. 233.

36. Leveson-Gower, *Hary-o*, p. 203.

37. Mayne, *Lady Byron*, p. 94.

38. Moore, *Life*, p. 253.

39. Ibid., p. 257.

40. Broughton, *Recollections*, pp.156–7.

41. Moore, *Life*, p. 259.

42. Mayne, *Lady Byron*, p. 102.

43. Ibid., p. 103.

44. Ibid., p. 104.

45. Moore, *Life*, p. 263.

CHAPTER FOUR (pp. 58–92)

1. Una Pope-Hennessy, *Durham Company* (Chatto & Windus, 1941), pp. 54–5.
2. Langley Moore, *Ada*, p. 24.
3. Moore, *Life*, pp. 266–7.
4. Ibid., p. 263.
5. Ibid., p. 265.
6. Elwin, *Lord Byron's Wife*, p. 219, footnote 1.
7. Hodgson, *Memoir*, vol. 1, p. 294.
8. Viscount Esher, ed., *The Girlhood of Queen Victoria, A selection from Her Majesty's Diaries between the years 1832 and 1840* (2 vols, John Murray, 1912), vol. 1, p. 341.
9. Mayne, *Lady Byron*, p. 122.
10. Ibid., pp. 212–13.
11. Ibid., p. 123.
12. Ibid., p. 125.
13. Ibid., p. 127.
14. Ibid., p. 131.
15. Prothero, *Works*, vol. 3, p. 78.
16. Broughton, *Recollections*, vol. 2, p. 198.
17. Ibid., vol. 3, p. 49.
18. Ibid., vol. 1, pp. 191–5.
19. Ibid., vol. 1, p. 195.
20. Moore, *Life*, pp. 271–2.
21. John Jolliffe, ed., *The Diaries of Benjamin Haydon* (Hutchinson, 1990), p. 96.
22. Mayne, *Lady Byron*, p. 160.
23. Harriet Beecher Stowe, *Lady Byron Vindicated* (London, Sampson Low, Sons, and Marston, 1870), pp. 304–10.
24. Ibid., pp. 169–70.
25. Pope-Hennessy, *Durham Company*, p. 71.
26. Doris Langley Moore, *The Late Lord Byron* (John Murray, 1961), p. 299.
27. Mayne, *Lady Byron*, p. 161.
28. Elwin, *Lord Byron's Wife*, pp. 268–9.
29. Ibid., p. 340.
30. Mayne, *Lady Byron*, p. 162.
31. Ibid., p. 165.
32. Stowe, *Lady Byron Vindicated*, p. 36.
33. Hodgson, *Memoir*, vol. 2, pp. 7–13.
34. Mayne, *Lady Byron*, p. 172.
35. Moore, *Life*, p. 276.
36. Ibid., pp. 279–80.
37. Mayne, *Lady Byron*, p. 174.
38. Hodgson, *Memoir*, vol. 2, pp. 13–15.
39. Mayne, *Lady Byron*, pp. 175–9.
40. Elwin, *Lord Byron's Wife*, p. 311.
41. Hodgson, *Memoir*, vol. 2, pp. 16–17.

42. A.G. L'Estrange, the Reverend, *The Literary Life of the Reverend William Harness Vicar of All Saints Knightsbridge and Prebendary of St. Pauls* (Hurst and Blackett, 1871), p. 23.
43. Morpurgo, *Leigh Hunt*, pp. 252–3, 288.
44. Moore, *Life*, pp. 279–81.
45. Mayne, *Lady Byron*, pp. 180–1.
46. Ibid., p. 183.
47. Ibid., p. 185.
48. Broughton, *Recollections*, vol. 1, p. 323.
49. William Parry, *The Last Days of Lord Byron with his Lordship's Opinions of various subjects particularly on the state and prospects of Greece* (London, Knight and Lacey, 1825), p. 217.
50. Foster, *Two Duchesses*, pp. 408–9.
51. Marguerite, Countess of Blessington, *Journal of the Conversations of Lord Byron with the Countess of Blessington* (Henry Colburn, 1834; Princeton University Press, 1969), p. 80.
52. Stowe, *Lady Byron Vindicated*, pp. 304–10.
53. Blessington, *Conversations*, p. 83.
54. Hodgson, *Memoir*, vol. 1, p. 103.
55. L'Estrange, *Life of the Rev. W. Harness*, p. 35.
56. Moore, *Life*, p. 290.
57. Prothero, *Works*, vol. 3, pp. 293–4.
58. Broughton, *Recollections*, vol. 2, p. 359, Appendix B.
59. Lovelace, *Astarte*, p. 39.
60. Ibid., pp. 39–40.
61. Brougham, *Recollections*, vol. 2, p. 253.
62. Stowe, *Lady Byron Vindicated*, p. 294.
63. Broughton, *Recollections*, vol. 2, pp. 215–16.
64. Ibid., vol. 2, p. 202.
65. Ibid.
66. Lovelace, *Astarte*, pp. 40–2.
67. Broughton, *Recollections*, vol. 2, p. 207.
68. Ibid., vol. 2, p. 256.
69. Ibid., pp. 208–9.
70. Ibid., pp. 262–6.
71. Ibid., pp. 234–5.
72. Hodgson, *Memoir*, vol. 2, pp. 28–33.
73. Mayne, *Lady Byron*, p. 212.
74. Broughton, *Recollections*, vol. 2, p. 242.
75. Marchand, *Letters and Journals*, vol. 5, pp. 26–7.
76. Broughton, *Recollections*, vol. 2, pp. 244–5.
77. Prothero, *Works*, vol. 3, pp. 310–11.
78. Broughton, *Recollections*, vol. 2, p. 267.
79. Ibid., pp. 277–84.
80. Mayne, *Lady Byron*, pp. 208, 215.
81. Foster, *Two Duchesses*, pp. 412–14.

82. Langley Moore, *Ada*, p. 27.
83. Lovelace, *Astarte*, p. 322.
84. Foster, *Two Duchesses*, p. 413.
85. Lovelace, *Astarte*, p. 322.
86. Moore, *Life*, p. 303.
87. Lovelace, *Astarte*, pp. 51–2.
88. Broughton, *Recollections*, vol. 1, pp. 334–6.

CHAPTER FIVE (pp. 93–122)

1. Mayne, *Lady Byron*, pp. 242–3.
2. Ibid., pp. 242–5.
3. Langley Moore, *Late Lord Byron*, p. 317.
4. Mayne, *Lady Byron*, pp. 244, 317.
5. Marchand, *Letters and Journals*, vol. 5, p. 69.
6. Lloyd Sanders, *The Holland House Circle*, (Methuen, 1908), p. 278.
7. Broughton, *Recollections*, vol. 1, p. 337.
8. Ibid., vol. 1, pp. 341, 345.
9. Lovelace, *Astarte*, pp. 264–5.
10. Ibid., pp. 210–11.
11. Ibid., p. 61.
12. Ibid., pp. 264–5.
13. Ibid., pp. 64–7.
14. Ibid., pp. 271–3.
15. Ibid., pp. 273–4.
16. Ibid., pp. 283–5.
17. Ibid., pp. 268–70.
18. Ibid., pp. 69–71.
19. Ibid., pp. 287–8.
20. Leslie A. Marchand, *Byron, A Biography* (3 vols, New York, Alfred A. Knopf, 1957), vol. 2, p. 602.
21. Moore, *Life*, p. 307.
22. R. Glynn Grylls, *Claire Clairmont, Mother of Byron's Allegra* (John Murray, 1939), p. 64.
23. Ibid., p. 65.
24. Moore, *Life*, pp. 315–19.
25. Lovelace, *Astarte*, pp. 268–70.
26. Marchand, *Letters and Journals*, vol. 5, 162.
27. Buxton Forman, *Life of P.B. Shelley* (Oxford University Press, 1913), pp. 170–2.
28. George Paston and Peter Quennell, *'To Lord Byron'* (John Murray, 1939), pp. 224–5.
29. Ibid., pp. 226–7.
30. Prothero, *Works*, vol. 4, p. 123.
31. Moore, *Life*, p. 372.

32. Paston and Quennell, *'To Lord Byron'*, pp. 230–1.
33. Ibid., pp. 236–7.
34. Moore, *Life*, pp. 66–8.
35. Prothero, *Works*, vol. 6, pp. 313–16.
36. Ibid., p. 382, note.
37. Lovelace, *Astarte*, pp. 278–80.
38. Ibid., pp. 16–17.
39. Marchand, *Letters and Journals*, vol. 11, p. 165.
40. Prothero, *Works*, vol. 3, p. 329.
41. Moore, *Life*, pp. 383–6.
42. Marchand, *Letters and Journals*, vol. 6, p. 14.
43. Lovelace, *Astarte*, p. 68, note.
44. Hodgson, *Memoir*, vol. 2, pp. 53–4.
45. Iris Origo, *The Last Attachment* (New York, Charles Scribner's Sons, 1949), p. 40.
46. Marchand, *Letters and Journals*, vol. 6, p. 141.
47. Moore, *Life*, p. 397.
48. Lovelace, *Astarte*, pp. 290–1.
49. Marchand, *Letters and Journals*, vol. 6, p. 171.
50. Lovelace, *Astarte*, p. 294.
51. Moore, *Life*, p. 422.
52. Ibid., p. 410.
53. Ibid., p. 420.
54. Ibid., pp. 422–3.
55. Marchand, *Letters and Journals*, vol. 6, p. 231.
56. Lovelace, *Astarte*, pp. 295–7.
57. Moore, *Life*, pp. 246–7.
58. Lovelace, *Astarte*, p. 294.
59. Ibid., pp. 89–91.
60. Moore, *Life*, p. 366.
61. Prothero, *Works*, vol. 5, pp. 10–12.
62. Hubert E.H. Jerningham, *Reminiscences of an Attaché* (William Blackwood and Sons, 1886), p. 102.
63. Moore, *Life*, p. 451.
64. Prothero, *Works*, vol. 5, pp. 73–5.
65. Ibid., pp. 498–9.
66. Moore, *Life*, p. 501.
67. Ibid.
68. Iris Origo, *A Measure of Love* (Jonathan Cape, 1957), pp. 62–3.
69. Marchand, *Letters and Journals*, vol. 8, p. 226.
70. Lovelace, *Astarte*, pp. 306–9.
71. Marchand, *Letters and Journals*, vol. 9, pp. 56–7.
72. Moore, *Life*, p. 544.
73. Prothero, *Works*, vol. 5, pp. 493–4.
74. Origo, *A Measure of Love*, p. 67.
75. Jerningham, *Reminiscences*, p. 108.

76. Prothero, *Works*, vol. 5, p. 501.
77. Origo, *A Measure of Love*, p. 73.
78. Moore, *Life*, pp. 558–9.
79. Marchand, *Letters and Journals*, vol. 10, p. 68.
80. Prothero, *Works*, vol. 5, p. 497.

CHAPTER SIX (pp. 123–37)

1. John Edward Trelawny, *Trelawny's Recollections of the Last Days of Shelley and Byron* (Oxford University Press, 1931), p. 87.
2. Medwin, *Life of Shelley*, p. 407.
3. Moore, *Life*, p. 564.
4. Marchand, *Letters and Journals*, vol. 10, p. 11.
5. Moore, *Life*, p. 565.
6. Blessington, *Conversations*, pp. 5–6.
7. Moore, *Life*, pp. 580–1.
8. Ibid., pp. 585–6.
9. Ibid., p. 589.
10. Marchand, *Letters and Journals*, vol. 10, pp. 177–8.
11. Blessington, *Conversations*, p. 218.
12. Moore, *Life*, p. 594.
13. Charles Mackay, ed., *Medora Leigh: A History and an Autobiography With an introduction, and a commentary on Charges brought against Lord Byron by Mrs Beecher Stowe* together with *Appendix: Conversations with Lord Byron in Greece in 1832* (London, Richard Bentley, 1869), pp. 246–7.
14. Sir John Fox, *The Byron Mystery* (Grant Richards, 1924), p. 57.
15. Mackay, *Medora Leigh*, pp. 252–64.
16. Moore, *Life*, p. 608.
17. Ibid., p. 605.
18. Ibid., p. 611.
19. Parry, *Last Days*, pp. 74–81.
20. Ibid., pp. 31–2.
21. Ibid., pp. 41–6.
22. Ibid., pp. 69–70, 153.
23. Ibid., pp. 118–22.
24. Blessington, *Conversations*, p. 227.
25. Parry, *Last Days*, p. 113.
26. Moore, *Life*, p. 636.
27. Ibid., p. 637.
28. Ibid., p. 664.
29. Parry, *Last Days*, pp. 124–8.
30. Ibid., p. 148.
31. Broughton, *Recollections*, vol. 3, pp. 35–6.
32. Lovelace, *Astarte*, pp. 122–3.
33. Broughton, *Recollections*, vol. 3, p. 53.

34. L'Estrange, *Life of the Rev. W. Harness,* p. 23.
35. Broughton, *Recollections,* vol. 3, p. 68.
36. Ibid., pp. 69–70.

CHAPTER SEVEN (pp. 138–65)

1. Hodgson, *Memoir,* pp. 49–52.
2. Foster, *Two Duchesses,* pp. 430–1.
3. Lovelace, *Astarte,* p. 302.
4. Ibid., pp. 312–13.
5. Langley Moore, *Ada,* p. 22.
6. Ibid., p. 23.
7. Ibid., p. 36.
8. Earl of Ilchester, ed., *Journal of the Hon. Henry Edward Fox* (1923), p. 104.
9. Langley Moore, *Ada,* p. 32.
10. Dorothy Stein, *Ada, A Life and a Legacy* (The MIT Press, Boston, Mass., 1985), p. 34.
11. Mary A. De Morgan, *Threescore Years and Ten – Reminiscences of the late Sophia Elizabeth De Morgan – to which are added Letters to and from her husband the late Augustus De Morgan, and others* (London, Richard Bentley and Son, 1895), pp. 177–8.
12. Langley Moore, *Ada,* pp. 33–6.
13. Mayne, *Lady Byron,* p. 335.
14. De Morgan, *Threescore Years and Ten,* pp. 181–5.
15. Broughton, *Recollections,* vol. 4, p. 330.
16. Ilchester, *Hon. Henry Edward Fox,* p. 147.
17. Mayne, *Lady Byron,* p. 332.
18. Stein, *Life and a Legacy,* p. 52.
19. Medwin, *Life of Shelley,* p. 327.
20. Stein, *Life and a Legacy,* p. 52.
21. De Morgan, *Threescore Years and Ten,* pp. 198–200.
22. Mayne, *Lady Byron,* p. 433.
23. Mackay, *Medora Leigh,* p. 135.
24. Ibid., pp. 135–6.
25. Mayne, *Lady Byron,* p. 354.
26. Fox, *Byron Mystery,* p. 58.
27. Langley Moore, *Late Lord Byron,* p. 159.
28. Mayne, *Lady Byron,* p. 341.
29. Mackay, *Medora Leigh,* pp. 121–5.
30. Mayne, *Lady Byron,* pp. 315–17.
31. Moore, *Life,* pp. 661–3.
32. Ilchester, *Hon. Henry Edward Fox,* p. 109.
33. Langley Moore, *Late Lord Byron,* p. 335.
34. Haydon, *Diaries,* p. 142.
35. Hodgson, *Memoir,* vol. 2, p. 198.
36. Mayne, *Lady Byron,* pp. 340–8.

37. Mackay, *Medora Leigh*, pp. 127–30.
38. Ibid., pp. 130–2.
39. Mayne, *Lady Byron*, p. 350.
40. Ibid., p. 351.
41. Ibid., pp. 352–3.
42. Mackay, *Medora Leigh*, p. 137.
43. Langley Moore, *Ada*, p. 129.
44. Fox, *Byron Mystery*, pp. 50–1.
45. Mackay, *Medora Leigh*, p. 137.
46. Mayne, *Lady Byron*, p. 357.
47. Ibid., pp. 360–1.
48. Mackay, *Medora Leigh*, p. 139.
49. Ibid., pp. 149–50.
50. Ibid., p. 152.
51. Ibid., pp. 91–100.
52. Ibid., pp. 101–7.
53. Langley Moore, *Ada*, p. 188.
54. Mackay, *Medora Leigh*, pp. 107–10.
55. Ibid., p. 117.
56. Ibid., pp. 155–60.
57. Catherine Turney, *Byron's Daughter* (Charles Scribner's Sons, 1972), pp. 257–60.
58. Ibid., pp. 267–8.
59. Ibid., p. 274.

CHAPTER EIGHT (pp. 166–86)

1. Toole, *Ada Enchantress*, p. 425.
2. Broughton, *Recollections*, vol. 6, pp. 69–70.
3. Ibid., pp. 145, 150, 175–6.
4. Reverend Frederick Arnold, *Life of the Reverend Frederick Robertson of Brighton, with Some Notices of His Times and Contemporaries* (London, Ward and Downey, 1886), p. 170.
5. Toole, *Ada Enchantress*, p. 185.
6. Ibid., p. 161.
7. Ibid., p. 199.
8. Ibid., p. 305.
9. Ibid., p. 307.
10. Ibid., pp. 300–3.
11. Broughton, *Recollections*, vol. 6, p. 238.
12. Langley Moore, *Ada*, pp. 244–5.
13. E. Beresford Chancellor, *The History of the Squares of London* (Kegan Paul, Trench, Trübner, 1907), p. 96.
14. Toole, *Ada Enchantress*, p. 359.
15. Mayne, *Lady Byron*, p. 388.

16. Toole, *Ada Enchantress*, p. 369.
17. Ibid., pp. 378–9.
18. De Morgan, *Threescore Years and Ten*, pp. 213–16.
19. Toole, *Ada Enchantress*, p. 388.
20. Langley Moore, *Ada*, pp. 288–9.
21. Arnold, *Robertson of Brighton*, pp. 180–6.
22. Blessington, *Conversations of Lord Byron*, p. 99.
23. Hodgson, *Memoir*, vol. 2, p. 198.
24. Arnold, *Robertson of Brighton*, pp. 184–6.
25. Lovelace, *Astarte*, pp. 31–2.
26. Toole, *Ada Enchantress*, p. 412.
27. Ibid., p. 418.
28. Ibid., p. 420.
29. Ibid., p. 421.
30. Ibid., p. 320.
31. Arnold, *Robertson of Brighton*, p. 175.
32. Stein, *Life and a Legacy*, p. 423.
33. Arnold, *Robertson of Brighton*, pp. 176–7.
34. Mayne, *Lady Byron*, pp. 435–6.
35. Ibid., p. 437.
36. Arnold, *Robertson of Brighton*, p. 158.
37. Ibid., p. 161.
38. Stowe, *Lady Byron Vindicated*, pp. 300–4.
39. Ibid., pp. 153–62.
40. Ibid., p. 300.
41. Mayne, *Lady Byron*, p. 429.
42. Langley Moore, *Ada*, p. 37.
43. *Your Dear Letter. Private Correspondence of Queen Victoria and the Crown Princess of Prussia, 1865–1871*, ed. Roger Fulford (London, Evans Brothers, 1971), p. 258.
44. *Ralph, Earl of Lovelace, a Memoir*, ed. Mary Countess of Lovelace (London, Christophers, 1920), p. 27.
45. Jerningham, *Reminiscences*, pp. 102–3.

EPILOGUE (pp. 187–9)

1. Lytton, Earl of, *Life of Edward Bulwer, First Lord Lytton* (2 vols, Macmillan, 1915), vol. 1, p. 119.
2. Ilchester, *Hon. Henry Edward Fox*, p. 219.
3. Ehrsam, Theodore G., *Major Byron, the Incredible Career of a Literary Forger* (Charles S. Boesen, New York, 1951).
4. Moore, *Life*, pp. 50–1.
5. Prothero, *Works*, vol. 2, p. 45.
6. Paston and Quennell, *'To Lord Byron'*, p. 33.
7. Moore, *Life*, p. 153.
8. Burgess family files.

Bibliography

Place of publication is London unless stated otherwise.

Airlie, Mabell, *Lady Palmerston and her Times*. 2 vols, Hodder & Stoughton, 1922.

Armstrong, Margaret, *Trelawney, A Man's Life*. Robert Hale, 1941.

Arnold, Reverend Frederick (ed.), *Life of the Reverend Frederick Robertson of Brighton with Some Notices of his Times and Contemporaries*. Ward and Downey, 1886.

Babbage, Charles, *Passages in the Life of a Philosopher*. 1864.

Bessborough, the Earl of, *Lady Bessborough and her Family Circle*. John Murray, 1940.

Blakiston, Georgiana, *Lord William Russell and his Wife 1815–1846*. John Murray, 1972.

Blanch, Lesley (ed.), *Harriet Wilson's Memoirs*. Folio Society, 1964.

Blythe, Henry, *Caro, the Fatal Passion*. Rupert Hart-Davis, 1972.

Bos, Charles du, *Byron and the Need of Fatality*. 1931.

Burford, E., *Royal St James's, being a story of Kings, Clubmen and Courtesans*. Robert Hale, 1988.

Burnett, T.A.J., *The Life and Times of Scrope Berdmore Davis*. Oxford University Press, 1983.

Buxton Forman, H. (ed.), *The Life of Percy Bysshe Shelley by Thomas Medwin*. Oxford University Press, 1913.

Carman, W.Y., *British Military Uniforms from Contemporary Pictures*. Hamlyn, 1968.

Cecil, David, *Melbourne*. Reprint Society, 1955.

Chancellor, E. Beresford, *The History of the Squares of London*. Kegan Paul, Trench, Trübner, 1907.

Chapman, John S., *Byron and the Honourable Augusta Leigh*. New Haven and London, Yale University Press, 1975.

Cole, Hubert, *Beau Brummell*. Mason/Charter, New York, 1977.

Coleridge, Ernest Hartley (ed.), *The Complete Works of Byron*. 1878–1903.

Croucher, Barbara, *The Village in the Valley. A History of Ramsbury*. Croucher, Ramsbury, Wiltshire, 1986.

Dallas, R.C., *Recollections of the Life of Lord Byron from the Year 1808 to the end of 1814*. Philadelphia, 1824.

De Morgan, Sophia Elizabeth, *Three Score Years and Ten*. 1895.

Dorchester, Lady (ed.), *Recollections of a Long Life by Lord Broughton (John Cam Hobhouse) with additional extracts from his private diaries*. 6 vols, John Murray, 1911.

Ehrsam, Theodore G., *Major Byron, the Incredible Career of a Literary Forger*. Charles S. Boesen, New York, 1951.

Elwin, Malcolm, *Lord Byron's Family*. John Murray, 1975.

—— *Lord Byron's Wife*. New York, Harcourt Brace & World Inc., 1963.

—— *The Noels and the Byrons*. Macdonald, 1967.

Esher, Viscount (ed.), *The Girlhood of Queen Victoria, A selection from Her Majesty's Diaries between the years 1832 and 1840*. 2 vols, John Murray, 1912.

Finden, Edward and William, *Illustrations of the Life and Works of Lord Byron*. John Murray, 1833.

Foster, Vere (ed.), *The Two Duchesses*. Blackie & Son, 1898.

Fox, Sir John, *The Byron Mystery*. Grant Richards, 1924.

Fulford, Roger (ed.), *Your Dear Letter, Private Correspondence of Queen Victoria and the Crown Princess of Prussia, 1865–1871*. Evans Brothers, 1971.

Gordon, A.C., *Allegra: The Story of Byron and Miss Clairmont*. Methuen, 1927.

Gower, Lord Donald, *Stafford House Letters*. Kegan Paul, Trench, Trübner, 1891.

Gray, Austin K., *The Story of Byron's Last Mistress*. Harrap, 1948.

Grylls, R. Glynn, *Claire Clairmont, Mother of Byron's Allegra*. John Murray, 1939.

Gunn, Peter, *My Dearest Augusta*. Bodley Head, 1968.

Haslip, Joan, *Lady Hester Stanhope*. Penguin Books, 1934.

Haythornthwait, Philip J., *Uniforms of Waterloo*. Blandford Press, 1974.

Heath, Rebeka, *Memoirs* (Nottingham City Archives, Ref. DD1251/20/59).

Herold, J. Christopher, *Mistress to an Age, A life of Madame de Staël*. Readers Union, 1960.

Hodgson, Rev. James T., *The Reverend Francis Hodgson, B.D. – A Memoir by his son the Reverend James T. Hodgson, M.A.* 2 vols, 1878.

Holland, Henry Richard Vassall, 3rd Lord Holland, *Further Memoirs of the Whig Party, 1807–1821*. John Murray, 1905.

Howard, Alfred (ed.), *The Beauties of Byron consisting of selections from his works*. Thomas Tegg, 1826.

Ilchester, Earl of (ed.), *Journal of the Hon. Henry Edward Fox*. 1923.

—— *Elizabeth, Lady Holland to her Son – 1821–1845*. John Murray, 1946.

—— *The Home of the Hollands 1605–1820*. John Murray, 1937.

Jenkins, Elizabeth, *Lady Caroline Lamb*. Sphere Books, 1972.

Jerningham, Hubert, E.H., *Reminiscences of an Attaché*. Edinburgh, 1886.

Jolliffe, John (ed.), *Neglected Genius, The Diaries of Benjamin Haydon*. Hutchinson, 1990.

Lamb, Lady Caroline, *Glenarvon*. 3 vols, 2nd. edition, Colburn, 1816.

Langley Moore, Doris, *The Late Lord Byron*. John Murray, 1961.

—— *Lord Byron Accounts Rendered*. John Murray, 1974.

—— *Ada, Countess of Lovelace*. John Murray, 1977.

Leconfield, Lady Maud, *Three Howard Sisters*. John Murray, 1955.

L'Estrange, the Reverend A.G., *The Literary Life of the Reverend William Harness, Vicar of All Saints Knightsbridge and Prebendary of St. Pauls*. Hurst and Blackett, 1871.

Leveson-Gower, Sir George and Palmer, Iris (eds), *Hary-o, The Letters of Lady Harriet Cavendish, 1796–1809*. John Murray, 1940.

Locker-Lampson F., *My Confidences. An autobiographical Sketch addressed to my descendants. 1896.*

Longford, Elizabeth, *Byron*. Hutchinson, Weidenfeld & Nicolson, 1976.

Lovelace, Mary Countess of (ed.), *Ralph, Earl of Lovelace, a Memoir*. Christopher, 1920.

Lovelace, 2nd earl of, *Astarte, A Fragment of Truth concerning George Gordon Byron, Sixth Lord Byron. New Edition with many additional letters*. Christopher, 1921.

—— *Lady Byron and the Leighs*. 1887.

Lovell, Ernest J. Jr. (ed.), *His Very Self and Voice, Collected Conversations of Lord Byron*. New York, Macmillan Company, 1954.

—— *Lady Blessington's Conversations of Lord Byron*. Princeton University Press, 1969.

Luttrell, Barbara, *The Prim Romantic*. Chatto and Windus, 1965.

Lytton, Earl of, *Life of Edward Bulwer, First Lord Lytton*. 2 vols, Macmillan, 1915.

Mackay, Charles (ed.), *Medora Leigh: A History and an Autobiography With an introduction, and a commentary on Charges brought against Lord Byron by Mrs Beecher Stowe* together with *Appendix: Conversations with Lord Byron in Greece in 1832*. Richard Bentley, 1869.

Marchand, Leslie A. (ed.), *Byron's Letters and Journals*, 12 vols, John Murray, 1973–82.

—— *Byron, A Biography*. 3 vols. New York, Alfred A. Knopf, 1957.

—— *Byron, A Portrait*. The Cresset Library, 1971.

Massie, Alan, *Byron's Travels*. Sedgwick & Jackson, 1988.

Massingham, H.J., *The Friend of Shelley – A Memoir of Edward John Trelawny*. Cobden-Sanderson, 1930.

Maurois, André, *Byron*. New York, D. Appleton and Company, 1930.

Maxwell, Sir Herbert (ed.), *A Selection from the Correspondence and Diaries of the late Thos. Creevey, M.P.* 2 vols, John Murray, 1904.

Mayne, Ethel Colburn, *The Life and Letters of Anne Isabella Lady Noel Byron*. Constable, 1929.

—— *A Regency Chapter, Lady Bessborough and her Friendships*. Macmillan, 1939.

—— *Byron*. Methuen, 1912.

Medwin, Thomas, *Journal of the Conversation of Lord Byron noted during a residence with his Lordship at Pisa in the years 1821 and 1822*. 1824.

—— *A Life of Percy Bysshe Shelley*. 2 vols, 1847.

Messenger, Charles, *History of the British Army*. Bison Books, 1986.

Moore, Thomas, *The Life, Letters and Journals of Lord Byron*. John Murray, 1838.

Morpurgo, J.E. (ed.), *The Autobiography of Leigh Hunt*. The Cresset Press, 1949.

Origo, Iris, *The Last Attachment*. New York, Charles Scribner's Sons, 1949.

—— *A Measure of Love*. Jonathan Cape, 1957.

Park, S.J. and Nafziger, *The British Military, its System and Organization 1803–1815*. 1983.

Parry, William, *The Last Days of Lord Byron with his Lordship's Opinions on Various Subjects particularly on the state and prospects of Greece*. Knight and Lacey, 1825.

Paston, George, and Quennell, Peter, *'To Lord Byron'*. John Murray, 1939.

Pierson, Joan, *The Real Lady Byron*. Robert Hale, 1992.

Pope-Hennessy, Una, *Durham Company*. 1941.

Pratt, Willis W., *Byron at Southwell*. Texas, 1948.

Priestly, J.B. (ed.), *Tom Moore's Diary*. Cambridge University Press, Cambridge, 1933.

Prothero, Rowland, E. (ed.), *The Works of Lord Byron. A New Revised and Enlarged Edition, with Illustrations*. 6 vols, John Murray, 1901.

Quennell, Peter, *Byron, a Self-portrait*. 2 vols, John Murray, 1950.

—— *Byron in Italy*. St James's Library, 1941.

—— *Byron, the Years of Fame*. Reprint Society, 1943.

Rowse, A.L., *The Byrons and Trevanions*. Weidenfeld & Nicolson, 1978.

Sadleir, Michael, *Blessington D'Orsay, A Masquerade*. Constable, 1933.

Sadleir, T. (ed.), *Henry Crabb Robinson, Diary, Reminiscences and Correspondence*. 1869.

Sanders, Lloyd, *The Holland House Circle*. Methuen, 1908.

Shelley, Lady Frances, *The Diary of Lady Frances Shelley*. Ed. by Richard Edgcumbe, 2 vols. John Murray, 1912.

Smith, Nowell C. Sidney (ed.), *Selected Letters of Sidney Smith*. Oxford University Press, Oxford, 1981.

Spark, Muriel and Dereck Stanford (eds), *My Best Mary*. Alan Wingate, 1953.

Stein, Dorothy, *Ada, A Life and a Legacy*. Cambridge, Mass., MIT Press, 1985.

Stocking, Marion Kingston and David Mackenzie Stocking (ed.), *The Journals of Claire Clairmont*. Cambridge, Mass., 1968.

Stowe, Harriet Beecher, *Lady Byron Vindicated*. Sampson Low, Sons, and Marston, 1870.

Strickland, Margo, *The Byron Women*. 1974.

Stuart, Dorothy Margaret, *Dearest Bess*. Methuen, 1955.

Thompson, E.P., *The Making of the Working Class*. Pelican, 1968.

Toole, Dr Betty A., *Ada, The Enchantress of Numbers*. Strawberry Press, 1992.

Trelawny, John Edward, *Trelawny's Recollections of the Last Days of Shelley and Byron*. Oxford University Press, Oxford, 1931.

Turney, Catherine, *Byron's Daughter*. New York, Charles Scribner's Sons, 1972.

Villiers, Marjorie, *The Grand Whiggery*. John Murray, 1939.

Walford, Edward, *Old London: Westminster to St James's 1825–1897*. Alderman Press, 1989.

Walker, Violet W., *The House of Byron. A History of the Family from the Norman Conquest 1066–1988*, revised and completed by Margaret J. Howell, Quiller Press, 1988.

White, R.J., *Life in Regency England*. Batsford, 1963.

Wilson Knight, G., *Lord Byron's Marriage*. Routledge & Kegan Paul, 1957.

Index